D0323516

*Dictionary of Television
and Audiovisual Terminology*

Dictionary
of Television
and Audiovisual
Terminology

by

MOSHE MOSHKOVITZ

McFarland & Company, Inc., Publishers

Jefferson, North Carolina, and London

British Library Cataloguing-in-Publication data are available

Library of Congress Cataloguing-in-Publication Data

Moshkovitz, Moshe, 1950–
    Dictionary of television and audiovisual terminology / by Moshe
Moshkovitz.
      p.   cm.
    ISBN 0-7864-0440-X (library binding : 50# alkaline paper) ∞
    1. Television—Dictionaries.   2. Television broadcasting—
Dictionaries.   I. Title.
TK6634.M67   1998
791.45'014—dc21   98-2945
                                                                              CIP

Manufactured in the United States of America

McFarland & Company, Inc., Publishers
  Box 611, Jefferson, North Carolina 28640

In memory of my father,
Yitzhak Mayer Moshkovitz

Acknowledgments

I would like to express my deep appreciation to my good friend Ronald Basford who helped, advised and encouraged me all the way and without whom there would be no book in the first place.

Thanks go to my family—my wife Shunamit, my son Liran and my daughter Naama—who had less of me for the last few years and all of whom were highly supportive and understanding.

Finally, I would like to thank Lior Razin, who helped me with audio terms.

Contents

Preface

The world of television is half a century old and has rapidly spread into almost all areas of our lives. It has continuously renewed its tools and technology, especially during the last decade. With the increased use of computers and the advancement of modern electronics, equipment and production methods change rapidly. New technology brings new terminology, making it difficult to keep pace with new inventions and methods.

The same terms are used almost everywhere in the "global village" this world has become, with television programs being distributed worldwide in real time by satellites. Common terminology is vital for the exchange of material between individuals, companies and stations worldwide. Program material comes in the form of film, recorded tapes or through transmission, all needing standards, formats and measurement methods agreed upon by both the sender and the receiver.

Collected and defined in this volume are the terms used by professionals in everyday work and professional publications of the television and telecommunications industry worldwide. The information in this work relies on more than two decades of hands-on experience in television work, teaching and research.

This work started when I was teaching a college-level television technology course. It was at first a modest attempt to collect a list of common television terms and their explanation (in Hebrew) for the benefit of my students. Soon I realized that there are thousands of such terms and that this is not a small task.

An attempt has been made to capture the essence of each and every term and to give it the appropriate space. The length of each definition depends on its complexity on the one hand and the term's importance on the other hand. Explanations tend not to include in-depth physical or mathematical analysis but deal with the practical usage rather than the theory of operation.

1

This is a reference book intended for professionals in the different branches and subjects of television, for students of television and other telecommunication studies and for amateurs and hobbyists interested in audio, video and related subjects. Professionals will find in this book, apart from the classical terms, the latest innovations and trends in television technology.

Many of the terms have quite different meanings in general usage. The reader should note that this dictionary defines all terms only as they relate to television or audiovisual terminology, while other meanings are ignored.

Both audio and video terms are explained in this book. Audio deals with recording, mixing, editing, playback and transmission of sound signals, as well as the various instruments and processes used. Video terms deal with the production, lighting, shooting, recording, editing, switching, test and measurement and transmission of visual signals, as well as all the instruments used in the process, standards and methods. Terms from other closely related fields are also included, as are certain basic terms from electricity, electronics and computer science. Some definitions refer the reader to other terms that are related or can shed additional light on the subject.

It is my hope that this work will be useful to anyone who is interested in television or already involved in the industry, as well as to general readers who encounter this sometimes bewildering terminology.

Moshe Moshkovitz
Spring 1998

The Dictionary

A Ampere. A unit of electrical current. The amount of current that consists of 6.29×10^{18} electrons.

AAAA American Association of Advertising Agencies.

ABC-ROLL Similar to AB-ROLL, the difference being that there are three players: player A, player B and player C. This configuration enhances the possibilities and makes the editing system more efficient. Complex effects take fewer "generations" or runs to make. A dissolve or wipe between A and B and graphics from C superimposed can be done in one run in an ABC-ROLL editing room. In AB-ROLL it would take two runs. Another advantage is that more raw material cassettes can be loaded into VCRs and less shuffle is needed.

aberration Distortion of an image due to an imperfection of an optical device such as a lens, prism or mirror. Common aberrations are astigmatism, chromatic aberrations, coma, spherical aberration, barrel and pincushion.

AB-ROLL A complex videotape editing system consisting of two players, VCR A and VCR B, and one recorder, VCR C. It is possible to add a character generator, an effects-generator and additional audio and video equipment to enhance the possibilities of the system. An "editing controller," which is a computerized apparatus that controls all the active devices in the system, maintains communication (usually RS-422) to get information from the different devices in the editing system such as current time code and status of machines (play, stop, rec) and to send instructions to perform different tasks such as cut, dissolve, wipe (to the video mixer) or play, rec, stop (to a VCR).

This configuration enables different kinds of audio and video transitions such as wipes, dissolves and crossfades between the two players, as well as superimpositions of several signals (e.g., characters over live video). The video signals from the two players and other video sources are fed to a video mixer that makes the video transitions and superimpositions. The result is recorded on the record VCR. The audio tracks are fed to an audio mixer and from there sent to the record VCR.

An AB-ROLL editing system is expensive but offers a variety of possibilities not found on simpler cut-to-cut editing systems. Because of the expensive nature of the AB-ROLL system, off-line editing is usually used to make all the edit decisions on a simple, low-cost system. The editing list (EDL) is then brought to the AB-ROLL suite together with the unedited tapes. The EDL is loaded into the editing controller, which does most of the editing automatically, with great speed and precision. This way, costly AB-ROLL suite time is saved. *See also* **on-line editing**.

absorption loss Decrease in signal strength caused by absorption of light in fiber-optic lines. Absorption is caused by imperfect light reflection within the fiber or by impure glass. The attenuation of the signal is measured in dB per km. *See also* **fiber optics**.

A-B test Comparative measurement of one signal in relation to another reference signal.

AC Alternating current, electric current changing its amplitude and its polarity in a periodical way (usually a sine wave). Utility system voltage is AC. In the U.S. the frequency of the utility system voltage is 60 Hz (cycles per second) and its voltage is 110 volts. AC is used by large or medium-sized electric motors, lighting and other power devices, but small motors and electronic equipment usually use DC (direct current). Automotive electrical systems use DC as well. *See also* **DC**.

access time (a) The time required to reach every point on a magnetic disk or a magnetic tape in order to retrieve data. Access time is limited by the speed of the mechanical systems that drive the disks, tapes and heads. The access time is significant to the overall speed of a given computerized system. Access time is measured in milliseconds for magnetic disks, whereas for magnetic tapes the access time can take up to several minutes. (b) Time when affiliated TV stations transmit non-network programs or local material, normally from 7:00 P.M. until 8:00 P.M.

achromatic (a) Color with no saturation or hue, consisting of white, gray or black. (b) Lens treated to eliminate chromatic aberrations.

acoustic baffle A partition used to absorb and block the passage of sound to unwanted directions. Used mainly in recording studios.

acoustic center The place from which sound originates in a loudspeaker or loudspeaker system.

acoustic delay line A long tube with a speaker in one side and microphone at the other. The longer the tube, the longer the delay will be. Obsolete today due to electronic delay lines that deliver better quality and a large range of delay times.

acoustics The creation and behavior of sound waves in different environments. Acoustic conditions, mentioned in relation to TV studios, theaters, concert halls and sound rooms, refer to: (a) Ways to prevent the penetration of sound from the surrounding environment, such as noise from cars and airplanes; (b) The concealment of unwanted noise from internal sources such as air conditioning; (c) The reflections and absorption of sound by walls, floors, ceilings and furniture.

active video   The part of the video signal that contains the actual picture information. The video signal contains additional information, such as synchronizing pulses and time code. *See also* **video**.

active window   One of the windows in a windows-based software application that is currently operational or active. Usually appears in front of other, nonactive windows. In single-task operating systems, the active window represents the only application currently running, working or computing. In multitask operating systems, however, computing can take place simultaneously in both active and nonactive windows. *See also* **operating system**.

ACTV   Advanced compatible television. An advanced television standard or system such as high-definition television (HDTV) or PALplus with the ability to be displayed on regular NTSC or PAL home receivers as well. Lack of such compatibility of new TV systems will make all existing TV receivers obsolete.

AD   **(a)** Assistant director. **(b)** Associate Director.

A/D   Analog to digital conversion. The conversion of analog signals such as video or audio to digital form. Conversion is done by measuring the amplitude of the analog signal at any given moment and expressing this value with a binary number. The accuracy of the conversion depends on the sampling rate (the number of measurements taken per second) and on the number of digits (bits) in the binary number (number of levels).

ADA   Audio distribution amplifier. An amplifier with one audio input and many outputs of the same signal. The purpose is to distribute exactly the same signal to different instruments. The amplification is small—just enough to compensate for losses due to long cables. The number of outputs is usually between four and ten.

adaptation for television   Transformation of a play, story or novel into a television script. Parts left to the reader's imagination in a literary work must be converted to visible scenes in TV. Detailed description of characters, scenes, audio and video components must be written in the conventional form of a script for TV.

additive color system   A system in which the three primary colors red, green and blue (RGB) are mixed in different variations to get different colors from black to white, with a full range of every hue and saturation between. In professional TV cameras, three light sensitive devices such as tubes or CCD units are employed, one for each of the primary colors. The three output signals from these devices are mixed together to form the output video signal of the camera. TV color picture tubes have an array of many small red, green and blue dots on the screen that form the color picture. *See also* **subtractive color system; camera (video)**.

additive mix   Addition of two or more video signals in a video mixer, with no attenuation of any of them. The result might exceed standard video levels.

address   A location of certain information inside a computer memory or disk, defined by a number or set of numbers. The address is used internally by the computer and rarely accessed by the user. Each piece of information in the computer has a unique address (many computer errors are caused by wrong addresses). The address is transferred via a specialized address bus, connecting the CPU with memory chips or disk drives. *See also* **bus; CPU**.

adjustment   A change in voltage, current, frequency, pressure and so on, inside an electrical or mechanical instrument, in order to improve performance. Adjustment is done either periodically according to manufacturer's recommendations or when performance is deteriorating. Most components change their accuracy over time, and adjustment compensates for these changes.

AES   Audio Engineering Society (USA).

AES/EBU   A standard for digital audio that defines the sampling rate for different machines handling audio, such as CDs (44.1 kHz) and other postproduction equipment.

AF   Audio frequency. The audio frequency range between 20 Hz and 20,000 Hz. This portion of sound waves is the part that the human ear can detect or sense—usually not all of it and not at a uniform level.

AFC   Automatic frequency control, an electronic circuit that keeps a certain frequency in an electronic instrument stable by changing voltage or another parameter in the circuit to compensate for the change. AFC circuits

are common in radio and TV receivers where they are used to keep the tuner circuits from drifting or moving away from a specific transmission channel. *See also* **frequency**.

AFT   Automatic fine tuning. A circuit in TV receivers that adjusts the correct tuning after a station has been selected.

AGC   Automatic gain control, an electronic circuit that keeps a certain level in an electronic instrument stable by changing voltage or another parameter in the circuit to compensate for the change. AGC circuits are common in radio and TV receivers to compensate for differences in audio level between different stations. *See also* **gain**.

air time   The planned or performed transmission time of a program or other transmitted item.

aliasing   An undesirable effect caused mainly by digital equipment used to produce or process video signals. It appears as twinkling lines or stepped borders between areas of different brightness or color. In advanced systems, anti-aliasing circuits are used to filter out those effects. *See also* **anti-aliasing**.

alignment   Adjustment or tuning of components in an apparatus (usually done according to manufacturer's recommendations) to enhance performance.

alignment tape   Test tape. A tape recorded with precision audio or video test signal used for adjustment of tape machines.

alpha channel Key channel. A channel in a digital format (4:4:4:4) or an effects generator that holds key information related to the video signal. *See also* **key**.

alphanumeric Every character or symbol that is either a letter or a digit. To distinguish from other symbols, such as !@#$/}?+),%^&*. The term is used mainly in computer jargon.

AM *see* **amplitude modulation**

ambience Audio background noise typical to a certain environment, sometimes referred to as "room tone." Usually a mixture of sounds and reverberations. Ambience is characteristic to every room, hall, studio or open space. Ambience changes according to the different sound sources and acoustical conditions. *See also* **room tone**.

amplitude Magnitude or intensity of a waveform or signal such as video or audio. Amplitude of electrical signals is measured in volts peak to peak (PP) or volts RMS. Amplitude has no meaning in reference to DC. *See also* **peak to peak; RMS**.

amplitude modulation A signal such as audio or video modulates or changes the intensity of a fixed frequency wave or carrier by way of summation or multiplication. The result is a carrier with changes in intensity that relate directly to the changes in the intensity of the video or audio signal. The carrier is transmitted and after it reaches its destination, the original signal is retrieved by demodulation. Amplitude modulation is very common in radio and TV transmissions.

See also **demodulator; frequency modulation; modulation**.

analog The opposite of digital, an analog signal is a signal that is continuously changing its level, periodically like a sine wave, or following one or more physical sizes like brightness of a picture or sound waves. All natural waveforms are analog, unlike man-made digital signals.

angular field of view One of the important specifications of a lens. Measured in degrees horizontally and vertically. Fixed lenses have one set of numbers used to describe the lens' field of view (such as 47 × 36). Zoom lenses have two sets of numbers, specifying the widest position of the lens and the narrowest. The field of view parameters are necessary to know the coverage and range of the lens. These parameters are also needed in calculations concerning the size of a scene and the distance from the lens in order to plan scenery and shooting distances for a given studio and lens.

animation Creation of the illusion of movement, made from a series of images. Usually still objects or drawings are captured on film or video and changed or moved slightly for every frame. In the early days of animation each picture was drawn by hand, by a group of artists. This method was slow and tedious. Today, animators use computers that supply the artist with new tools, abilities and possibilities. Animation is used for children's programs (cartoons), scientific movies and special effects.

animation camera Film or video camera mounted steadily over an animation stand or table. Film camera must have provisions for single frame shooting and frame counters. For a video camera a videocassette recorder with single frame and time code is used.

animation stand   A large and rigid stand equipped to hold and move artwork in a controlled way. Precise horizontal, vertical and rotation movements are provided. Registration pins fix the location of artwork sheets. The camera is mounted on a column above the stand that allows vertical movement of the camera.

antenna   A metal rod or wire used to collect electromagnetic waves from the environment or to transmit them. There are many kinds of antennas to suit different frequencies and power requirements. The higher the frequency, the smaller the antenna. There are directional and nondirectional antennas. Dishes are used for antennas with a very narrow distribution pattern.

anti-aliasing   Measures taken to conceal the aliasing effect by filtering or narrowing the frequency response of the system. *See also* **aliasing**.

antiphase   In stereo audio, if one of the channels is reversed in phase (two wires crossed), the left and right channels will cancel each other if mixed together, and if the two channels are sent separately to two corresponding speakers, some mutual cancellation will take place.

aperture   A general term used to describe the ability of a lens to gather light or the maximum diameter of a light beam passing through the lens. *See also* **f-number**.

arc   An electric lamp using a bridge or arc of strong electric current between two electrodes to produce light. Many large film projectors use arc lamps. Color temperature is similar to daylight and the intensity of light is high. These attributes make arc lamps suitable for outside work in film or TV during daylight.

art director   A person in charge of all the aspects in a motion picture that determine the final appearance ("look") of the movie. The art director is involved in decision-making about lighting, scenery, wardrobe, makeup and props. There are art directors also in commercial-making and in some TV programs.

artifacts   Defects in a video signal caused by certain electrical circuits in the process of video-making and processing. Professional equipment contains circuits and filters to eliminate artifacts. Most artifacts are visible, although they are not covered by conventional measurement methods. *See also* **cross color; cross luminance**.

artificial light   Light produced by means of electrical equipment, as opposed to daylight. In film, sometimes artificial light is a name for light with a color temperature of 3,200° Kelvin or for film made to be used in this kind of light.

ASA   American Standards Association. Also a common unit of sensitivity of film to light.

ASCII   American Standards Committee for Information Interchange. ASCII is a standard code in which each character is represented by a number between 0 and 127. ASCII is used in computers as a standard form of transmitting textual data that is completely machine independent. However, ASCII is not intended to be used to transmit graphical information. ASCII includes both visual characters (letters, digits and symbols) and control characters (new line, form feed, space, tab, backspace and alarm). As computers grew more powerful and widespread, a need for more special characters arose. An extended ASCII code was written. The extended code includes 256 characters relating to mathematical symbols, charts and letters for several languages. The extended code is not completely standard.

ASIC   Application specific integrated circuit. A nonstandard circuit designed to perform a specific complex task and replace a number of other standard circuits. The benefits are savings in space, energy consumption and enhanced speed and simplicity of assembly. They are, however, expensive. ASICs are used mainly in portable equipment to reduce size and weight and to save battery consumption.

aspect ratio   The proportion between the width and height of a TV or film frame. In conventional TV, the aspect ratio is 4:3 (1.33:1). In future formats such as HDTV and PAL-PLUS, the width of the frame will be larger, resulting in an aspect ratio of 16:9.

asperity noise   Inherent noise in unrecorded magnetic tapes. Asperity noise increases after a tape has been recorded, mostly near both sides of the recorded frequency.

assemble edit   A method of video editing in which video, audio tracks, time code and a control track are added on the tape to an existing segment in sequence, without interruption, to make a smooth edit. Assemble edit does not require a prior continuous recording on the tape. It is usually used in rough editing because of its superior speed, but it does not allow more complex edits, such as audio overlaps. *See also* **insert edit**.

assembly language   A computer language in which each line the programmer writes translates into one computer instruction, thereby giving absolute control over the computer. This therefore makes assembly the most powerful and fastest language. However, it is a very difficult language in which to write programs.

asynchronous   A video signal that is not locked to the rest of the system; e.g., a satellite feed coming into a studio is not synchronized to the rest of the equipment in the studio, such as cameras. A frame-synchronizer is used to synchronize the incoming feed with the studio. Asynchronous signals are stand-alone and cannot be mixed or superimposed onto other signals. Also used to describe digital circuits that do not include or use a clock pulse. *See also* **synchronizer**.

ATR   Audio tape recorder. Machine used for recording and playback of audio signals. Most common are ¼" tape machines. Wider tapes are used for multitrack machines. Today most audio recording equipment is based on cassettes, either analog or digital, and disk recording.

ATSC   Advanced Television Systems Committee. An American committee that develops standards for high-definition television (future standards). *See also* **HDTV**.

attack   In audio instruments, the time taken to respond to an incoming signal. For example, in an audio compressor the attack time is the time taken until the device responds to a high input signal and starts to attenuate.

attenuation pad *see* **pad**

attenuator   A circuit or component that reduces level of a given signal. Used mainly for audio signals. Attenuators are used in order to avoid damage to sensitive equipment. A good attenuator should consist of resistive load only to avoid distortion and changes in frequency response. Usually measured in dB. *See also* **dB**.

audio   (A) An electronic signal that carries sound information by translating the air vibrations into corresponding voltage changes. (B) The theory and practice of recording, editing and playing sound signals. Used in radio, television, cinema, public address and home entertainment. Radio was the first instrument made to carry high fidelity sound over long distances. Most of the audio equipment was originally developed for use in radio recordings and broadcasting. The next stage in audio equipment was the development of home entertainment devices such as record players and tape recorders. In TV, audio has a significant role. Sound waves are picked up at the scene by microphones, processed and mixed by complex equip-

ment and transmitted along with video information to the home TV set. Making a good audio recording or transmission is a complex job that requires the proper equipment and expertise.

audio amplifier   Amplifier specially built to amplify audio signals. Professional amplifiers are normally divided into distribution amplifiers, preamplifiers and power amplifiers. Most amplifiers are dual channel or stereo. Distribution amplifiers have unity gain and multiple outputs to feed various devices (typically four to ten outputs). Preamplifiers are used to raise microphone signal levels of several millivolts to line level (1 volt). Power amplifiers are used to drive audio monitors from a line level feed. The power provided starts at approximately 30 watts per channel, up to hundreds of watts per channel.

At the consumer level, amplifiers are normally part of a home stereo system, including both the preamplifier and power sections. Inputs are provided for the different audio instruments such as CD, tuner, tape machines, TV input and an auxiliary input. Switching between the inputs is built into the amplifier. Power output of consumer amplifiers ranges usually between 20 and 150 watts per channel. Sometimes the amplifier is part of a larger system.

audio console   A device used to mix, filter and control a large number of audio sources. An audio console has a large number of audio inputs, ranging usually from 8 to 256. For every input there is a channel that has many functions, such as input attenuation or amplification, filtering, assignment to groups, panning to left and right and a fader that controls the output from the channel. The output from all the channels can be mixed to the left and right outputs or to groups. Audio consoles are used to mix and control the signals from a large number of microphones, tapes, CDs, remote feeds and VCRs. The audio console is used in sound studios, TV studios and for public address in concerts.

audio follow video   The ability of a mixer to switch audio and video together at the same stroke of a button. Used mainly in master control rooms of cable and TV stations to switch video sources with the corresponding audio. Audio follow video is also found in routing switchers.

audio jack   A connector commonly used in audio facilities. It connects three wires for balanced signals.

audio mixer   A device used to mix a number of audio sources into one output signal. Small mixers are used in field recordings of news, documentaries and commercials (three to eight inputs). Small mixers have one output for mono sound and others have left and right outputs for stereo. Stereo mixers also have the ability to send each input to both outputs by means of a "panning" button. Bigger mixers are referred to as "audio consoles." *See also* **audio console**.

audio monitor   A loudspeaker or loudspeaker system used to listen to audio signals in control rooms, audio recording studios and TV studios. Professional audio monitors must be of good quality and deliver the full bandwidth of the audio in order to reflect the quality of the audio signal monitored. The same applies to the amplifier driving the loudspeaker.

audio track   Part of a magnetic tape or film devoted to sound. In film and video tape, one or more tracks of sound are used beside the larger part containing the picture. Location and width of sound tracks are precisely defined for each film or tape format. Some common videotape formats such as Betacam have four sound tracks. In less professional equipment, two sound tracks are usually used for stereo sound.

auto assembly   Automatic editing of video and audio material by an edit controller in an edit facility. Editing is performed according to an EDL (Editing List) put together in a simpler editing room. *See also* **AB-ROLL; off-line editing; on-line editing**.

automatic changeover   An arrangement used to switch between sources of signal or power automatically, in case of signal loss or power failure. Automatic changeover is faster than human response and also used in remote or unattended locations such as transmitter and switching sites.

auto transition   In video mixers a function that enables the operator to do a transition such as a wipe, dissolve or fade by one keystroke. The length of the transition is determined in advance, in frames. Auto transition ensures smooth transition, independent of the hand movement of the operator.

auxiliary bus   A row of buttons used to switch video or audio sources (or both). Usually part of a video switcher and can be located on the main control panel or separately. Used to switch sources into devices such as effects, keyers' monitors and much more.

auxiliary send (AUX) In audio consoles, a function that enables inputs to be sent into one or more auxiliary outputs. On every input module there is a button for each AUX output. The AUX outputs are used to send groups of sources to devices such as earphones, public address monitors and recording equipment. *See also* **audio console**.

axis **(A)** A set of imaginary lines used in digital effects to determine the location and movement in three-dimensional space. The x-axis is a horizontal line across the screen. The y-axis is a vertical line. The z-axis is a line going into the depth of the screen, usually representing the size of a frame. **(B)** In optical equipment, the line on which one can find the center of a lens or set of lenses or other optical devices and also the center of the focal plane.

Az/El mount Azimuth Elevation mount. A mount used for satellite dish antennas to allow controlled manual or electric movement in horizontal (azimuth) and vertical (elevation) directions.

azimuth In magnetic tape recorders, the angle of the recording or playback head gap in relation to the tape movement direction.

baby A small spotlight with power rating usually between 500 and 1,000 watts.

baby legs *see* **baby tripod**

baby tripod A tripod with short legs for low-angle camera shots.

back focus A basic adjustment of a TV lens. In this adjustment the focal plane is moved in order to get the sharpest image possible. This adjustment is used only after replacing a lens or when using optical attachments to the lens that change focus, such as a wide-angle attachment.

background generator A circuit used mainly in video switchers to generate a unicolor video output. The brightness, saturation and hue can be adjusted to get any desired color. Some advanced background generators are able to produce more sophisticated backgrounds, with colors changing continuously both in horizontal and vertical. The product of the background generator is called a "matte." This signal is used to color characters, backgrounds and different areas in the picture created by some other sources. Background generators usually work in conjunction with key circuits. *See also* **key; matte; video switcher**

backlight A light beam used to separate a person's or object's image from the background. The light is aimed at the person's head and shoulders from the upper back. Backlight is one of the three major lighting directions used in TV and cinema. *See also* **fill light; key light.**

back porch The part of a video signal between horizontal synchronization pulse and the beginning of active video. The color burst is found on the back porch.

back projection Projection of an image from a cinema, slide or video projector onto the rear of a screen. Back projection is used to avoid obstruction of the beam of light by the viewers or to hide the presence of a projector. A special semitransparent screen is used for back projection. Some of the light is absorbed by the screen when passing through and therefore this kind of projection is less efficient in term of contrast and brightness. Back projection is also used in large-screen TV sets that use a video projector instead of a picture tube (CRT).

backspace edit A system of editing used in portable VCRs. A clean edit is made whenever recording is stopped and later continued from the same position on the tape. The VCR goes backward for pre-roll and playing and goes into recording at the frame where the stop button had been pressed. The result is a quick but imprecise edit. See also **editing.**

back timing Timing of a program or scene when the required length is known in advance; the counting goes backward from the full length to zero. This way the momentary time count is always the time left to the end of the time period or slot planned. The floor manager can tell the talent how much time is left to the end of the program, which is helpful to finish live transmissions on time. Special studio timers are normally used with the capability to be preset to a certain time and count back to zero.

backup copy A copy of film, audio or videotape made and kept safe. The backup copy is used in case of loss or damage to the original.

backup supply A second power supply used to enhance the reliability of a given system. Power supplies are

crucial to the system, but are subject to failure more than other circuits. Usually the backup supply is operated automatically if a malfunction of the main supply occurs.

balance (a) In audio, adjusting the relative levels of different audio channels of musical instruments, performers or other sources in a mixing console to get a mix that will sound natural. Balance is normally done prior to recording or transmission of a program or before and during rehearsals. (b) In video, a quality of pleasant composition. (c) To adjust the center of gravity in a camera mounted on a camera head to allow easy tilt up and down.

balanced (a) In an audio system, having three-conductor wiring, two for the signal and a separate one for the ground. This system is used for small signals, where interference and noise must be kept very low, such as microphone lines. Most professional audio equipment uses balanced wiring. (b) The state of a camera after a mechanical adjustment is made to the camera head so that the center of gravity will be exactly above the tilt axis. This will make it easy to tilt the camera up and down during shooting with little effort and added stability.

ballistics In audio, the ability of a meter needle to move exactly according to the momentary level of the audio signal under measurement. Some meters are designed to respond to signal peaks (PPMs) and others to a mean value of sound (VU meters). See also **PPM, VU meter.**

band pass filter A device that allows only a narrow part of the spectrum to pass through. There are optical filters that allow only a certain frequency (or color) of light to pass and there are electronic circuits that allow only a certain frequency or band of frequencies to pass through.

bandwidth   A range of frequencies limited by a device. The bandwidth of a device is the range of frequencies it is able to handle. When used outside this range, attenuation will occur. Bandwidth is specified by the highest and the lowest frequencies in which attenuation is less than 3 dB and measured in Hz. The bandwidth of a system is determined by the device with the narrowest bandwidth. The wider the bandwidth, the more information can be handled and the more expensive the device will be. The bandwidth of sound waves that a human ear can perceive is between 20 and 20,000 Hz. The bandwidth of a PAL video signal is between 50 Hz and 5.5 MHz. Many instruments lose bandwidth due to degradation in performance of components, causing loss of information. In a TV set, smaller bandwidth in video circuits will result in less detail in the picture.

bargraph   A kind of display usually used to show audio levels by displaying a vertical bar the height of which is proportional to the strength of the signal.

barn doors   Metal flaps used to limit and shape the light flow from a lamp or a studio light. Barn doors come in many shapes, the most common being trapezoid-shaped flaps surrounding the light output.

barrel   An aberration in a lens or picture tube that makes parallel lines

in the frame appear to move away from the center. This effect creates a shape similar to the curved appearance of a barrel. *See also* **aberration.**

base   Plastic film coated with an oxide or a metal particle layer to create a magnetic tape.

base band   An electronic signal before it has been modulated. Usually used in reference to a device that has both modulated and unmodulated signals (such as transmitters and receivers).

baseline   distortion   Low-frequency changes in the DC level of a video signal.

base station   The part of a distributed system containing the static, heavier parts of the system. In a studio camera chain the base station contains power supplies, amplifiers and control boards. The base station is connected by cable to the camera head. All the connections for power, video, intercom and control are connected to the base station. *See also* **camera (video).**

basic tracks   In audio multitrack work, the first tracks to be recorded, normally the rhythm section.

bass reflex enclosure   An audio monitor with an opening in the front for low-frequency sound waves reflected from the inside of the loudspeaker housing.

battery   A device providing electrical power. It consists of a chemical cell or cells, made usually from metal electrodes inside a solution. Batteries produce only DC (direct current).

Some batteries are rechargeable. The battery power is measured by the voltage it provides and the amount of power that can be drawn from the battery, measured in amperes per hour (Ah). Batteries come in all sizes, from a truck battery providing 500 Ah in 24 V to a watch battery providing less than 1 mAh in 1.2 V.

battery belt   A wide belt worn around the waist into which batteries are built. This belt is used to power different devices in the field, such as cameras, lighting and recorders. This way more batteries are conveniently carried hands-free and the weight is distributed in a healthier way.

battery charger   An electrical power supply fed from mains, used to recharge batteries. Some units charge one battery at a time and others can charge four or six batteries at the same time. The more advanced units sense when the battery is fully charged and then cut off the power to prevent overheating of the battery, which causes long-term damage.

battery pack   Several battery cells, usually rechargeable, packed together to form a unit for powering portable cameras, recorders, monitors and other portable equipment. Sometimes battery packs are built into a specially made belt. *See also* **battery belt.**

baud rate   The speed at which information is transferred from one digital device to another. Baud rate is measured in bits per second. Higher baud rate means faster communication, but it is limited by the bandwidth of the line and speed of the components on both ends. Data compression enables moving more data under the same baud rate.

beam   A ray of light or electrons. A beam has a certain diameter, direction and speed. A beam can be focused, reflected, deflected, split and absorbed. In a picture tube (CRT), a focused electron beam is being sent from an electron gun to the screen, where it hits a fluorescent coating that produces light. The beam is deflected to scan the entire screen area.

beam splitter   An optical device used to divide the light coming through the lens into three basic colors (RGB). Used in professional color TV cameras. These cameras use a separate light-sensitive device for each color. A beam splitter consists of two dichroic-coated prisms.

best boy   First assistant to the electrician in film and TV production.

Betacam SP   A Sony registered name for a format of component videocassette recorders using ½" tape. This format includes a large variety of machines for playing, recording and editing. Betacam SP is a successful and widely used format due its professional quality and to the fact that it has the complete range of equipment, from sophisticated editing machines to lightweight field recorders. There are two types of cassettes in Betacam format: small (up to 30 minutes) and large (up to 90 minutes), both having four audio channels. Portable recorders use only the small cassettes.

Betamax   A format for home, nonprofessional videocassette recorders used during the 1980s. The Betamax cassette housing is the same as today's small Betacam cassette.

B-Format A professional standard for videotape machines that used 1-inch tapes. B-Format was used in the 1980s in limited numbers, mainly in Germany and Austria. This standard was resistant to vibrations due to its small head wheel diameter. Unlike other formats such as C-Format, every turn of the head scanned a small number of lines and not a full field. This made it very difficult to do freeze frames and slow-motion, but picture and audio quality was very good. B-Format was in use at the same time as C-Format, but sold in much smaller numbers.

BG Background.

bi-amplification A process in which two amplifiers are used to amplify two separate parts of the audio bandwidth.

bias A magnetic field applied to a recording head separate from the field created by the audio or video signal to improve the nonlinear characteristics of magnetic coating on tapes. Bias may be applied as a steady-state DC current or as high-frequency AC.

bias light A small lightbulb inserted into a video camera pickup tube to improve the linearity of the output signal and the camera performance in dark scenes.

bias oscillator In audio recording equipment, an oscillator producing the bias current. *See also* **bias; bias trap.**

bias trap In audio recording equipment, a filter used to remove bias frequency from the playback signal coming from the playback head. *See also* **bias.**

bi-directional (mike) A microphone sensitive to sound coming from two directions, the front and the back. This kind of microphone is useful in radio studios where people are located on two sides of the table with the microphone between.

big mac Large fresnel spotlight, usually with 10 KW of power.

binary Mathematical representation of numbers in base 2 as opposed to the base 10 we normally use. The binary system was invented and put to practical use in order to simplify calculations on machines such as computers and calculators. All data in the computer are stored in binary and all programs are presented to the computer and executed in binary form. Representation in binary form requires a larger number of digits than the base 10 (decimal) numbers. For example: the number 12 in binary is 1100.

binaural jack Audio jack used for connection of binaural earphones (each ear gets to hear one audio channel).

binaural sound Sound recorded on two separate tracks, each intended for one ear.

binder Material that binds oxide or metal particles onto plastic tape to form magnetic tape. Magnetic tape binder has to be stable for many years and has to be resistant to wear due to contact with heads and other mechanical parts.

bipolar An electric current or voltage that has positive and negative amplitudes.

bird's-eye view Camera shot taken from a point high above, from a place such as a crane, tower, helicopter and so on.

bit The basic information unit used by a computer. A bit can have either the value of 1 or the value of 0 (sometimes called "on" and "off"). Two bits represent four levels of combinations, three bits eight levels, eight bits 256 levels. All data in every binary system consists of sets of bits. *See also* **binary; byte.**

black A composite video signal that contains horizontal and vertical synchronizing pulses and bursts for color reference. It contains color information that causes the screen of a TV set or monitor to be black. Most programs and commercials start and finish with black. Black is used as a background and for recording on tapes prior to insert editing. It is also used as a reference signal fed to many kinds of video devices so that they can lock to it. Black (color black) is distributed in video facilities such as studios and TV stations to cameras, VCRs and frame synchronizers to lock and time all of them together.

black balance Alignment of the red, green and blue channels of a video camera so that when no light is coming into the camera (cap is closed), the video picture will be black, with no additional colors. If the black balance is not correctly adjusted, dark areas in the picture might have all kinds of colors instead of black. This adjustment is usually done on a daily basis or before starting to shoot, together with white balance. *See also* **white balance.**

black burst *see* **black**

black level The level of 0.3 volts from the sync tip in a standard video signal is referred to as the black level. Picture information that will be in this level will appear black on a TV set or picture monitor.

blanking A signal used to create blanked areas in a video signal. This signal is standard and usually supplied by a sync generator. Blanking is needed to turn down the scanning beam—that is, the "fly back" period, when the beam has finished scanning one line (horizontal) or field (vertical) and starts to go back quickly to scan the next one. At the blanking intervals, the beam intensity is brought down so that it will not be visible on the screen. The exact length of blanking intervals is defined by the different transmission standards, such as NTSC.

blimp Housing used to silence equipment noise on the set. A special kind of housing is used for every kind of equipment. Film cameras and power generators are usually blimped.

blooming A distortion of the picture on a video monitor or TV set causing excessive white areas to defocus and "swell."

blowup (a) Enlargement of film in the lab to larger format, such as from 16 to 35 mm. This process decreases quality, but allows projection on 35 mm projectors. (b) Large prints of still pictures used in TV as part of scenery.

blue One of the three primary additive colors (RGB) used in TV to produce all other hues.

Blumlein pair A pair of microphones mounted for stereophonic pickup.

blur Disfigurement and defocus of film or video image due to a swift movement of the camera or the object being shot.

B-MAC A broadcasting system based on MAC, using two digital channels for stereo audio. *See also* **MAC.**

BNC A connector commonly used for video coax cables and other high-frequency signals. BNC is a bayonet-type connector, with a center lead and a housing connected to the screen of the coax cable.

board (a) Printed circuit board. An electronic circuit mounted on a partinax board, with copper printed leads and components soldered to it. Most components of electronic equipment are mounted on boards. (b) Control panel of equipment in a control room.

body brace An arrangement for operating a portable camera, attached to the operator's shoulder and waist. Helps to distribute the camera weight and adds stability. *See also* **shoulder pad; Steadicam.**

boom A long pole, hand-held or mounted on a special construction, used to hold a microphone above the studio or outside location. Booms are used to pick up sound where there is a lot of movement on scene and sta-tionary microphones cannot be used. The boom operator is able to follow the actor's movement and get clean sound. Booms present problems on the set because sometimes they show in the long shots and they make it difficult for the lighting director to avoid the shadows they cast. Today, with the improvement of light and wireless microphones, booms are used less.

booster (a) An electrical device that increases utility system voltage for use with specific lighting equipment, usually for outside work. (b) An arc light used usually in daylight to fill shadows.

boot In a computer, an operation that starts the operating system from the very beginning, as if the power has just been switched on. There are two kinds of boot. In a "warm boot," the operation is done by striking certain keys on the keyboard and is performed by software. A "warm boot" does not erase computer memory and is therefore ineffective in certain cases. In a "cold boot," a reset button is pressed that resets the computer CPU and memory. Sometimes booting is the only way to continue work if the computer has frozen.

bounce (light) Light is bounced (reflected) for one of the following purposes: (a) to soften the light by using a rough surface as a reflector. (b) to change color temperature of the light by using a colored surface. (c) to use sunlight in outside locations by bouncing it onto the scene.

bouncing tracks In audio multi-track recording, a method in which two or more audio tracks are mixed and the result is recorded on another track on the same tape. This process can be repeated several times. This way synchronization between tracks is always accurate. The channels already mixed can be reused.

bow Distortion of a video picture in which straight lines bend in horizontal or vertical directions. Bow distortion can occur in tube video cameras, and circuits are placed to correct it. It also occurs in TV sets and picture monitors and is corrected by the use of magnets and coils, creating a magnetic field that changes the deflection of the electron beam to minimize this distortion.

bow tie A test signal, shaped like a bow tie, used in component analog video systems for measurement of component channel gain and delay inequalities.

brace A support, usually wooden, to keep scenery erect.

break (a) Station break: a suspension in a radio or TV program for station identification or notice. (b) Commercial break: a pause in a program for a group of commercials. (c) A pause in a recording session or rehearsal.

breakdown (a) An analysis of a script to list all necessary personnel, equipment and locations needed for shooting each scene in the script. Breakdown is used for planning the work process, facilities and funds needed. (b) A detailed schedule for shooting a film or TV program, including all necessary personnel and equipment.

breathing (a) In audio recordings, periodical changes in background noise level. In severe cases, it may become noticeable. (b) In videotape recordings, periodical changes in RF level. It may sometimes cause picture distortion. (c) Any unwanted, periodic or slow change in audio or video parameters.

bridge An audio or video segment used to soften or fill the transition between scenes or programs.

bridging connection Connection of an audio, video or data signal over an existing connection, usually for measurement or distribution purposes. The bridging is normally high impedance not to load or change the signal in any way.

brilliance In audio, a quality of sound that is clear and distinct.

broad (light) A large floodlight used in film and TV studios for widespread, unfocused light.

broadcasting (a) Transmission of radio or TV programs on the airwaves to a wide audience. The broadcast is open to anyone with a receiver; normally the broadcaster has no control over the audience that listens to or views his programs, unless they are encrypted or sent over cable to subscribers. (b) A comprehensive name for all aspects of radio and TV programs and facilities, including ownership, production, transmission and sales.

broadcast journalism Radio and television journalism, as opposed to newspaper journalism. Characterized by live coverage of events from the field.

broadcast quality (a) A grade of audio and video signals and recordings that conforms to broadcast standards and regulations. (b) Quality of equipment used in radio and TV production, postproduction, transmission and reception. Usually the highest end of equipment quality above industrial and consumer levels.

broadcast spectrum The frequency range designated for radio or TV transmission.

brute Old kind of carbon arc lamp with high-power light output. Used in feature films. Today more efficient lighting is in use.

bucket Name for studio floodlight.

buffer (a) A digital device capable of storing and regulating the flow of data. For example, if a buffer is connected between device A and device B and device A is sending data faster than device B can handle, the buffer will store parts of the data until B is ready for it, then release it. (b) A protective sleeve or coating used to guard optical fibers carrying information.

bug A software malfunction caused by a human error that occurred when the software was written. The higher the quality of a software, the fewer bugs it will usually have. New software usually has some bugs. Considerable test and usage are needed to detect all bugs in a software.

bulk eraser A device using a strong magnetic field to erase magnetic tapes, consisting of a large coil connected to utility system voltage and sometimes also a mechanism to move the tape through the magnetic field. Tapes are erased (degaussed) in a matter of seconds.

bumper Short transition between a program and commercials in radio and TV. In some countries bumpers are obligatory to avoid a situation where commercials can be mistaken for part of a program.

burn A defect in camera picture pickup tubes, caused by pointing the camera at a strong light source or a stationary scene for a long time. After several hours of work, depending on the amount of burn, the tube returns to normal. Sometimes permanent damage is caused. A similar defect occurs in computer screens showing the same image for a long time. In computer screens, however, the burn damage is irreparable. To avoid this, screen savers (programs that pop up when the computer is not in use for some time and show a moving display) were developed.

burn-in In video camera tubes, damage caused by intensive light. Bright objects or light sources the camera has been focused on for a long time will cause dark areas in the camera picture. Sometimes the damage is permanent. Almost nonexistent in modern CCD video cameras.

burnt-in time code Time code superimposed on a video picture. Time code becomes part of the picture information of the video signal and cannot be removed. Burnt-in time code is used for work copies of raw material or for off-line editing. The apparatus making the superimposition is called "time code inserter."

burst Seven to nine cycles (NTSC) of a sine wave located at the beginning of every active TV line. It is used as a reference for the color information of that line. The phase difference between every part of the picture information and the burst determines which color it will have on the screen. Burst amplitude is 0.3 volts and is in subcarrier frequency (approximately 3.58 MHz in NTSC). If there are no bursts in the video signal at the beginning of each line, the picture will be in monochrome.

burst flag (BF) A pulse coming out of a standard TV pulse generator used to determine the exact position of the bursts in the video signal.

burst gate Same as burst flag.

bus A group of wires or conductors inside a computer that carries parallel digital information such as data or addresses. The number of conductors in a bus matches the number of bits— usually multiples of eight (8, 16, 24, 32, 64).

butt splice Joining together two film or tape pieces. There is no overlap in material. The film is cut between frames and joined together by adhesive tape.

buzz track A sound track of background sound or room-tone. Used when mixing sound tracks as background and fill sound.

BW *see* **bandwidth**

B – Y One of the three color difference signals in component video. A subtraction of Y (luminance) from B

(Blue channel). *See also* **color difference signal; component video.**

bypass An operation in which an electrical apparatus is taken out of use in a larger system without interrupting the flow of signals or current. Usually a relay is used to switch the input signal directly to the output through an alternative route, manually or automatically. This is done in case of failure of the normal operation of the apparatus or for maintenance purposes.

byte A group of eight bits that together make a binary number. A byte can consist of a number ranging from 0 to 255. Memory arrays are built to store data arranged in bytes and computer data is processed in bytes. When large amounts of data are involved, size is measured as shown:

Kilobyte (KB)	=	1,024 bytes
Megabyte (MB)	=	1,048,576 bytes
Gigabyte (GB)	=	1073,741,824 bytes
Terabyte (TB)	=	1,099,511,627,776 bytes

See also **bit.**

cable A number of conductors usually made of copper, isolated from each other and grouped together, used to carry electrical power or signals. There are countless types of cables according to the task. Cables differ in the number and width of conductors, length and kind of end connectors.

cable equalization Compensation done by an amplifier for changes in frequency response caused by a cable. The longer the cable, the more compensation is needed.

cable television A television system distributing TV channels to consumers by a cable network. Cable television makes it easy to distribute a large number of channels. Every consumer has to be connected individually to the cable network. Cable networks are common in large cites and connection is done by subscribing. Cable television can offer advanced services such as two-way communications and video on demand. The difficulties presented by a crowded spectrum of TV channels transmitted on air in dense residential areas are solved by cable television. On the other hand, building the cable network is expensive and subscribers have to pay monthly for this service.

cache *see* **digital cache**

calibration **(a)** Adjustment of equipment or an apparatus to achieve better performance according to set standards or manufacturer's recommendations. Calibration can be performed for electrical, mechanical or optical performance. Most analog TV equipment needs periodical calibration as part of maintenance. Digital equipment needs very little calibration, if at all. **(b)** Scales or markings found in mechanical, electrical and optical equipment such as f-numbers on lenses or a dB scale on a mixing console's fader.

call letters Initials used for identification of broadcast stations or networks such as BBC, CBC and CNN given by communications authorities.

camcorder A combination of a video camera and a videocassette recorder in one unit with the same housing. This combination eliminates the connecting cables between the two units, making it simpler to operate. The number of members in a camera

crew can be reduced by one. This innovation was possible because of reduction in equipment size and weight.

camera (video) A device that captures images and translates them into an electronic signal. The video camera is the most fundamental piece of equipment in the television industry. There are many kinds of TV cameras, ranging from small, hand-held amateur cameras to large and sophisticated professional studio cameras. The price ranges accordingly—from several dozens of dollars to over $100,000 per camera. The performance of a camera is measured by: **(a)** The fidelity of the output picture to the various shades and colors of the scene under varying light conditions. **(b)** The amount of detail in the picture (resolution).

The requirements from professional cameras are high because of the large number of viewers watching the product of the camera. Another reason is the fact that the signal's quality deteriorates during processing and transmission and therefore only the highest quality signals can produce good quality at the end of the path. This need of such high quality makes professional cameras very complex and expensive, both to purchase and maintain.

In the early days of television, cameras were only black and white. Only in the late 1950s did cameras with full color come into use.

Every camera has a lens. The lens gathers light coming from the object and produces an image. The camera converts the image into an electronic signal by means of light-sensitive devices. At first the light-sensitive devices consisted of bulky vacuum tubes such as the Image-Orthicon. Over the years the imaging devices became smaller and better, such as the family of Plumbicon tubes. These days most video cameras employ CCD devices instead of tubes. CCDs are smaller, lighter and require less current. They are also less sensitive to vibration and excessive light and have a very long life.

The different devices scan the image line by line and convert the brightness of every dot in the picture (pixel) into a corresponding electric current. This current is amplified and processed into the form of a standard video signal. In black and white cameras, only one light-sensitive device is needed. In order to reproduce full color, one must use three such devices, one for each primary color (red, green and blue, or RGB). In color cameras the light coming from the lens is separated into the three primary colors by an optical device called a beam splitter. The three signals from the light-sensitive devices can be processed into one signal (composite) by means of an encoder circuit. In some systems the three color signals are handled separately (component).

Professional television cameras are produced in two sizes: portable, hand-held cameras and large studio cameras. Portable cameras weigh usually up to 20 pounds, while studio cameras weigh much more. A small black and white picture monitor called a viewfinder is attached to the camera showing the output picture; it is used to aim and handle the camera accordingly. Every kind of camera has an appropriate support system such as a lightweight tripod or a studio pedestal.

Studio cameras are divided into subsystems located in different places in the studio: the camera head with the lens is located in the studio on the mount. The camera head is connected by cable to a base station, which consists of the power supplies and some additional circuits and is located in a nearby engineering room. The base station is connected to the outside world and has video outputs, reference inputs for genlock purposes and connections for intercom and tally light. Another subsystem is a control panel connected to the base station used to control the different parameters of the camera: iris opening (contrast), black level (brightness), color balance, gamma settings and more.

Most studios and OB trucks have a number of cameras—usually 3 to 5, and sometimes up to 12. The parameters of all cameras in the same location are controlled together by one person to maintain uniformity in the color balance and other picture qualities. In modern cameras there are specialized computers to aid the vision control (camera control unit—CCU) operator to change parameters for all cameras at the same time. Camera control is a specialized job that requires knowledge and experience.

Most hand-held cameras can be connected to a base station in a studio configuration. Usually one hand-held camera is kept in the studio for shooting angles the studio cameras cannot get to, such as very low angles from the floor or lying on one side. *See also* **beam splitter; camera mount; camera sensitivity; encoder; gamma; knee function; lens; pixel.**

camera car   A vehicle used for taking moving shots. Usually several camera mounts are installed.

camera card   Cards containing the shooting list used by studio camerapersons. The card is attached to the camera so that the cameraperson can see it while operating the camera. Each card contains the number of the shot and the description of each one of them, such as "Steve extreme close-up" or "long shot."

camera chain A complete camera system that includes all subsystems: camera head and lens, base station, control panels and connecting cables.

camera control unit (CCU) (a) The equipment used to control the different functions and parameters of the camera. **(b)** The job of person or engineer controlling the cameras. *See also* **camera (video).**

camera coverage *see* **field of view**

camera crane *see* **crane**

camera crew A crew that operates the camera in outside production. The number of crew members differs according to the task but usually includes a director, camera operator, soundman and assistant camera operator. Sometimes additional crew members are added, such as electricians, gaffers and makeup artists.

camera head The part of a camera that contains the most vital parts: the lens, beam splitter, imaging devices, power supply and corresponding circuits. In portable cameras, usually the entire system is included in the camera head. In studio cameras, the system is split into subsystems. *See also* **camera (video).**

camera helmet Video camera mounted on a helmet for use mostly in sports and sometimes in news. The camera is small and light in weight, usually also remote-controlled and equipped with a transmitter that sends the video signal back to a control center. In sports events, such cameras are used to give the viewpoint of the performer, such as a motorcycle racer or parachutist.

camera light Small spotlight mounted on top of hand-held or studio cameras. Such a light is used to eliminate shadows from people's faces in front of the camera, especially around the eyes, and thus it is also called an "eye light." Camera lights are sometimes used in the studio, but more frequently in news.

cameraman/woman *see* **camera operator**

camera mount Any of various devices used to support the camera and enable the camera to perform the basic movements. Usually consists of a base and a pan and tilt head. The common devices are: **(a)** Tripod: consists of three legs connected together, usually foldable and lightweight. **(b)** Pedestal: a support system equipped with rubber wheels and a column enabling the camera to move up and down. The operator can move the camera on the studio floor in all directions. **(c)** Dolly: similar to a pedestal but moves on special track, similar to a small train track. **(d)** Crane: a long arm that can take the camera high above floor level and can also move freely above the studio set and audience.

Camera mounts are built to support the weight of the camera and allow smooth movement with as little vibration possible. The camera weight is balanced so that a little effort is needed to move the camera. *See also* **crane; dolly; pan and tilt head; pedestal; tripod.**

camera movement   There are several basic camera movements used in television work. All of them have to be performed in a smooth and continuous way: **(a)** Pan: a horizontal movement, right to left or left to right. **(b)** Tilt: a vertical movement, up and down, around an axis under the camera center of gravity in the tilt head. **(c)** Pedestal up and down: a vertical movement; the camera and tilt head are carried up and down by the pedestal column. **(d)** Dolly in/out: movement of the camera and pedestal toward the object or away from it. **(e)** Track: movement of the camera and pedestal or dolly from left to right or from right to left while the camera is aimed in the same direction. **(f)** Tongue: a crane movement from left to right or right to left. **(g)** Crane: movement of the crane arm including the camera up and down.

Two or more camera moves can be combined during shooting to form more complex and interesting camera work. *See also* **camera mount; pan and tilt head.**

camera obscura   Literally, "dark chamber." A darkened room or box with one small opening. The light coming from outside forms an upside-down image on the wall opposite the opening. The larger the opening, the brighter and less focused the image will be. A converging lens placed in the opening will enhance both brightness and focus. If photographic film or paper is placed where the image is formed, the image can be captured. The history of the camera obscura dates back to the eleventh century. The camera obscura is the ancestor of the modern still camera.

camera operator   Cameraman/woman. The person operating the camera, a job that requires artistic and technical skills. The camera operator aims the camera at the object, sets the framing, adjusts the focus and zoom and performs different and sometimes complex camera movements. In single-camera work when there is no CCU, the camera operator is also responsible for adjustment of iris, white and black balance, use of filters and additional adjustments. When a camcorder is used, the camera operator also operates the recorder. Often in ENG work the camera operator is the one to set up the lighting. *See also* **black balance; camcorder; camera movement; camera control unit (CCU); ENG; white balance; zoom in; zoom out.**

camera rehearsal   A rehearsal of a program to be taped or transmitted, including full cast and all camera shots and movements; also to check lighting, sound, props and costumes.

camera sensitivity   The amount of light needed by the camera to produce a specific video signal level. Sensitivity is one of the camera's most important attributes. There is no single way to specify a camera's sensitivity. A common way to measure broadcast-quality camera sensitivity is under the following conditions:
—The camera video gain is set to 0 dB.
—Gamma and knee function circuits are switched off.
—A 60% reflective white card is put in front of the camera and illumi-

nated with 1,500 lux of 3,200 °K white light.

—The lens iris is opened until a 1-volt video signal is obtained.

The iris position at this point indicates the sensitivity under these conditions. Normal sensitivity for modern studio CCD TV cameras is in the range of f4 to f8 at 1,500 lux.

camera speed In film cameras, the number of frames exposed per second. The standard speed for a cine camera is 24 pictures per second (PPS). Higher speeds are used to get slow-motion effects when projected at normal speed.

camera system *see* **camera chain**

camera tube A vacuum tube used as a pickup device to convert an optical image to a video signal. In a black and white camera there is one tube, but in color cameras three tubes are needed, one for each primary color—red, green and blue.

The first commercial camera pickup tube was the Iconoscope, developed by Zworkin and put to use in 1933 in the first electronic TV camera. The second generation was the line of Image-Orthicon tubes. They presented some improvements in resolution and sensitivity, but they were still very large and bulky and too big to put three of them to form a color camera in a housing of a practical size. The next generation was the large Plumbicon family of pickup tubes. Plumbicons are still used today and come in four different diameters—½", ⅔", 1" and 1-¼"—to fit all camera sizes. Plumbicons are capable of producing HDTV pictures (High Definition TV).

Camera tubes have a limited life usually not exceeding 5,000 working hours. Today there are many additional types of picture tubes for specialized needs. Most television cameras built today use CCDs instead of tubes.

cancellation When two identical or similar audio signals are mixed, if one of them is in reversed polarity, the result will be a strong attenuation. The same will happen to sound from a set of two stereo monitors; if one is reversed in polarity, cancellation will occur.

candela *see* **foot candle**

candid camera A name for scenes or programs taken with a hidden camera, where the objects of the camera are not aware of its existence.

candid shot A spontaneous camera shot, neither posed nor rehearsed.

cap (a) A cover used to guard a camera lens from dust, dirt and physical damage when it is not in use. (b) An internal metal flap used to block the light input to the camera to guard the optical system from excessive light. Also helps to guard the system from dust when not in use or when the lens is taken off.

capacitor An electrical device used in most electronic circuits. The capacitor can hold electrical energy. This ability is measured in micro-Farads or pico-Farads. The capacitor is one of the fundamental building blocks of electronic circuits. It is built from two parallel metal plates that do not touch each other. An insulating material is placed between the metal plates.

The bigger the plates, the bigger the capacitance. The capacitor allows the flow of alternating current and blocks direct current.

capacitor microphone *see* **condenser microphone**

capstan In magnetic audio or videotape recorders, the tape is held between the axis of an electric motor from one side and a rubber wheel from the other side. As the axis turns, it moves the tape at a constant speed inside the machine between the supply reel and the takeup reel, past the tape heads. The capstan is used only in play or record mode, when movement accuracy is required. During fast-forward or rewind, the rubber wheel moves away from the metal axis to enable fast movement of the tape. *See also* **reel.**

capstan idler *see* **pinch roller**

capsule The vital part of a microphone, which translates sound waves into small electric currents. The capsule is placed in shielding housing, sometimes together with a preamplifier and battery. *See also* **microphone.**

caption Lettering or titles added to a TV picture. Captions are usually created by an electronic character generator or, in the earlier days of television, by letters printed or drawn on paper put in front of the camera.

caption camera A camera dedicated to shooting captions. This kind of camera is usually installed on a special stand, above a surface on which the caption is placed. Most of the time a black and white camera is enough to

do the job; the coloring can be added later by the vision mixer.

cardioid A pickup pattern of a microphone shaped like a heart (upside down). This is a common unidirectional kind of microphone. A cardioid microphone is less sensitive to sound coming from the sides.

carrier to noise ratio (CNR) A measurement of noise used in RF (radio frequency). The noise is measured relative to peak carrier wave level and the ratio is expressed in dB. *See also* **signal to noise ratio (S/N, SNR).**

carrier wave An electromagnetic wave that is modulated by another wave. The carrier wave is transmitted while carrying the shape and information included in the modulating wave. Once the original information modulating the carrier is recovered at the receiving end by a demodulator, the carrier wave has finished its function. *See also* **modulation; demodulation.**

cart machine A machine that handles cartridges (shortened to carts) or cassettes automatically. The machine consists of a mechanical or robot arm that moves carts from a storage area to players and back, all inside the machine and under control of a management system that is usually computerized. The management system stores all the data relevant to the system, such as the play list, the inventory of the cassettes inside the machine and data regarding the material inside each cassette. The management system also controls the mechanical arm, the VCRs and a switcher that switches the relevant VCR signals to the output of the system. Every cart has a bar-code identification number. The mechanical arm identifies carts by means of a bar-code reader. The capacity of the storage is dependent on the length and capacity of items to be played. Using cart machines is the best way to handle transmission of large numbers of cassettes per hour and therefore is widely used for transmission of commercials in commercial television. A cart machine is an expensive system that includes many subsystems. Its cost and maintenance requirements are high, but it makes a frame-accurate transmission with reduced labor. Since the human factor is considerably reduced when transmitting from a cart machine, many faults are avoided.

cartridge　　Plastic case usually containing ¼" audiotape in a loop. Cartridges (carts) are used in radio and television stations to play back commercials or short pieces of audio. The cart is automatically rewound to the beginning to be ready for the next time it will be played.

cascade　　Arrangement of a number of circuits or components (usually identical) in which the output of one circuit is connected to the input of the next one. Cascades are used to multiply the effect of a single circuit.

cassette　　A housing holding magnetic tape. The cassette contains a supply reel, a take-up reel and the tape. The cassette guards the tape from dust, smoke, humidity and other physical damages. The invention of the cassette made it possible to load tape machines in one quick action by nonprofessional staff, without touching the sensitive magnetic tape and with-

out having to thread the tape through all the guides and wheels in the machine, as in tape machines.

cassette recorder　　A machine that uses cassettes for recording of audio or video, as opposed to a tape recorder that uses tape on open reels. Most equipment today uses cassettes rather than open reels. *See also* **cassette.**

cast　　All actors and performers in a film, radio or TV program, or recorded audio program.

casting　　The process of selecting actors or performers for the parts in a production. Auditioning is frequently used to select the cast from the available applicants for each role.

casting director　　Person in charge of casting for a film, program or series.

catchlights　　Reflections of strong light sources seen in the eyes of performers, usually of studio lights. Catchlights are highly visible in close-up shots.

cathode ray tube (CRT)　　Picture tube. A glass tube with a flat rectangular surface on one side. On the flat inside surface there is a luminescent layer. An electron gun on the other narrow side of the tube creates a fine electron beam that scans the luminescent surface. From every point where the beam hits the luminescent material, light is emitted and seen from the outside of the picture tube. The intensity of light is proportional to the intensity of the electron beam. In TV, the electron beam is deflected to scan the entire screen area line by line, frame by frame. Where a bright area should be, the electron beam intensity is increased, and in dark areas the intensity is lowered.

There are many kinds of CRTs; some display a black and white picture and others a full-color picture. The size of the picture area in the tube ranges from a one-inch diagonal to 33 inches. CRTs used in test and measurement devices such as oscilloscopes usually produce a green picture. The CRT is used to display pictures in TV receivers, video monitors, computer screens and oscilloscopes.

To produce color pictures, three electron guns and three kinds of luminescent material are used: red, green and blue. The correct blend of these three primary colors can produce every necessary color or hue.

The CRT is bulky, fragile, power consuming, expensive and needs a large array of supporting circuitry such as high-voltage generators and deflection circuits to produce the picture. Efforts are being made to replace it with a flat, more efficient and simple-to-operate display such as the LCD.

cathode ray tube projector   A video projector that uses three cathode ray tubes to produce a high-intensity video picture and project it with the aid of three lenses onto a screen.

CATV *see* **cable television.**

catwalk   Narrow platform high above studio or stage floor used for access and maintenance of air conditioning, electrical equipment, sound systems and lights. Access to the catwalk is by a ladder attached to the wall or a door from a higher floor.

CAV   **(a)** Constant angular velocity. Used in relation to video disks. The disk rotates at a constant speed. The outer tracks recorded on the disk are much longer than the inner tracks, but the speed is constant and so is the amount of data in each track (every track holds the data of one frame). The disadvantage is that a lot of capacity is wasted in the outer tracks. The advantage is that it is easy to play back a single frame (still frame). *See also* **CLV. (b)** Component analog video. An analog video format in which video is handled and distributed, divided into three signals: one for luminance (Y) and two for color difference (B – Y) and (R – Y). In this method, better picture quality than composite is obtained, but equipment, wiring and maintenance are more complicated and expensive.

CAV was an improvement on the composite video signal and was related to the introduction of the two major ½" videotape recording formats during the mid–1980s that used CAV. *See also* **luminance, B – Y, R – Y.**

C-band   A frequency band of 4GHz for satellite transmission used mainly in North America and in Russia.

CC   **(a)** Closed circuit. *See also* **CCTV. (b)** Closed captioned. A symbol for a TV program with subtitles that needs a special decoder to be displayed on-screen. Normally produced for the hearing-impaired, sometimes for multilingual translation. **(c)** Color correction.

CCD   Charged coupled device. A light-sensitive device that transforms light into voltage and stores samples of analog signals. In practice, CCDs convert the image coming from the lens into a video signal. CCD is the heart of modern video cameras. Advantages over picture tubes used in earlier cameras include longer life, higher sensitivity to light and absence of aberrations such as bow, linearity, trapeze burn and lag. CCDs also have no registration problems and they need no warm-up time, unlike tube cameras. CCD cameras are very stable in performance and need little adjustment. CCDs are also used in telecines as the light-sensitive device.

A CCD unit is built from tiny cells, each of which converts light to voltage. The higher the number of cells, the better the quality of picture it will produce. Broadcast cameras employ three CCD units, one for each primary color. Each of the CCD units has some 500,000 cells. Amateur video cameras employ a single CCD.

CCIR Comite Consultatif International Radiocommunications. A standards committee no longer active. Has been absorbed by the ITU, which is a United Nations body. Many standards set by the CCIR are still in use today worldwide.

CCIR 601 An international standard for component digital video signals. Also known as ITU-R BT.601-2, CCIR 601 defines a 4:2:2 sampling rate of 13.5 MHz and 720 samples per active line for luminance. Recommendation 601 defines both RGB and Y, B – Y and R – Y component digital systems in 525/60 (525 horizontal scan lines per field, 60 fields per second), as well as 625/50 systems and 8- or 10-bit digitizing. Eight-bit digitizing gives 16,777,216 different colors

defined by the Y, Cr, Cb digital color video signal. CCIR 601 is the high-end digital standard used today by the television industry for production and postproduction. *See also* **4:2:2; luminance; RGB; B – Y; R – Y.**

CCIR 656 Known also as ITU-R BT.656. Recommendation 656 defines parallel and serial connections for CCIR 601 signals, as well as electrical characteristics of the digital signals such as multiplexing methods, sync, blanking and connectors structure.

CCITT International Telegraph and Telephone Consultative Committee. European body that formerly set standards for the telephone industry. Replaced by the United Nations body, ITU (which also replaced other similar regulatory bodies). *See also* **ITU.**

C-clamp A metal clamp used in lighting to connect studio lamps to scenery, furniture and scaffolds. The clamp is shaped like the letter "C," hence the name.

CCTV Closed circuit television. Simple television systems in which signals are not transmitted to a large number of users, but sent by cable to a small number of picture monitors and VCRs. CCTV is used in educational and other institutions, hospitals and for security and surveillance. The level of equipment used is usually not broadcast, often black and white and therefore less expensive.

CD *see* **compact disk**

CD-ROM Compact disk read-only memory. A use of compact disk technology for storing and distributing digital data. Digital information is recorded on the disk as a series of microscopic dots. In the player a laser beam is used to read the information off the disk. Compact disks are highly durable and if treated properly can last for a lifetime, much longer than magnetic media. The standard 120 mm digital optical disk has a capacity of approximately 656 MB. Data transfer rate is 1.8 MB/s and is improved all the time. CD-ROM players are becoming a standard accessory for home and office computers. Software is often sold on a CD-ROM, rather than a series of floppy disks.

C-format   A standard for 1" video and audio open-reel tape recording. It was the industry standard for broadcast quality recording worldwide in the late 1970s and early 1980s. C-format 1" VTRs were manufactured by several major companies. This format came after the bulky 2" format and was a large step forward in reducing size and costs. Some C-format machines are capable of recording three-hour tapes, and there was a portable machine with 20 minutes of recording (no longer in use). A lot of archive video material is still on C-format, and 1" machines are still found in video facilities. This format was the last one of the open-reel video recording formats. Operating 1" machines was more complicated than today's format because of tape threading and adjustments that had to be done for every record or playback operation. After the C-format, different analog and digital cassette formats took over.

CG *see* **character generator; computer graphics**

CGI   Computer generated image.

channel (CH)   **(a)** A signal path within an instrument that handles more than one signal, such as an audio mixing console or a digital effects unit. **(b)** One of many equal parts in the television broadcast spectrum assigned to a specific TV station. A broadcast channel is wide enough to accommodate the full bandwidth of the modulated video and audio signals, which in NTSC is 6 MHz.

channel separation   The degree of separation between the left and right channels in a stereo audio device such as an amplifier, measured in dB. Separation is the absence of crosstalk. *See also* **crosstalk.**

character generator (CG)   A specialized computer or standard computer with some modifications, used to produce titles or subtitles for video and television in all sizes, shapes and colors. The characters in the titles usually have a border or shadow to separate them from the background. Titles can be moved in different standard ways, such as rolled up or down the screen and scrolled to the side. Character generators are used in studios and editing rooms and characters usually are superimposed on other video signals. CGs are capable of producing their own background, including some that produce background graphics. CGs are standard equipment in today's TV environment.

checkerboard assembly   Auto assembly of audio and video material in an editing facility, performed in the order in which the edits from one playback tape are edited and then edits from the next tape, not according to the order of the cuts in the edited tape.

This means that some parts will stay blank between edits, until material is taken from all playback tapes. This method saves tape loading and unloading time.

chest mike *see* **lavaliere mike**

chip Integrated circuit. A very small electronic circuit with many built-in components used as building block for larger, more complicated circuits.

chroma crawl *see* **cross-luminance**

chroma gain In an amplifier or other circuit handling video signals, the gain or amplification of chrominance. Chroma gain affects the saturation of the color of the picture produced on a TV set or monitor. Increased chroma gain in an amplifier will increase the chroma level of the signal handled by this amplifier. *See also* **chroma level.**

chroma key A method used in television to replace the background of a figure in a TV picture. This is done by a special circuit inside a video switcher or a separate unit. Areas of a particular color in the picture are replaced with picture information coming from another source (fill). For example, a news announcer is placed in front of a blue curtain or wall. The blue background is taken out by the chroma keyer and a picture of a particular scene replaces the visible background. The result is an illusion, as though the announcer is in front of the particular scene. Chroma-key effects can be operated with all colors as long as they are saturated enough for the chroma keyer to detect them. Blue gives the best results when separating the human skin tone from the background.

There are linear and nonlinear chroma key circuits. The early circuits were nonlinear and there was switching that sometimes did or did not change the background as desired. This method often caused problems in certain areas of the picture where the hue or the amount of saturation was not conclusive. Later came the improvement of linear key, which mixed the two picture signals in the border areas between the background and the fill.

chroma level The level of the subcarrier in composite video or the color difference in a component video signal. These levels determine the saturation of chrominance in the picture produced from the video signal.

chroma phase In a composite video signal, the phase of color information (subcarrier) is measured in degrees in reference to the burst. This relationship determines the actual color that the information in the video signal will produce on a TV screen. *See also* **burst; phase; video.**

chromaticity The color of light, consisting of hue and saturation, with no reference to the intensity.

chrome dioxide tape Magnetic recording tape with characteristics superior to ferric oxide tape.

chrominance The information included in the video signal of the actual color in every pixel in the TV picture produced. Chrominance contains the hue and saturation information. The luminance information is excluded.

chrominance channel A recorded or transmitted channel that contains chrominance information.

chrominance/luminance delay inequality A time difference between chrominance and luminance parts of the video signal occurs when passing through a system or instrument. The difference is usually expressed in nanoseconds. This time difference causes smearing of picture detail at the edges of objects.

chrominance/luminance gain inequality Gain difference between chrominance and luminance parts of the video signal. Occurs when passing through a system or instrument. The difference is usually expressed in dB or a percentage. Such gain difference causes incorrect color saturation in the TV picture.

chrominance/luminance intermodulation Cross-modulation. Changes in the level of the luminance signals when superimposed on chrominance signals, caused after passing through a system. The change in luminance level will affect brightness and contrast of the TV picture.

CIE Commission Internationale de l'Eclairage. An international commission that sets standards for colors of illumination for still photography and television. The CIE publishes a chart that is used for objective measurement of illuminate and surface colors as a function of the three primary colors viewed in defined conditions by the "standard observer."

cinemaScope A common widescreen format used in cinema. The picture is projected from a 35 mm film through an anamorphic lens, producing on the screen a picture with an aspect ratio of 2.35:1. During production the image is squeezed by an anamorphic lens. *See also* **aspect ratio.**

circuit The interconnection of electrical components to form an instrument that performs a certain electrical or electronic task.

clamping The process of restoring the DC level of a video signal. Sometimes low-frequency interference changes the original DC level. The clamping process adjusts the sync tip or blanking level according to an external reference level.

clapboard A board on which the scene and take number are written. The board has a small stick hinged to it. When the camera starts rolling, the board is put in front of the camera and the stick is clapped against the board to make an audible and visible cue point at the same time. The clapboard is used in film production to identify the scene and take and to allow synchronization between sound track and picture.

Clarke Belt Geostationary orbit of telecommunications satellites (named after Arthur C. Clarke). *See also* **geostationary orbit.**

Class A time Prime time. Normally the time between 9:00 and 11:00 P.M. when the number of listeners or viewers is the greatest. *See also* **prime time.**

clean edits Transitions that are accurately placed in terms of horizontal phase, subcarrier phase and color framing.

clean feed (a) In audio, a monitoring feed providing a participant in a program all sound except his own sound signal. (b) An output of a video switcher without downstream key.

client (a) One of the computers in a network that receives services from the server computer. (b) A firm or individual that buys air time in radio or TV to place commercials.

clip (a) In a video switcher, the trigger point or threshold at which the key will take place; also the knob or control that adjusts the action of keying. (b) In digital picture manipulators, an option that blanks part or side of an image when it is turning and moving in and out of the frame to avoid seeing the "wrong side" of a picture. (c) A cutoff in program sound. (d) A short part of film footage cut out during editing. (e) A short video or film footage used as insert during editing or transmission.

clipping An action taken to limit an audio or video signal's level from exceeding a standard level. Exceeded levels can cause damage to equipment such as amplifiers and transmitters and can cause distortion.

clipstrip A row of studio lights used to light up the background or cyclorama in the studio or onstage with uniform light.

clock frequency A stable periodic pulse or waveform used to synchronize or trigger the operation of electronic circuits such as computers.

clock jitter Variations in clock phase due to inaccuracy of the clock circuits or to interference.

clone An instrument or equipment created by copying attributes and features of another. Usually small manufacturers copy equipment of the large and famous.

closed-loop gain Amplification (gain) of an operational amplifier circuit determined by the feedback (loop) elements.

close-up A basic shot used in cinema and TV in which the face and shoulders (or sometimes face only) fill the screen. The close-up is the most common shot used in TV, especially in talk shows.

CLV Constant longitudinal velocity, used in relation to video disks. CLV is one way of making video disks, in which the outer tracks recorded on the disk carry three times as much information as the inner ones. The rotation speed of the disk changes to keep the relative speed between the head and the track constant. Reading still frames from the disk is very difficult and usually not a feature included in such laser disks. Playing time of the disk is much longer than the alternative kind of video disk, CAV. *See also* **CAV.**

C-mount A standard for mounting CCTV lenses onto the camera (screw mount).

coaxial cable (coax) A cable in which two conductors share the same axis: a center lead and a noise shield surrounding it. A nonconductive isolation separates the two, with a protective sleeve on the outside. Coaxial cables are widely used in TV for video and other high-frequency signals.

There are some standards that specify different parameters of coax cables, such as diameter and impedance.

codec   Coder-decoder. Converts audio and video to digital form, to be sent over transmission lines such as coax, fiber or on air and able to convert received signals back to analog.

coding   In the process of converting from analog to digital, the representation of each level of the analog signal by a number.

coercivity   Magnetic flux or signal level for which magnetic recording tape is designed and made.

coherence   Polarity between two signals, not necessarily identical, such as two audio signals.

coincident pair   An arrangement of two microphones used to make stereo recordings. The microphones are mounted close together with a 90-degree horizontal angle between them.

cold lighting   A new range of fluorescent lighting used for television. Fluorescent lighting for TV has an accurate color temperature (normally 3,200° K). Most fluorescent lights are floodlights. Some lights use special grilles to control the direction of light output. Fluorescent spotlights are still in the development stage.

Cold lighting power consumption is considerably lower than conventional lighting, introducing several major advantages: smaller utility system power supply and installation, less heat build-up in the studio and consequently a reduced need for air conditioning.

cold start   Start up of equipment by switching on the power, usually some time after it was switched off and cooled down.

color background   A full-field color video containing a solid uni-color signal. Used as background in video pictures or to fill certain areas, such as character graphics, with color. *See also* **background generator.**

color balance   Adjustment of the gain of the three color channels in a video camera to get the best fidelity of colors in reference to the actual scene. Usually a gray-scale test chart is used to adjust the high levels (white), low levels (black) and mid-levels (gray) to exactly match.

color bars   A standard video test signal containing eight vertical bars of color: white, yellow, cyan, green, magenta, red, blue and black. This order of colors is used also as a gray scale: if the chrominance is removed, the luminance level is left and is arranged according to the brightness of the colors from white to black in eight steps. Color bars are standard worldwide and used to measure hue, saturation and brightness in recorded and transmitted video signals. Color bars are recorded at the beginning of videotapes as a rule, so that the operator can match the playback levels to the standards and to the original recording even if the playback is done at a different time and environment from the recording.

color black *see* **black**

color black locking   Synchronizing of equipment such as VCRs or CGs to an incoming black reference.

color burst *see* **burst**

color contrast viewing filter A filter used by lighting artists and engineers to determine hot spots, highlights and shadows in a set. The set with lighting on is viewed through the filter, which reduces the dazzle of studio lights and gives the viewer an impression similar to the studio camera's output.

color correction Correction of color balance in video signals. Often used in postproduction to correct recordings done in the field in poor conditions or in film to tape transfers to compensate for variations in film color. A "color corrector" is the device performing the color correction.

color difference signal The result of the subtraction of luminance signal from a primary color signal. Two of the three parts that make a component video signal are color difference signals. The common color difference signals are $B - Y$ and $R - Y$. *See also* **B – Y; component; R – Y.**

color filter A piece of glass or gelatin that changes the color of light passing through it. *See also* **filter (optical).**

color frame A sequence of four fields (NTSC) or eight fields (PAL) that make a complete cycle of all sync and color information. Color framing has to be taken into consideration while editing composite video signals. Editing fields in an incorrect sequence will result in vertical picture shift and color changes.

color frame identification An electrical pulse generated by standard TV pulse generators. This pulse identifies the beginning of the first field in the 8- or 4-field sequence. *See also* **color frame.**

colorization A computerized process in which color is added to old (and usually classic) black and white films.

color saturation *see* **saturation**

color television Improvement of the black and white television systems by adding full color reproduction to the television image. The introduction of color made broadcast and consumer equipment much more complicated and expensive, but the result justifies the effort.

The production and delivery of color images starts in the color TV camera. Three channels of the primary colors red, green and blue are employed to produce a composite video signal. The signal can be recorded, processed and transmitted live to home color TV receivers. At the end of the path, the signal containing the three primary colors is used to drive three electron guns in the home receiver, producing a color display on the screen.

Three major color transmission systems are used at the moment: NTSC is used mainly in North America and Japan, PAL mainly in Europe and SECAM mainly in France. All other countries use one of these standards or combinations of them. Efforts are being made to introduce improved digital or higher resolution transmission as well as wider aspect-ratio pictures. *See also* **DVB; HDTV; PAL-plus.**

color temperature A convention of measuring the delicate hue differences between various "white" light sources. Color temperature is measured in degrees Kelvin. Standard studio lighting for television is 3,200° K, daylight is approximately 5,600° K and a standard lightbulb below 100 W is 2,600° K. The higher the color temperature, the bluer the light will appear. The lower the color temperature, the more yellow the light will appear. Color temperature of lighting equipment changes with the voltage supplied to the device. If the voltage supplied is lower than the rated voltage, the color temperature will be lower as well. Video and film cameras are highly sensitive to the color temperature of light in the scene. Filters can be used to correct color temperature. *See also* **camera (video); filter (optical).**

color temperature meter A measurement device used to accurately determine the color temperature of light. The color temperature meter gives a reading in degrees Kelvin and is usually combined in the same instrument with the light meter that measures the intensity of light. Color temperature meters are used, among other things, to determine which filters to use with a specific light. Accurate color temperature setting is important for testing and measurement of color video cameras.

color timing Adjustment of two or more video signals in such a way that the bursts of each one will coincide in terms of phase and timing. Color timing adjustments are used in studios, editing and all other places where video switching is used. Color timing is important for avoiding color shifts during switching of different video sources.

comb filter An electrical circuit that relays frequencies with a constant deviation between them, such as F, 2F, 3F and 4F. The frequencies between are blocked. The frequency response curve of the filter looks like the teeth of a comb. Comb filters are used to take out a certain frequency with its harmonies from a more complex signal. In video equipment, comb filters are often used to separate the chrominance signal from the luminance.

combiner A circuit or device that enables two or more digital effects channels to operate as one and enhance the possibilities of the system. The combiner coordinates the operation of the different channels and sets the boundaries and priorities in such a way that one visual effect can contain signals from all channels involved and move as one. An example is a cube moving in three-dimensional space, where each face is a live video picture coming from a different effects channel.

comet tail An undesired side effect created in camera picture tubes. Light areas in the picture leave trails when the picture frame moves (due to camera movement or zoom). Modern CCD picture elements do not produce comet tails.

commentator Someone who makes announcements and comments during a live event or recorded program. The voice of the commentator is heard mixed with the sound of the program. The commentator is usually not seen on the screen.

commercial Advertisement broadcast on radio or television. Large numbers of commercials are broadcast on commercial stations, often in groups during "commercial breaks." Normally a large artistic effort is made and considerable funds are spent to make the commercials attractive and esthetic. The commercial has to appeal to the target audience and deliver a specific message that will help to sell a product.

The length of commercials is normally no longer than one minute and the price for transmission of the commercial is determined by a number of variables, the most important of which is the number of viewers at the time of transmission. This kind of advertising is considered efficient and a large part of advertising budgets is usually spent on radio and TV commercials, mainly by large firms and corporations.

commercial television A television station or network that is financed (fully or partly) by selling air time for transmission of commercials (advertisements).

common mode An amplifier or other electrical circuit that has signals applied to its two input terminals. The signals are equal in terms of frequency, phase and amplitude.

common mode rejection The ability of a differential amplifier to reject signals that appear at the same time and phase on both input terminals. Common mode rejection is measured in decibels (dB).

communication satellite *see* **satellite communication**

compact cassette The most popular standard for home stereo audiocassettes. The width of the tape inside the cassette is ⅛ inch. Playing time is usually up to 90 minutes, although 120-minute tapes are available, including both sides. Four tracks can be recorded on the tape, two for each side.

compact disk (disc) A standard home digital stereo audio recording format. The disks are based on an optical system, which, unlike cassettes, cannot be rerecorded (write once). The information is written on the master by means of a laser beam. Another laser beam in the player retrieves the information. The main advantages of compact disks (often abbreviated CDs) are high quality of sound, random access and nondeteriorating quality. This standard was adopted by the computer industry as a read-only memory due to its vast capacity of information and small dimensions. The compact disk is also used as a professional playback medium. *See also* **CD-ROM.**

compander A system used for noise reduction in audio signals. The process includes compression and decompression of the audio signals.

compatibility Matching of systems, standards or protocols to enable coexistence of different systems or instruments. When TV first started broadcasting in color, black and white TV receivers could still reproduce a picture from the color signal and color receivers could produce a picture from black and white signals. This was due to compatibility between the two systems.

complementary color   One color of light is complementary to another if the two mixed together make white light. Usually in relation to video signals and cameras, complementary colors refer to magenta, cyan and yellow, which are the complementaries of the primary colors red, green and blue. Some test patterns contain complementary colors. Filters are transparent to their own color and absorb their complementary color. *See also* **color bars.**

complimiter   A combination of an audio compressor and an audio limiter. This combination is common in recording studios, editing and control rooms. A complimiter or compressor-limiter is used to control and limit audio levels to stay within certain standards or preset limits. *See also* **compressor; limiter.**

component analog   Component video in analog form. Usually refers to a system using Y, B – Y, R – Y. *See also* **component video.**

component digital   Component video in digital representation or form, usually Y, B – Y, R – Y. Component digital is the signal that delivers the highest picture quality and allows for more generations of recording and playback than other forms of video signal. The component digital standard is defined by the following: CCIR 601, ITU-R BT.601-2. The parallel interface is defined by CCIR 656, ITU-R BT.656 and SMPTE 125M.

component video   A video signal that is separated into three different signals such as RGB or Y, B – Y, R – Y.

Component video signals produce a better picture quality than composite signals. Unwanted effects such as cross color that result from mixing luminance and chrominance information are avoided.

composite analog   A complex, single signal that contains all the necessary information to reproduce a color picture: luminance (brightness and contrast), chrominance (hue and saturation) and synchronizing pulses (line and field). *See also* **composite video.**

composite digital   A digital form of the composite video signal. This kind of signal is not used as much as other video signals because it suffers from all the shortcomings of composite video, with the addition of some transcoding footprints. Composite digital signals allow for multiple generations with less loss of quality than analog signals.

composite sync   A set of synchronizing pulses containing the complete information for synchronizing the TV picture both horizontally and vertically.

composite video   A video signal in which chrominance information is superimposed on the luminance. Composite is a single signal containing all of the picture information, including synchronization pulses. The different transmission standards such as NTSC and PAL each have a precise definition of the levels, frequency and structure of the signal. Composite video was created, among other things, to solve the problem of compatibility between the old black and white television and the new color television when it was first developed.

The action of combining the RGB signals from a camera to a composite signal is called "encoding," and the opposite action of separating the color signals from the composite video is called "decoding." Composite video is the most common form of video signal and is the only form that most TV sets all over the world can use to display pictures after the video signal has been separated from the carrier by demodulation.

Composite video is a complex waveform. Other kinds of information such as teletext, test signals and time code can be added. *See also* **composite analog; video.**

compression (audio)   A process of making an audio segment shorter without changing the pitch of the sound.

compression (data)   A general name for techniques used to reduce the size of digital data. Every device using data has data storage limitations, such as the size of the disk. Using compression allows more efficient use of available storage space. Compression of data shortens the time needed to transfer data files in local networks and over telephone lines. Compression also reduces the bandwidth of digital transmission channels and can considerably enhance the capability of costly satellite channels. Some compression methods that remove redundant data produce files reduced in size without any loss of data, while others that also remove noncritical data can cause partial loss of data. Special compression techniques such as JPEG and MPEG were developed for the compression of digital video signals. *See also* **JPEG; MPEG.**

compression (image)   Reduction of highlights in the video signal to allow a large contrast range into the standard video signal. One of the modern circuits that performs such image compression is the "knee function." *See also* **knee function.**

compression (video)   A distortion caused by nonlinear behavior of video circuits.

compression artifacts   Small defects that appear when compressing and then decompressing digital data. In decompressed video signals, artifacts such as noise, busy edges and distortions of moving objects are present. The higher the compression rate, the more artifacts there will be.

compression ratio   The ratio between the amount of data before and after compression. The compression ratio differs with the different compression techniques. In broadcast-quality video signals, compression is usually no more than 1:3. For other purposes, such as off-line editing, and home video editing, compression ratio can be as much as 1:15. Higher compression ratios often lead to lower quality.

compressor   A device used to constrain or reduce audio signals. Modern compressors can compress audio according to given parameters, such as the level at which the compression will start (threshold), the amount or ratio of the compression (gain) and how fast the compression will start (attack) and end (decay).

computer   A machine capable of running programs that tell it how to perform different tasks. Computers can do numerous things, all based upon the ability to perform mathematical calculations and logical operations at high speed. By using combinations of simple and basic operations, more complex operations can be utilized, which in turn can be used to perform even more complex operations. Computers use binary notation, meaning that all the computer can understand is a series or a combination of zeros and ones.

The main difference between various computers is their speed and data-storing capability. They are divided into four main categories, from smallest to largest: personal computers, minicomputers, mainframes and supercomputers.

In broadcast equipment, almost every major item such as a camera, a character generator or a VCR is controlled by microcomputers or built-in computer chips. Computers are also used to control editing systems, lighting systems and automated transmission centers. Networking is used by computers to share large databases, software and to pass information between different users of the network. *See also* **binary.**

computer graphics Graphics generated with the aid of appropriate software on a computer. There is a variety of software that helps create the less artistic and more technical part of graphics, such as coloring, drawing lines, polygons and circles, copying, moving, changing size and proportions and much more.

Computer graphics are frequently used in TV for making animation, backgrounds, captions and even commercials or programs. Graphics are immediately translated by a video card installed inside the computer into a video signal that can be recorded, mixed and processed with other signals.

Some software can be used with standard home computers, while other more sophisticated and more powerful programs need stronger and more expensive workstations. The power and sophistication of graphics software are constantly growing with the development of computers.

condenser microphone A microphone that is based on a capacitor that changes its capacitance when subjected to sound waves. Unlike dynamic microphones, condenser microphones need a steady supply of voltage to operate. Some models use batteries and others are fed directly from the recorder or mixing console with "phantom" powering. Condenser microphones have a small preamplifier built in and are highly sensitive. Sound quality of condenser microphones is usually very good. *See also* **phantom power supply.**

console A desk or large control panel used for mixing or switching signals such as audio and video. *See also* **audio console.**

consumer When applied in an audio-video context, a lower degree or level of sophistication, quality, durability and price as opposed to the higher industrial and broadcast levels. *See also* **broadcast quality; industrial.**

contact microphone A microphone attached to a musical instrument such as a violin or piano. Sound is picked up mainly by mechanical vibration from the instrument's structure.

continuity   **(a)** In the process of making a movie or a TV program, the avoidance of accidental changes in lighting, props, dresses, makeup, audio quality and camera work between scenes. Polaroids are used to help rebuild scenes after a break. If continuity is disrupted, odd things can happen. Objects can jump from place to place, actors suddenly look different and so on. **(b)** Material transmitted on the air between programs such as announcements, promos and commercials that make a complete transmission schedule.

continuity cutting   Traditional film editing in which care is taken to keep the action continuous in terms of time, place and objects.

continuity studio   A small studio or announcing booth in a radio or TV station used for announcements between programs.

contouring   Unwanted effects that look like posterization. Contouring occurs when not enough quantization levels are used or if a partial loss of data has occurred. *See also* **posterization, quantizing.**

contrast   The range between the brightest and darkest areas in a picture. Most TV sets have a button that controls the contrast.

control room   A place from which decision makers such as directors, producers and engineers supervise and manage the activity in studios, transmission centers and switching stations. Control rooms contain monitoring, remote control equipment, switching equipment, test and measurement equipment and communication equipment. Control rooms are always built as close as possible to the process being controlled. Different control rooms are built according to the task at hand.

control track   A sine wave or other periodical waveform recorded on magnetic tape in order to reproduce the original recording speed and head tracking during playback. In insert editing, the control track remains untouched along the edited tape and thus contributes to the continuity of the recording. *See also* **insert edit.**

convergence   In color video cameras, TV sets or monitors, the accuracy of the reproduction of the three elementary colors in such a way that the colors will perfectly overlap each other, creating a sharp image.

copyright   Ownership of literary material, musical script and composition, audio and video recordings and programs, photographs and creative or artistic work of all kinds. Copyright can be registered to assure the author's or creator's rights. In the U.S., copyrights are registered at the U.S. Copyright Office, which is a section of the Library of Congress. In other countries different arrangements exist to register copyrights. Copyright of works created after January 1, 1978, is for the lifetime of the author and an additional 50 years. After that period the work enters the public domain.

corner pinning   In some digital effects units, the ability to take a live picture and to reposition the picture anywhere in a 3-D space, by determining new positions for the corners of the picture. This process is done in real time.

costume Wardrobe. A set of clothing made specially for a character or performer in a TV program, cinema, theater or opera and other shows. The costume includes all accessories and jewelry.

costume designer The person who creates new costume design, selects the material and oversees the manufacturing, fitting and selection of accessories.

countdown A count backward to the beginning of a program, take, playback or other event in studio work concerning several people. Normally the countdown is announced by the assistant director over the intercom system. Countdown helps all parties involved to know exactly when to do their part. It is also used to coordinate switching of transmission from one source to another.

Sometimes a countdown is recorded at the beginning of a film or videotape. Numbers decrease from 10 in one-second intervals until the beginning of the recorded material— sometimes three seconds before the beginning.

counterprogramming Programming of a transmission schedule in a station or network that is planned to respond to competitive programming in other stations.

coverage (a) Activity of a radio or TV station to record, report and broadcast from where news events occur (news coverage). (b) The number of houses or size of area in which a certain radio or TV station's transmission can be received. (c) The use of several cameras to "cover" an event from different angles.

cover shot A wide camera shot that covers the complete area where an event is taking place. A cover shot is normally used to give the viewer the feeling and orientation of where things are happening. Cover shots are usually used at the beginning of programs and from time to time during the program. Sometimes called "establishing shot" or "orientation shot."

CPT Cost per thousand. A term from advertising, it refers to the cost of a specific advertisement for every thousand viewers, listeners or readers.

CPU Central processing unit. The part of a computer where instructions are interpreted and carried out. The power of a computer is determined mainly by its CPU. However, a CPU cannot work alone and must be connected to peripheral equipment such as memory, display, data storage equipment and other support circuitry in order to be useful.

crab Sideways movement of a camera. The new camera position is parallel to the old one. This movement is performed by the camera mount and not by the camera itself. *See also* **camera mount; pan.**

crab dolly A camera mount on wheels that can be steered in different directions. Rubber wheels are used in-house and track wheels outside, on specially built tracks.

crane A long arm that carries the camera, sometimes also the cameraman, from the floor level to high above the audience and scenery. Cranes come in different sizes, some up to 40 feet long. A crane can perform complex camera moves. Some are balanced by lead weights and moved by hand, while others are electrically or hydraulically moved.

credits List of participants and other information appearing at the start or end of a TV program or film.

cropping Reduction of image size by cutting parts from the edges.

cross color Unwanted visual effect in an encoded video picture. Appears as moiré or lines in changing colors. Cross color effects are usually noticeable when the talent wears a striped jacket or shirt. Cross color occurs in encoders and decoders that misinterpret luminance information with certain frequencies as chrominance information. Known also as "cross chrominance."

cross-fade A transition frequently used in production and postproduction in which one audio signal slowly disappears while at the same time another one appears. During the cross-fade the two signals overlap in an ever-changing ratio. Cross-fades are used to soften the transition between two signal sources. A cross-fade of video signals is called a dissolve. *See also* **dissolve; fade.**

cross light Stage or studio lighting coming from the sides of performers.

cross-luminance Known also as chroma crawl or dot crawl. Unwanted visual effect in an encoded video picture. Areas of high color saturation are interpreted by the decoder circuit as luminance information. The result is colored dots moving around the edges of objects.

crossover network An electrical circuit that is usually built into speaker systems (audio monitors) that separates the audio signal into several frequency bands before being fed to the loudspeakers. Each kind (or size) of speaker is built to deliver a different frequency band. The crossover network feeds each speaker with the appropriate frequencies.

cross point A point in an array of source and destination lines where a connection can be made. In some patch-panels, source lines go through horizontally and destination lines vertically, or vice-versa. A mechanical connection can be made between one or more lines where the lines cross. The same principle applies to electronic routing switchers, where connection is made electronically.

crosstalk Unwanted transmission of electrical signals from one circuit or cable to another one nearby. Crosstalk appears mainly in, but is not limited to, multichannel equipment such as video mixers or audio mixing consoles.

CRT *see* **cathode ray tube**

CU *see* **close-up**

cue card Large poster-size cards on which text is written, used in the studio for the benefit of talent who do not know their text by heart. Text is written in large letters and the cards are placed close to the camera lens so that the person does not have to turn his or her eyes away from the camera while reading.

cue light A term used in Britain for tally light. *See also* **tally light.**

curie point   The temperature at which magnetized metal loses its magnetic orientation. This phenomenon is used in magneto-optical disks, where a laser beam heats a point on the disk to ease the polarity change of the magnetic field.

current   A stream of electrons in a conductor. Measured in amperes. Electrical current delivers the power needed for most devices in an easy and cheap manner. There are two kinds of electrical current: direct current (DC) and alternating current (AC). *See also* **AC; ampere; DC.**

current limiter   An electrical circuit that limits the amount of current flowing through it to a certain known amount.

cut   An abrupt transition between two video sources. The actual switching between the sources takes place in the vertical blanking interval, between frames.

cutaway   A fast transition away from the action to an establishing or reaction shot.

cutback   A fast transition back to the action from an establishing or reaction shot.

cut-in   Interruption of a program or transmission for an unplanned announcement or news flash.

cut-off frequency   In filters, the frequency at which the output level is down by 3 dB.

cutter   Film or video editor.

cutting   Editing of film or video material. The name originates from the actual cutting used in film editing. *See also* **editing.**

cut-to-cut   A simple editing system with two VCRs, one of which serves as the player and the other as a recorder. Even though basic, most of the editing work can be done in cut-to-cut editing systems rather than more complex editing systems such as AB-ROLL.

cyc   Abbreviation for cyclorama.

cyclorama   A curtain surrounding the studio walls from the inside. Used as background for studio shooting. Three basic colors are used for the cyclorama: black to have an unnoticeable background, blue for chroma key and off-white on which to display lighting effects.

cyclorama light   A special quartz lamp used to light the cyclorama. The cyclorama usually has to be lit evenly, and lamps with special reflectors are used. An array of cyclorama lights placed four to ten feet away from each other, either on the floor of the studio or near the upper side of the cyclorama, will do the job.

D1   A standard format for digital component videotape recording. D1 is built according to CCIR 601 and 4:2:2 standards. Cassettes with tape 19 mm wide are used and the maximum playing time is 94 minutes. D1 is ideally suited for multigeneration postproduction work. D1 is a high-end, high-priced recording standard and is not in widespread usage.

D2 A standard format for digital composite (NTSC or PAL) videotape recording, conforming with SMPTE 244M. It uses 19 mm tape cassettes and the maximum playing time per cassette is 208 minutes. Using only eight bits to sample the coded signal reduces amplitude resolution and increases the amount of contouring artifacts. D2 is often used to replace the older 1" VTRs. Being a composite format, it suffers from all the inherent shortcomings, such as color framing sequences and cross color. (D2 is incompatible with D1 and D3).

D3 A standard format for digital composite (NTSC or PAL) videotape recording sampled at eight bits, conforming with SMPTE 244M. It uses ½" tape cassettes in three cassette sizes and the maximum playing time per cassette is 245 minutes. Performance is similar to D2 format. The reduced format allows for the same format to be used all along the production chain: there are camcorders, studio recorders and editing machines all using the same family of cassettes.

D5 A standard format for digital component videotape recording. D5 is built according to CCIR 601 standards at ten-bit resolution. The tape cassettes used are the same as D3, allowing the playing of D3 tapes using internal decoding. Because the signal is uncompressed digital component, it makes superb quality similar to D1. Some D5 machines have provisions for recording HDTV signals using compression.

D6 A recorder for HDTV signals using D1 tape.

D/A Digital to analog conversion. *See also* **DAC.**

DAC Digital to analog conversion. The transforming of digital data into analog signals. Many devices (such as video effects generators) convert signals from analog to digital for processing and then convert them back to analog. A digital stream of data is converted to corresponding voltages or currents and they are linked together to form a continuous analog signal. *See also* **A/D.**

DAT Digital audio tape. A common two-track or stereo digital audio format frequently used for mastering. DAT machines use technology based on a rotary head, similar in principle to video machines. Cassette size is small, about half the size of a standard "compact cassette," and playing time is up to 90 minutes. Helical scan is used and there are no longitudinal tracks. DAT tape machines use sampling rates of 32 kHz, 44.1 kHz and 48 kHz. "Consumer" DAT machines do not allow the use of the 44.1 kHz sampling rate to avoid digital duplication of commercial CDs. Some DAT machines have a time code recording capability.

day for night *see* **night effect**

daylight conversion A diachronic glass filter used to convert 3,200° K studio light to a daylight temperature of 5,600° K. The filter is usually installed on quartz lamps in outside locations.

dB Short for decibel. *See also* **decibel (dB).**

DB *see* **delayed broadcast**

DBS   Direct broadcast satellite.

DC   Direct current. Current that does not change its direction or amplitude. Direct current is used mostly in small devices. Most electrical circuits work in DC. Current drawn from a battery is always DC. *See also* **AC.**

DC component   The part of a signal that contains the direct current; also the average value or voltage of a signal.

DC coupling   A connection method between circuits that allows the DC component of the signal to pass from one circuit to another as well as AC component (variations). In most cases AC coupling is used. DC coupling is used for signals with negative energy such as component analog video signals (Y, B – Y and R – Y).

DC offset   A change in the required or correct DC level of a signal.

DC restorer   A circuit that recovers the DC level of a signal. The original DC level is usually lost after the signal passes through an AC-coupled device.

DCT   (**a**) Discrete cosine transform. A type of data compression of digital video pictures. DCT takes small parts of the picture, normally 8 by 8 pixels, and deals with the attributes of each part separately. JPEG uses DCT for compression of digital video data. (**b**) Digital Component Technology. A video recording format introduced by AMPEX. DCT VTRs use 19 mm tape cassettes not compat-ible with any other format. DCT uses 2:1 data compression.

DDR   Digital disk recorder.

dead   In reference to a studio or other confined environment, having negligible reverberation. This is usually a place where a lot of work has been invested to change the acoustical conditions.

decay time   The period of time taken until echoes and reverberation fade away.

decibel (dB)   A unit for comparing relative levels of voltage, current and power. The number of dB by which two power sources differ (in watts) is expressed by the following formula: $dB = 10 \log P2 / P1$. In terms of voltage: $20 \log V2 / V1$ and in terms of current: $20 \log I2 / I1$. Often V2 is the voltage at the output of an amplifier or amplifier stage and V1 is the input voltage.

Sometimes specific reference levels are used to simplify and standardize measurements. Suffix letters are then added to the dB abbreviation:

dBm in reference to 1 mW (1 milliwatt)

dBu in reference to 0.775 V (0.775 volts)

dBv in reference to 1 V (1 volt)

dBw in reference to 1 W (1 watt)

dBk in reference to 1 KW (1 kilowatt)

Decibels are very useful in broadcasting for expressing levels of audio, amplification of amplifiers, gain of antennas, signal-to-noise ratios and more.

decoder   A circuit that separates the component signals from a composite signal. Decoder circuits are used in TV receivers to recover the RGB signals from the composite video signal received after demodulation. The RGB signals are used to drive the three electron guns of the picture tube.

dedicated   In reference to a circuit or control, being designed to perform a specific job, unlike others that can serve several functions.

de-esser   A circuit used in audio to reduce sibilants such as the *s* sound.

default   A standard setup of a circuit or software set by the factory or loaded during startup. The default is usually the best or most used option or adjustment based on experience.

definition   The amount of detail in an image. *See also* **resolution.**

deflection   The process of causing a beam of electrons in a CRT or picture tube to move away from the center to scan the entire screen area. Deflection of an electron beam can be achieved either by a magnetic field created by current flowing in coils or by an electric field created by metal plates charged with electric tension. In TV receivers, deflection coils are used; in oscilloscopes, charged plates are used. The method of deflection depends on the angle needed. In CRTs, deflection angles of up to 110 degrees are used, while in oscilloscopes the deflection is no more than 60 degrees. Magnetic deflection presents more aberrations and consumes more power.

defocus   A situation in which a picture coming from a film or TV camera is taken out of focus. This situation can either be intentional or uninten-tional. Sometimes the image is defocused purposely to create a certain visual effect. Sometimes defocus is used as a transition in which the end of one scene is defocused; it dissolves to the next scene, which starts defocused and then becomes focused.

degausser   An instrument using a strong magnetic field to demagnetize different mechanical parts or magnetic tapes. AC current is driven through a coil and the current decays. TV receivers have a built-in coil around the screen that demagnetizes the picture tube on start-up. Buildup of undesirable magnetic fields causes distortion of color in the picture produced by the CRT.

In studios and editing rooms, bigger coils are used to erase magnetic tapes. Tapes are irreversibly erased in a matter of seconds.

degeneration   **(a)** Degradation of signals recorded on tape due to multiple generations of recording and playback. **(b)** Decrease of amplifier stage gain by applying a negative feedback to it.

delay   The time taken by a signal to pass through a device, transmission line or component. Even though electronic signals such as video travel at the speed of light or near it, the time it takes for the signal to travel from one continent to another via satellite, for example, is noticeable. Digital video equipment takes relatively long periods of time to process analog video into digital and vice-versa. Delay time for video is usually measured in microseconds or in nanoseconds. Delay time for audio is usually measured in milliseconds.

Delay between different signals in

studios, editing rooms and other facilities causes a major problem. In
order to mix or switch video signals,
they must be synchronized together.
If there are delays in the system, synchronization is lost. To gain the synchronization, other signals have to be
delayed as well to match the most delayed ones. Deliberate delay can be
obtained by the use of delay lines, or
for longer delay by frame synchronizers. *See also* **delay line.**

delay distribution amplifier   A
distribution amplifier equipped with
built-in delay line circuits to match the
signal output to other signals in the
system in terms of timing. *See also*
delay line.

delayed broadcast   A program or
live event transmitted after its occur-
rence because of time zone difference,
adaptation to an existing transmission
schedule, or to allow time for translation or censorship.

delay line   An electric circuit, usually passive, used to delay signals by
a given amount of time. Delay lines
usually consist of an array of resistors,
coils and capacitors. Some delay lines
are fixed and others have combinations of delay times such as 1, 2, 4, 8,
16, 32, 64, 128 and 256 nanoseconds.
The different combinations can be
connected or disconnected by jumpers;
in such a device, every delay time between 1 and 511 nanoseconds can be
obtained in 1-nanosecond increments.
Delay lines cause some distortion to
signals: the higher the frequencies involved, the higher the distortion. Distortion is also dependent on the
amount of delay and at some stage,
delay lines are no longer efficient.
There are active delay lines that use

amplification to compensate for loss
of level in certain frequencies.

delegate   To use one control or
control panel to operate a number of
similar or identical devices one at a
time. For example, a camera control
panel can control one of several cameras. A switch selects which of the
cameras will be controlled.

delta   A picture tube (CRT) in
which the arrangement of the three
electron guns for the three colors
(RGB) is in a triangle. The color dots
on the screen also form triangles.
Delta picture tubes have better resolution in the picture but less light output contrast than other kinds of CRTs.

demodulator   A circuit used for
separation of information from a
modulated carrier. Demodulation is
the opposite of modulation. The carrier can be modulated in AM (amplitude modulation) or FM (frequency
modulation). After demodulation, the
carrier's function is finished. Demod-
ulators are common in TV and radio
receivers. *See also* **modulation; modulator.**

demultiplexer   A device or circuit
used for separation of a number of information channels that were combined (multiplexed) to be sent through
a single channel such as telephone
line, fiber optic line or satellite channel.

depth of field   When a camera
lens is focused on an object, there is
an area closer to the lens and farther
away from the object that will still appear sharp. The size of this area is the
depth of field. Depth of field depends
on many variables. When you move

away from the sharpest image, how much blur is still acceptable as sharp? Other major variables are the aperture and the focal length of the lens and the object's distance from the lens.

depth of perception   The capability of a listener to perceive separately different instruments in a sound recording or transmission. Depth of perception can be improved by training.

deserializer   A device that converts serial digital information to parallel digital information.

desktop   A device such as a computer that is small enough to fit on a standard desk.

desktop video conference   Video conference through computer networking. One person or group of people can talk to another somewhere else in the world by means of picture and sound carried by telephone lines. Advantages of desktop video conferencing are that no special setup and no expensive two-way satellite communications are needed. Conferencing can be made from one's desktop computer. Communications networks such as the Internet and ISDN and data compression techniques such as MPEG make it possible to transfer a bandwidth wide enough for video and sound of an adequate quality for such use.

detector   A device that detects and converts one kind of energy into another kind. A microphone is a kind of detector that converts sound waves into an electric signal.

diagnostics   A troubleshooting facility that tests certain functions of a circuit or device and displays the result on either a special display or on one that already exists for other purposes. If built into the device to be tested, it is known as "self-diagnostics."

dialogue   Conversation between actors as written in the script and performed by actors in a film or TV program. Not to be confused with narration, which is a description of the content of the program by someone who is not usually seen on the screen.

diaphragm   **(a)** A device used to control the amount of light coming through the lens. It is usually a combination of some thin metal flaps that are mounted inside or behind the lens that can be moved together to create a larger or smaller opening for the light to pass through. In older cameras a metal plate with different sizes of holes was used; the plate moved to place the right size of hole in the light path. It is necessary to control the amount of light so that the light-sensitive element in the camera will get the exact amount of light it needs. **(b)** A thin layer of metal sensitive to vibration that forms the heart of a microphone. In a dynamic microphone, the diaphragm generates an electric signal in a coil. In a cardioid microphone, the diaphragm is part of a capacitor and vibrations change the capacitance, which is translated into electrical signals.

dichroic filter   A clear glass filter with special coating that absorbs a certain color of light. Dichroic filters are used in lighting to change the color temperature of the light from artificial light 3200 degrees Kelvin to 5600 degrees Kelvin daylight. The filter absorbs part of the yellow light, thus making it bluer.

dichroic mirror   A clear glass with a special coating used as a mirror. The coating reflects a certain color, while all the other colors pass through. Dichroic coating is used in beam splitters for video cameras. *See also* **beam splitter.**

differential amplifier   An amplifier stage circuit that has two inputs and only differences in voltage between the inputs are amplified. The advantage in differential amplifiers is that every noise or hum present equally in both inputs will be ignored, not amplified and not passed to the next stage.

differential gain   A difference in color saturation between areas of different luminance. This distortion of the video signal is tested by an equally modulated luminance ramp. The subcarrier level is checked to be equal all along the signal path.

diffusion   Dispersion of light when it hits a surface or goes through a material. Some of the light continues to travel in the same direction and some will travel in different directions. Undiffused light casts harsh shadows and enhances wrinkles on a person's face and therefore is unsuitable for many kinds of photography. Diffusers are used to diffuse light coming from lamps and to soften images.

diffusion filter   Filters used to soften the image in TV, still and cinema cameras. In TV studio cameras

the filter is mounted on a filter wheel behind the lens inside the camera body. In other cameras the filter can be mounted on the front of the lens.

digital audio workstation (DAW)
A computer based, digital, nonlinear audio editing system. This kind of workstation employs a visual and friendly way of editing audio. Numerous digital audio tracks are stored on disk and can be mixed or cut and arranged in any desirable order. The order and length of segments in the edited tracks are stored on disk but not the actual edited tracks as a whole.

The amount of audio that can be stored in the workstation depends on the size of hard disk or other storage devices employed. Disk storage allows fast random access to sound segments, which makes the editing very fast relative to tape editing.

Usually a "timeline" is used to display the audio tracks and sound segments. Additional functions such as panning, equalizing, and virtual buttons for play, rewind, fast forward, record and pause can also be placed on-screen and operated by the mouse. Several versions of an audio mix can be created without any change in the original source tracks.

A basic audio workstation consists of a computer, special audio editing software, some additional hardware—usually an interface board installed inside the computer—and monitors (usually two). In more complex systems, additional hardware is used, such as an interface box for live audio and external control panels.

A DAW is a relatively inexpensive audio editing system that allows accurate and high quality production and postproduction work. *See also* **timeline.**

digital Betacam A ½" eight-bit digital component recording format based on the Betacam-SP cassettes. Having a compression rate of 2:1, it is used mainly for high-end editing. Some models of digital Betacam players can play analog Betacam cassettes and produce a digital output signal. This allows modern digital facilities to use existing analog Betacam-SP cassettes.

digital cache System using an array of hard disks or computer memory chips for storage of audio and video. Digital cache systems are used for storage and fast, random access retrieval of material in transmission and editing.

Most cache systems use hard disks and have a capacity of several hours of audio and video, depending on the amount of disk storage, compression algorithm and ratio used and fail-safe techniques used. Digital cache systems are usually not suitable for long items such as feature films, but they offer several advantages over videotape technology for shorter items such as commercials or news reports. The advantages include random, nonlinear access to recorded items, highly reliable operation, multiple input/output enabling read and write simultaneous operation and multiaccess to a single event, multigeneration and low maintenance costs.

In editing facilities, digital cache systems are used to replace several or all VCR machines. The cache system is controlled by the editing controller in the same way VCRs are normally controlled and also connected as a number of VCRs depending on the number of inputs/outputs available.

In transmission facilities, the cache system works under the control of the cart machine with the aid of special software, storing a large number of events, playing to air and recording at the same time. Several channels can be played to air simultaneously, replacing several VCRs.

The audio and video capacity of digital cache systems continues to grow rapidly with the increase in magnetic disk storage capacity and with the improvement in compression techniques.

RAM-based cache systems are still expensive and have small capacity, but due to constant improvement and lower prices in RAM computer chips, RAM-based digital cache systems with considerable capacity will probably be introduced in the near future.

digital effects Visual effects made with a digital device that moves, shapes, changes size and processes video signals. Digital effects can flip, tumble and rotate, move and resize pictures in 3-D space and also create effects such as posterization, solarization, mosaics, forced monochrome, crop and shadow. Some digital effects are also capable of reshaping a video picture into geometrical shapes such as cubes, cylinders, cones, rings and more.

"Key frames" are used by the digital effects to create continuity in movement from one position of the effects to another and make effects that have a given length and complexity as needed. Often more than one effects channel is used to enhance the possibilities and get more complex effects. A "combiner" is used to coordinate the operation of two or more digital effects channels. *See also* **combiner; key frame.**

digital mixing   Editing of digitized TV signals. Each signal is represented by a stream of digital data, normally 8-bit words. The result of the editing will be a 16-bit word that has to be reduced again to a standard 8-bit word. To avoid unwanted visible artifacts, dynamic rounding techniques have to be used. *See also* **dynamic rounding.**

Digital S   Digital Super VHS. A ½-inch digital metal-particle tape format. Tape speed is 57.8 mm/s and maximum play time is 104 minutes. Video is sampled at 8 bits, 4:2:2. The 166 Mbps component video data stream is compressed to 50 Mbps (3:3.1 ratio) using a DCT intraframe compression. The cassette housing is based on the VHS format but cannot be loaded into conventional VHS decks. The Digital S format utilizes two 16-bit digital audio channels with 48 kHz sampling. Digital S is a new member in the family of ½-inch digital VCRs. It seems that it will sell in prices considerably lower than the similar existing formats.

digitization   Replacement of analog signals by digital representation. *See also* **A/D.**

dimmer   Electronic circuit used to control the amount of electrical current drawn by an electrical device or circuit. Dimmers are used in TV studios to control the amount of light each lamp produces. The light output can be from zero to full power of the device, continuously. In large studios there are many dimmers, sometimes several hundred, and special lighting computers are used to control them. At the heart of the dimmer is usually a device such as an SCR or TRIAC. *See also* **lighting computer.**

DIN   Deutscher Industrie Normenausschuß. German standards institute.

dip switch   Miniature switch usually in groups of two, four or eight, in a dual in-line package. The package containing the switches is usually mounted on a printed circuit board to allow changes in the mode of operation. Dip switches are normally to be used by engineers for initial setup of circuits.

direct broadcast satellite   A satellite that transmits directly to viewers' homes. A special satellite dish antenna and receiver are needed. Some satellite broadcasts are encrypted so that unauthorized viewers will not be able to receive the signals properly.

direct mode   In an audio mixing console, direct connection from an input channel to a designated output, bypassing the normal path of the input channel and channel bus.

director   The manager of all the artistic and technical aspects in the process of making a TV program or feature film. A director must have a good basic knowledge of all aspects of television work such as script writing, camera work, sound, lighting, scenery, acting and editing. The director's work is always done under strict limitations of time and budget. Not only does the director have to manage and coordinate the work of many people in different jobs, he must also motivate everybody to give their best and work as a team. The director is responsible for the proper utilization of all the available production facilities. The director plans and performs the different stages of the pre-production, production and post-production.

director of engineering   In a TV station, network or other facility, the person in charge of all technical personnel, equipment, maintenance and operations that involve the use of technical equipment. Also the person in charge of short- and long-term planning of manpower, facilities and equipment renewal and acquisition.

director of photography (DP)
In a film production, head of the camera crew in charge of photography, lighting and composition.

direct pickup   Pickup of audio from an electronic instrument by connecting a direct line to the mixing console input. This kind of connection delivers a clean signal and eliminates echoes and surrounding noise.

direct sound   Sound that travels from the source directly to the listener, without any intermediate medium or echo.

direct wave   An electromagnetic signal such as a TV broadcast that is transmitted directly to the end user in one direct path, usually a line of sight path.

discharge lamp   Any of a family of lamps in which a gas is encapsulated in a glass tube with two electrodes. When the gas is heated by an arc between the electrodes, it starts to emit light. The lamp is connected to the power supply via special control circuits. Discharge lamps are efficient and can produce up to 45 lumens per watt and more. There are several gases used in discharge lamps, such as mercury vapor, sodium vapor and xenon. The intensity and efficiency of the lamp depends on the kind of gas used and its pressure. The exact composition of gases determines the spectral characteristics of the light emitted. Discharge lamps have a spiky spectral response in which large parts of the energy are emitted in discreet bands. Some of the more advanced kinds of discharge lamps such as xenon are used for lighting in cinema and TV productions. Xenon lamps are also used for motion picture projectors.

Fluorescent lamps are also discharge lamps that use invisible radiation in the ultraviolet region to cause special coating of the glass tubes to fluoresce visible light. This principle makes fluorescent light highly efficient.

dish   A device used for highly directional transmission and reception of electromagnetic signals. Terrestrial and satellite microwave links use dishes. The dish is a round parabolic structure surrounding the antenna, reflecting waves to the antenna from a certain direction or from the antenna to a certain direction. The bigger the dish, the more efficient the reception or the gain of the dish.

disk editing   Editing of audio and video material on a computerized workstation. This kind of editing is digital, nonlinear and random access. The workstation consists of a powerful computer equipped with a large storage, interface boards for audio and video and special editing software. Monitoring for audio and video are also provided. Audio and video segments of program material to be edited are copied to the disk. Analog material has to be digitized. Normally the material is also compressed to save disk space.

Disk editing is faster and more friendly than the traditional electronic tape-to-tape editing. Segments are accessed immediately. Several versions of the edited program can be produced, and changes to the edited material can be easily made at any point of the edited program.

At the disk editing workstation, material can be displayed on-screen by means of a timeline or by a large number of small frames each taken from one segment. Video effects such as dissolve, wipe, key, creation of characters and many more can be created within the workstation. Not all effects are made in real time; some take time to render. The number of audio tracks that can be attached to a video program is very large—sometimes unlimited. Usually two large computer monitors are used in such workstations. Live video can be displayed on the monitors in different configurations, together with other information or without. Normally two audio monitors are connected to the workstation—left and right. The actual editing is performed from the computer keyboard or with a mouse. Different icons and buttons are displayed on the screen, each one performing a different task.

Some disk editing systems do not have broadcast-quality video and are used for off-line editing to produce an editing list (EDL), which is then taken to a cut-to-cut or AB-Roll editing room for on-line editing. More expensive systems offer broadcast-quality video and edited material can be used for transmission. Audio quality in disk editing systems is normally CD quality and presents no problem.

Disk editing systems are advancing rapidly with the development of computers, video compression algorithms and storage devices. *See also* **EDL; nonlinear editing; off-line editing; on-line editing; random access; timeline.**

diskette   Name for removable floppy disk, used in computers. *See also* **floppy disk.**

disk recorder   A magnetic or optical disk used to record audio or video. The advantage of disk is the random access capability. Disk recorders usually have much smaller capacity than tape, especially for video recording. Disk recording of video signals is far more expensive than tape recordings, therefore disk recording is used only for special purposes such as high-end editing and automated transmission. Compression techniques are usually used to increase the capacity of disks. *See also* **compression (data); random access.**

display tube   Picture tube, or cathode ray tube (CRT). The TV screen. *See also* **cathode ray tube.**

dissolve   A smooth transition between two video signals. One signal slowly disappears while at the same time another one appears. During the dissolve the two signals overlap in an ever-changing ratio. Dissolves are used to soften the transition between two video sources. The length of the dissolve is normally in the neighborhood of one second, depending on the rhythm of the program. *See also* **fade.**

distance fog   Haze or fog characteristic of long-distance camera shots.

distortion   A change in a signal's characteristic, shape of image or waveform, usually unintentional. Distortion results from a less than perfect performance of all equipment involved in acquisition, processing, transmission and reception of radio and TV signals. Electrical, optical and mechanical equipment which is misaligned, overloaded, misused or defective in any way will in most cases distort signals. Care must be taken by operators and engineers every step of the way in order to avoid distortion. One of the benefits of modern digital equipment is that it is less subject to deterioration in performance and therefore causes less distortion to signals handled. Sometimes sounds or images are distorted intentionally in a controlled manner to create an artistic or other effect such as posterization and solarization.

distribution amplifier (DA)   An amplifier with one input and many outputs of the same signal. The purpose is to distribute exactly the same signal to many different instruments. The amplification is unity gain. The number of outputs is usually between four and ten. The DA is an important building block of studios, editing rooms and transmission facilities. Some distribution amplifiers also include cable equalization and delay capabilities. *See also* **cable equalization, delay.**

D-MAC   A transmission standard based on MAC, with the addition of NICAM digital audio. *See also* **MAC; NICAM.**

DMD   Digital micromirror device. A CMOS chip with a large number of microscopic mirrors mounted on the surface. Developed by Texas Instruments as a new projection method for use in video projectors. The number of mirrors in a video projector chip is approximately 500,000 and each can be moved to reflect light either to the screen or away from it. Each mirror can move three times during one frame to switch each one of the three primary colors of light separately. Light comes from a bulb, through a lens and a filter wheel.

dockable camera   A portable video camera designed in a way that a small portable VCR can be mechanically and electrically connected to it. Both units feed from the same battery or power supply and no interconnection cables are needed. This kind of setup makes it easy for the two units to be operated by one person.

Dolby   Name of the company that developed the audio noise reduction circuits known as "Dolby." The circuits they make are installed in home and professional audio equipment. A suffix letter such as B or C is added to the name "Dolby" such as B or C to denote the kind of circuit.

Dolby tone   A test signal usually recorded at the beginning of a tape containing Dolby-encoded material.

dolly   A camera support on wheels that enables the camera to move in any desired direction. The dolly is operated by persons other than the cameraperson. Also the name of the movement toward the object or away from it.

dolly shot   A camera shot taken in motion. The camera is mounted on the dolly and moved smoothly by dolly operators and camera crew. Sometimes a dolly movement is used to follow other movements such as a person walking and other times to move past stationary objects or persons.

domsat   Domestic satellite. Satellite transmission within a country, such as news broadcast from the field to the studio via satellite (SNG).

Doppler effect   A physical effect regarding waves of all kinds. If you move away from the source of the wave at a certain speed, the frequency of the wave you experience will decrease; and if you move toward the wave source, the frequency will increase.

DOS   Disk operating system. An operating system for personal computers created by Microsoft for IBM. DOS was developed to enable loading of the operating system from a floppy disk instead of from punched cards. DOS is a single-task, single-user system, but still a very popular operating system.

double cut   An edit of video material in which some frames appear twice. Double cuts can occur because of inaccuracy of editing equipment.

double exposure   In film, exposing the frame twice to get a double image. This can be made in the camera or in the lab. The same effect in video is obtained by an electronic mix of two video signals and is called superimposition or dissolve.

double system   A system in which the picture was recorded on film and audio on a special magnetic tape with the same width and perforation as the film. The double system was in use for many years in television and presented many problems. The handling of films and program material is complicated and it is common to have synchronization problems in which sound does not go together with the corresponding picture.

doubling   In audio, to create an effect of double the amount of singers or musical instruments in a recording, a slightly delayed signal is mixed with the original signal.

down converter   A circuit that converts certain frequencies to lower ones. A common down converter is one that converts high-frequency satellite transmission to a UHF-band frequency for the use of a home TV receiver.

downlink   A communications link from a satellite to a terrestrial station or a link from a transmitter to the studio. *See also* **uplink.**

downstage   The front of the stage; the part of the stage or studio close to the camera.

downstream keyer   A keyer in a video switcher placed after the mix-effect circuits at the end of the path of the signal. Background video can be changed while there is a key on air.

downtime   Period of time when equipment is taken for service or maintenance or when the equipment is out of service due to a fault. Unplanned downtime of equipment can cause increased production duration and costs.

DP (a) Director of photography. (b) Dramatis personae.

DRAM Dynamic random access memory. Every bit of data is stored in one transistor and a clock signal has to be supplied for the normal operation. Dynamic RAM has the largest capacity but not the fastest solid-state memory. *See also* **RAM, SRAM.**

dramatis personae Dramatic personnel. The actors and performers who appear in a play, film or program.

drift Continuous change in value of components and, as a result, changes in circuit parameters.

drop-frame time code Since there are 29.97 frames a second in NTSC signals, it introduces a difference between time code numbers and real time of 3.6 seconds per hour of program. To solve the problem, two time code numbers are dropped every minute.

dropout Defects in magnetic tape that cause momentary loss of signal during playback. Dropouts appear on video recordings as black lines in the picture. The more you use the same magnetic tape, the more dropouts you get. *See also* **dropout compensator.**

dropout compensator A circuit that is usually part of videotape recorders and videocassette recorders. Information is copied from neighboring lines in the video signal to replace missing picture information.

drop shadow An effect in which shadow is added to visual effects generated by effects generators and video switchers. Usually the shadow is below and to one side.

drum A mechanical assembly in helical scan videotape recorders such as Betacam, containing the headwheel (wheel with video heads mounted on it).

dry recording An audio recording without added artificial reverberation.

dry sound Sound that is unnatural due to insufficient reverberation or lack of low frequencies.

dry run A rehearsal for a TV program without recording or transmission.

DSP Digital signal processing. Internal camera signal processing. Modern broadcast TV cameras employ digital processing, which offers improved stability and reduced daily camera alignment time.

DT (a) Digital television. A television system that is digital all the way from the camera to the home receiver. Not yet available. The more complex part is to develop new transmission standards and to change the existing TV receivers. Work is being done on DT by many organizations and manufacturers, although major technological, economical and political problems are involved. There is no doubt, however, that the future belongs to digital television. *See also* **DVB.** (b) Dynamic tracking. A technology employed in many VCR machines to produce broadcast-quality slow motion and still frame. *See also* **dynamic tracking.**

DTH   Direct to home. Satellite transmission directly to the home viewer. The satellite signal is received by means of a small dish and a special home satellite receiver. *See also* **direct broadcast satellite.**

D-type connector   A standard for connectors used mainly for digital information in the computer industry. Also used frequently in TV facilities. Typically the numbers of pins are 9, 15, 25, 40 or 60.

dub   **(a)** To copy a recorded tape to another one in order to make an identical copy. **(b)** A copy of a video- or audiotape.

dubber   A recording and playback machine for 16 mm or 35 mm magnetic tape. Usually used in conjunction with telecine or film projectors. The dubber handles the audio part in a double system, while the picture is handled by another device. Dubbers are also used in the process of mixing many audio tracks to a final sound track of a feature film.

dulling spray   Canned spray used in studio lighting to reduce glare from shiny surfaces and objects.

dummy load   A load connected to a device instead of the normal load or equipment connected. A dummy load is connected to avoid damage during test or maintenance, normally to power outputs of amplifiers or transmitters or to maintain proper impedance at the end of a line or equipment output.

dupe   A copy of a film (duplicate). Normally used to make working copies for editing or for distribution to cinemas.

DVB   Digital video broadcasting. A project developed by a group of over 200 organizations and manufacturers all over the world. The DVB group is developing standards and practical methods for an all-digital television system that will use digital delivery techniques via cable, satellite and terrestrial transmitters. DVB is intended to use MPEG-2 to distribute improved sound and picture to the viewer at home as well as new digital services and text. It is planned to be able to deliver a number of quality levels from a limited 240 TV line level to full wide-screen HDTV quality with eight audio channels (or four pairs of stereo). DVB will include a series of standards for various all-digital applications:

DVB-C, a 7 MHz to 8 MHz bandwidth cable TV delivery system; DVB-T, a 7 MHz to 8 MHz terrestrial transmission system; DVB-S, a satellite delivery system designed to use 11-12 GHz band; DVB-SI, a service information system to be used by the DVB decoder; DVB-TXT, a teletext standard format, not linked to the vertical interval.

DVC   Digital videocassette. The latest in consumer formats, intended also for ENG work. The first working units were presented in 1995. DVC is a cooperation between Hitachi, JVC, Matsushita, Mitsubishi, Philips, Sanyo, Sharp Thomson and Toshiba, and will probably be adopted by many others.

The format is based on a 6.35 mm-wide tape in two sizes of cassettes, a 4.5-hour cassette ($14.6 \times 78 \times 125$ mm) and a 1-hour cassette ($12.2 \times 48 \times 66$ mm). It is built to record 525/60 4:1:1, 625/50 4:2:0 and HDTV television signals. DVC records 5:1 compressed 13.5 MHz 8-bit digital video signals. Video recording rate is 25 Mbits/sec. Audio is recorded in two channels of 16-bit 48 kHz or 44.1 kHz.

Based on the DVC format, there are professional-quality formats such as the DVCAM from Sony and the DVC-PRO from Panasonic. Each of these formats has a family of recorders for acquisition, editing and studio work. The professional versions are not always compatible with each other, and tape play times are different.

DVD   Digital video disk. A new standard for optical disks that is being developed to increase the capacity of the existing Compact Disc or CD-ROM. The DVD has been adopted by manufacturers in the broadcast and computer industries. DVD format will include a family of products that will be compatible with current CDs.

A single-layer disc will hold 4.7 GB of information, a double-layer single-sided disc will hold 9.4 GB, and a double-layer, double-sided disc will hold 18.8 GB. Write once and rerecordable media versions will be introduced.

The advantages of DVD are obvious for data storage, multimedia and storage of long video segments such as programs and feature films.

DVE   Digital video effects. *See* **digital effects.**

DVTR   Digital videotape recorder. DVTRs are more complex and expensive than analog VTRs, but they deliver better recording quality in both audio and video and multiple generation.

There are many DVTR formats: D1, D2, D3, D5, DCT, DVC and Digital Betacam. D1 was the first commercial digital VTR and it was first introduced in 1986. Some machines such as DCT, Digital Betacam and DVC use data compression to record the CCIR 601 on tape.

The multiple generation capability of digital machines is not without limits. New artifacts are introduced after a large number of generations, depending on the format. DVTRs employ complex error concealment circuitry to compensate for loss of data due to tape wear. *See also* **D1; D2; D3; D5; DCT; digital Betacam; DVC.**

dynamic cutting   As opposed to continuity cutting, in dynamic cutting during editing some sequences are placed in a nonsequential order to create a dynamic and nonconventional rhythm and structure.

dynamic microphone   A microphone widely used by sound engineers. The pickup device consists of a coil attached to a diaphragm and a fixed magnetic field. When sound waves move the diaphragm, the coil moves inside the magnetic field, creating small electric currents. Dynamic microphones are rugged and don't need internal or external powering, but they are less sensitive than condenser microphones.

dynamic range   The range or variation between the strongest and the weakest signals a device can handle. Dynamic range is limited by various mechanical and electrical factors. The lower end of the dynamic range is usually limited by the unwanted inherent noise of the device. Dynamic range is measured in decibels and is frequently used in conjunction with audio equipment.

dynamic rounding During some kinds of digital video processing such as mixing of two signals, multiplication of two 8-bit words occurs. The result—a 16-bit word—has to be reduced to 8 bits again. Dropping the 8 least significant bits causes visible contouring artifacts. Dynamic rounding is used to mathematically truncate the number of bits to 8 in a way that will result in a smooth picture.

dynamic signal processing Signal processing that is dependent on the signal parameters such as audio and video limiters and compressors and audio expanders.

dynamic tracking (DT) A feature that allows video recordings to be played in speeds different than normal play speed. In such players special video heads are used to follow the track during nonstandard speeds. The head can also jump from one track to another during playback. DT heads are mounted on a piezoelectric crystal that allows controlled movement of the head perpendicular to the tape movement direction. The piezoelectric device is controlled by a servo system in the VCR. *See also* **variable play.**

E-to-E Electronics to electronics. A function of audio and especially video recording machines. The signal applied to the input of the machine can go through the machine circuits and appears on its output when the machine is not playing. This option allows the operator to know what is connected to the input of the machine. Normally there is a two-position switch to operate the E-to-E option; the other option is "tape."

earth station A terrestrial transmit-receive station that maintains communications with satellites using microwave dish antennas. Usually earth stations are part of a large communications network linked to terrestrial relay stations and broadcast stations via microwave, cable or fiber-optical links. Small mobile earth stations are used to transmit from the field to the studio via satellite. *See also* **satellite communications; SNG.**

EBU European Broadcasting Union. An organization that consists of European broadcasters located in Geneva, Switzerland, dealing among other things with coordination of production and technical aspects, especially of the 625/50 European standard.

echo (a) Visual effect in which an image appears many times in a video picture. (b) Audible effect of repetition. *See also* **reverberation.**

echo return In an audio mixing console, circuitry, connections and switches involved in the return of a signal from an external echo or reverberation unit.

echo send In an audio mixing console, circuitry, connections and switches involved in sending a signal to an external echo or reverberation unit.

ECU *see* **extreme close-up**

edit The assembly or joining together of two sequences of audio, video or both either by physical cutting of the tape or film or by selective copying from one tape to another. *See also* **editing.**

edit controller A device used in editing rooms to regulate the operation of the different devices involved in the editing process such as VCRs, switchers, effects machines and audio mixers. The editor or operator of the editing room loads the edit information and commands either manually or from a computer file into the edit controller, which is a complex computerized device. The edit controller is connected to other devices in the editing room by a communications protocol such as RS-422 and via the protocol controls the other devices in the room to perform the edits. Often when edits involve simultaneous operation of several devices, such as a dissolve from player A to player B together with audio cross-fade, the edit controller has to calculate when exactly to run the different machines and to give the correct orders to the video switcher and audio mixer. Edit controllers can also perform a long series of edits according to an editing list (EDL) prepared somewhere else. *See also* **AB-ROLL; edit suite; EDL.**

editing The process in which a film or TV program is assembled from many segments. Editing is used to cut out faulty parts of the program or to use the best take of a scene out of many. Editing is also used to create a certain atmosphere and rhythm. Film editing is done by cutting the film and splicing the segments in a different way or order. Video is edited electronically by copying segments of picture and sound from one tape to an-other. Music, sound effects, video effects and titles can be added during editing. When a recorded program is longer than its airtime slot, editing is used to shorten it accordingly. An edited program can be joined together from many kinds of material, such as documentaries that use archive material from many sources and studio-recorded material as well. Normally editing is a time-consuming process and except for live transmission programs, almost every program goes through the editing process. *See also* **AB-ROLL; assemble edit; cut-to-cut; edit; edit controller; editor; editing suite; insert edit; off-line editing; on-line editing.**

editor **(a)** The person who performs the process of editing. Artistic as well as technical capabilities are required for the function of an editor. **(b)** A term sometimes used for an edit controller. *See also* **edit controller.**

edit suite A room where the editing equipment is located and the editing is performed.

EDL Editing decision list. A list of edit information including the number of the edit, number of reel or tape, edit points for the player and recorder, kind of edit or transition (cut, dissolve, wipe), duration of the transition and more.

There are some standards for EDL structure—usually every large manufacturer of editing equipment has one. An EDL can be made and stored on a floppy disk in one editing room during off-line editing and used to execute the final editing in the on-line editing room at another time. Once the EDL is complete, the final editing process becomes a technical routine. *See also* **off-line editing; on-line editing.**

EDTV Extended definition television. A general term for TV transmission standards such as High-Definition Television (HDTV) that have higher picture definition than the conventional NTSC or PAL standards. EDTV normally employs progressive scan and wide-screen techniques. *See also* **HDTV; PALplus; progressive scan, wide-screen.**

educational broadcasting Broadcast of classroom or general educational programs. Educational broadcasting is usually noncommercial and funded by the government and donations.

educational television TV station or channel intended for educational broadcasting only. *See also* **educational broadcasting.**

effects filter Glass filter mounted on the front of the camera lens or on a filter wheel behind the lens in large studio cameras to create visual effects. *See also* **filter (optical); filter wheel.**

effects library A collection of sound effects indexed and ready for use, recorded on tape or disk. Sound effects are mixed into film, radio and television programs to make the sound more realistic and rich. Effects libraries normally include domestic, city, nature, industry and transportation sounds.

Recording of sound effects can be a time-consuming and specialized job, and the availability of ready-to-use effects saves time during production and postproduction.

effects track An audio track in a multitrack machine or videotape used for audio effects only. This track is later mixed with other tracks to produce the final mix of the program. Effects track includes sounds such as car noise, footsteps, door slams and backgrounds such as street noise, restaurant noise and factory noise.

EFP Electronic field production. A video production made outdoors, usually by an outside broadcasting vehicle equipped with several video cameras.

EHF Extremely high frequency. Frequency band of 30,000 to 300,000 MHz. Wavelength is in the range of 1 cm.

EIA Electronic Industries Association. An American organization that publishes test procedures and standards for 525/60 TV.

8 bits (a) The video signal is quantized in serial digital video to eight bits of digital signal. (b) A standard data "word" is eight bits long. *See also* **bit.**

8 mm A consumer standard for audio and video recording on a compact cassette only 8 mm wide.

EIRP Effective isotropic radiated power. In a satellite downlink, the sum of the output power amplifier and the gain of the transmitting antenna expressed in dBW.

E.J. Electronic journalism. Journalism created and distributed by electronic media such as radio and TV, as opposed to newspapers. Electronic journalism in general has the advantages of being faster than written journalism and being able to deliver sounds and sights in real time.

electron gun A cathode in a picture tube that, given the right conditions, will emit a stream of electrons toward the screen or anode. *See also* **CRT.**

electronic editing Editing of video material by copying sequences selectively to a blank tape. In the first years of videotape machines, editing was done by cutting and splicing the tape. This method presented some problems: the splices used to break while the edited tape was playing to air, and the editing process was complicated and inaccurate. Nowadays electronic editing is accurate, reliable and keeps the master tape in one piece. No cutting of tape takes place in electronic editing. *See also* **editing.**

elevation The vertical angle of an instrument, such as a dish pointed at a satellite.

embedded audio Audio signal that is part of a serial digital data stream also containing a video signal.

Emmy Awards Annual awards presented by the National Academy of Television Arts and Sciences since 1949. Today the Emmy Awards are considered the most prestigious in the field of television. The awards are for achievements in news and documentaries, daytime programming, sports, engineering, community service and public service announcements.

encoded chroma key A chroma key circuit that uses an encoded video signal from which to take the color information. Since the encoded chroma key produces inferior results in comparison to the component chroma key, it is used only where a component signal is not available.

encoder A circuit that creates a single composite video signal out of several component signals such as RGB or Y, B – Y, R – Y. In a composite environment, cameras, character generators and other signal sources that produce component signals have to employ an encoder to submit a composite output. An encoder circuit can be part of another device, such as a camera, or a self-contained device in its own housing.

encryption Coding of data in such a way that specific information is needed to restore the original data. Encryption is employed to avoid access to data by unauthorized users.

endoscopic lens A lens used in medicine to be inserted into the body. The endoscopic lens is thin and flexible, sometimes composed of an array of optical fibers.

energy distribution curve In audio, a curve that describes the amount of amplitude or energy over the audio frequency range for a given sound source such as a musical instrument, voice or a combination (mix) of several sources.

ENG Electronic news gathering. Originated when the first portable hand-held professional video cameras were used, to distinguish from film news gathering. ENG normally refers to a news crew using a single portable video camera or camcorder. Also refers to the kind of equipment that is portable and self-powered.

engineering department Department in a TV station or other facility in charge of all technical aspects of planning, purchasing, operating and maintenance of equipment. At the head of the engineering department is the chief engineer.

envelope The outer shape of a waveform. Usually used in reference to modulated waves or waveforms that are more complex than a sine wave. *See also* **RF envelope.**

environmental sound *see* **room tone**

EOT End of tape. Message displayed by some tape recording machines as a warning that a short time is left for recording or playback on that tape.

EPG Electronic programming guide. A new and interactive way to present to viewers cable and TV program information. Program schedules are displayed on the screen, including the program, the channel and the time of transmission. The viewer can select a channel or preset a recording directly from the screen by one keystroke on a remote control. Additional services are sometimes provided such as on-screen weather, news, stock exchange and sports information. The programming guide information is either transmitted together with the TV channels (on air or in cable systems) or transmitted separately to air and picked up by a dedicated receiver.

episode One portion or program of a series of programs broadcast on TV.

EPROM Erasable programmable read-only memory. A kind of memory chip that does not need power to maintain data. The data can be erased usually by exposure of the chip to strong ultraviolet light. After erasure, new data can be programmed onto the chip. Normally an EPROM programmer is needed to load the data onto the chip.

EQ Short for equalization. *See also* **equalization.**

equalization Treatment given to signals to compensate for certain deterioration or loss of gain in specific frequencies, occurring when the signal has passed through equipment such as amplifiers, mixers, recorders and cables. In audio, equalization is also done in mixing consoles to compensate for insufficient microphone quality and less than ideal acoustical conditions. *See also* **audio console; cable equalization.**

equal loudness contours Graphs of the sensitivity versus frequency of the human ear for different loudness levels.

erase head An electromagnetic element in audio and video recording equipment that erases previously recorded tracks on tape. There are two kinds of erase heads: the stationary head, which usually erases the full tape width, and the flying erase, located on the head wheel and used to erase selected tracks from the tape.

erase oscillator An oscillator used in audio- and videotape recorders to supply erase current to erase heads.

error correction Error correction is used to restore lost data such as digital video information recorded on tape. Due to imperfection of the tape, small amounts of data are sometimes lost, causing signal degradation. Error correction is possible by making certain mathematical operations on the original data and recording the result on tape together with the data. If loss of data occurs, the lost data portion can be retrieved by a reversed mathematical operation. Error correction in serial digital video signals has to be performed very fast, in real time, since the stream of data is fast and continuous.

error signal A voltage proportional to a specific error such as an error in capstan speed, iris position or audio gain. Error signals are used mainly in servo systems to drive or trigger the correction process.

essential area *see* **safe area.**

establishing shot In film and TV, a wide camera shot used to show the surroundings of the scene. The establishing shot is used for the orientation and establishment of the place, time of day and general atmosphere of the place of scene. Normally, programs and scenes start with a long establishing shot and proceed later with closer shots. Establishing shot is also called orientation shot or cover shot.

ESG Electronic sports gathering. Similar to electronic news gathering. Coverage of sports events by means of electronic video equipment. The picture and sound are transmitted live or recorded for later use.

EST Eastern Standard Time. The farthest eastern time zone in the United States.

Ethernet Widely used computer network LAN (local area network). Computers are interconnected by twisted pairs, coax cables or fiber optic cables. Every computer connected to the network is equipped with a network interface circuit board. According to the requirements of the network, such as speed and distance between computers, hardware is selected. Ethernet networks are controlled by one computer, which is the "server." Sometimes more than one server is employed. The server is normally the fastest computer and the one with the biggest memory.

ETV *see* **educational television**

EURIKA A European institute that coordinates collaboration in research and development of new TV systems such as PALplus and HDTV within Europe.

Eutelsat A European organization for satellite telecommunications headquartered in Paris, France.

expander An amplifier in which the amplification grows as the signal amplitude grows. Expanders are used to increase the dynamic range of signal. They perform the opposite operation of a compressor, expanding the lower part of the signal from zero up to the threshold point.

expansion ratio In an audio expander, the ratio between input level change and output level change. Ratio is expressed in a number such as 1:4.

expansion threshold In an audio expander, the signal input level below which the expander will start to expand.

exposure   (a) Exposing film or any other light-sensitive material or device to light. (b) Bringing certain information to the knowledge of the media and public.

exposure meter *see* **light meter**

exposure setting   TV lens iris opening selected for specific light conditions. Iris setting determines the amount of light that will reach the light-sensitive device, picture tube or CCD. In film and stills, shutter speed is also crucial for the correct exposure (exposure time).

extender board   A circuit board with no components, used for troubleshooting. The extender board has connectors on both sides and connecting wiring or printed lines between the two sides. Normally circuit boards are densely packed inside appliances in such a way that it is not possible to service them while working. An extender board allows the mounting of a board for tests or adjustment outside the housing of an appliance and with the appliance turned on.

exterior   Scene or part of a program taking place outside the studio. Exterior scenes are subject to uncontrolled weather, lighting and sound conditions, which can sometimes cause extension of time schedules and budgets.

external broadcasting   Broadcasting services aimed at foreign countries, usually established by governments. Before the age of commu-

nication satellites, long-distance or global external broadcasting was done mainly by radio. Today satellites routinely distribute TV signals all over the globe.

external key   A video signal connected to a video switcher to be used only as key signal. Usually a special input is provided in switchers for external key. *See also* **key.**

extreme close-up   A very tight camera shot. Normally in a close-up, a person's face and shoulders will be included. In an extreme close-up only the face will be included—and sometimes only part of the face.

eyecup   A soft rubber cup placed on viewfinders to soften the contact of the eye with the viewfinder housing. It also prevents light entering from the sides.

eye level   A shot that is taken at the level of the performer's eyes.

eye pattern   A method of measuring the different parameters of serial digital video signals. The signal is displayed on an oscilloscope and measurements such as amplitude, rise time, jitter and unit interval can be performed. There are models of oscilloscopes specially made for eye pattern measurements, with special scales. The frequency of the digital "carrier" is high (143 Mb/s for NTSC, 270 Mb/s for CCIR 601) and the test equipment must be chosen accordingly. After the transformation of video and audio to a digital stream of data, there are very few measurements to make and the eye pattern supplies most of them.

eyepiece   Adjustable part of a viewfinder including usually a lens and an eyecup. The lens is used to enlarge and focus the viewfinder's picture. *See also* **eyecup.**

facilities person   A person employed as floor or stagehand or grip.

facsimile (fax)   Device used for transfer of pictures, drawings or printed material, usually through telephone lines. They are useful for fast transfer of scripts, contracts and other material during production.

fade   A transition in which the picture gradually disappears (fade out) normally to black or appears from black (fade in). In audio, sound going down to silence or coming up from silence. Many programs start with a fade-in of picture and sound and end with a fade-out of picture and sound. The length of the transition normally depends on the rhythm of the music at that point. *See also* **cross-fade.**

fade-in *see* **fade**

fade-out *see* **fade**

fader   Slider, part of a potentiometer in an audio mixing console used to control the level of audio channel or for fading audio in and out.

fader start   Starting a machine such as an audiotape machine by a contact attached to the fader in the mixing console that controls the level of that tape. This arrangement is efficient because one movement of the hand runs the tape and opens the channel while the other hand is free to perform other tasks. Very common in radio stations.

fall time   The time taken by an electrical pulse to decrease its level from 90 percent to 10 percent of its maximum amplitude. *See also* **rise time.**

fast motion   Projecting a film at a faster frame rate than it was shot or playing a videotape faster than the recorded speed to obtain an effect of rapid movement in the picture. *See also* **slow motion.**

FCC   Federal Communications Commission. Regulatory agency that sets standards and regulations for communications including telephone, radio and television in the United States. Seven FCC commissioners are appointed by the president for a seven-year period. FCC regulates and controls allocation and use of broadcast bands and frequencies. It also issues operator and station licenses and assigns call letters. The FCC is also involved in long-term planning of transmission standards and formats such as HDTV.

FDDI   Fiber data distributed interface. A fiber optic cable interface used mainly for computer networks. FDDI can deliver up to 100 Mbits/sec.

FDM   Frequency division multiplex. Technique for transmission of multiple signals on one channel or line. Subcarriers in different frequencies carry all modulated signals at the same time. NTSC, PAL and SECAM standards use FDM to send luminance, chrominance, sound and data at the same time through one channel or transmission line. Interaction between frequencies can cause unwanted effects such as cross color. *See also* **TDM.**

feed   An external TV signal source coming into a studio or TV station.

feedback   A situation in which part of an output signal from a system is fed back into the input of the system. Feedback is used in amplifiers to alter parameters such as gain and stability. In this case, feedback is accurately planned and controlled. Sometimes feedback occurs unintentionally and it can cause damage to equipment. For example, in sound systems where a microphone is connected to an amplifier and speakers, sound from the speakers can go back to the microphone, be amplified again and so on in an endless loop. In this case, audio levels will go up until they get to the upper limits of the system and burn fuses or cause damage to the amplifier and speakers, not to mention the ears of the audience.

fiber channel   High-speed computer network standardized by ANSI. It is planned to deliver 2 Gbits/second and more. Several major manufacturers are planning products for the all-digital, tapeless TV station. Regardless of the name, fiber channel can run on coax cable or twisted pair as well.

fiber optics   Very thin glass fibers used to transmit modulated light carrying information such as video. A fiber with a thickness of a human hair can carry information usually requiring thousands of copper telephone wires.

At both ends of a fiber optic line a special modulator and demodulator are needed to convert information such as audio, video or computer data into a modulated light beam and to restore the original information from the other end of the fiber line.

Being an optical medium, fiber lines are immune to crosstalk and electromagnetic interference of all kinds.

Optical fibers are usually grouped together in shielded cables that protect them from the environment. Usually fiber optic cables are joined to existing telephone infrastructure.

Fiber optics technology is replacing copper wires, coax cables and microwave links as a means for conveyance of large quantities of data.

fidelity   In recording of a signal such as audio, the accuracy of the reproduction of the signal in reference to the original signal. The higher the fidelity, the higher the quality of the recording will be. In the early days of home audio systems the term "high fidelity" (Hi-Fi) was used in relation to systems that gave a good reproduction of sound.

field   In a video signal, a single picture or frame is a combination of horizontal lines that scan the picture area from left to right. Every frame consists of two fields. Field one contains all the odd lines and field two contains all the even lines. The two sets of lines interlace to form a complete picture or frame. The number of fields per second in NTSC is 60 (50 in PAL). The number of lines per frame in NTSC is 525 and per field is 262½. *See also* **frame.**

field of view   The horizontal and vertical angles that confine the area visible through a lens. Field of view is one of the important attributes of a lens. Zoom lenses have a field of view that can be changed within specific limits. The proportion between the height and width for a specific lens is always fixed (3 to 4 in standard TV).

The field of view angles are important for planning of sizes and distances of objects and scenery in the studio and on the set.

field service   Maintenance given to equipment or software at the customer's site.

filler (fill)   Program material used to fill time intervals in a broadcast schedule. Live events sometimes end ahead of time, leaving time to be filled.

fill light   Illumination used to soften the strong contrast between the areas lit by the key light and other dark, unlit areas. The intensity of the fill light determines the contrast of the picture. If the fill light is dark, the outcome will be a dramatic picture with strong contrast. On the other hand, fill light with intensity close to the key light intensity will produce a "flat" picture. In the studio, floodlights are normally used to produce fill light. In daylight scenes, stronger light sources are usually needed, such as HMIs or reflectors that divert sunlight to the object. *See also* **backlight; floodlight; key light.**

film   Thin, long strips of celluloid or plastic coated with light-sensitive emulsion. The emulsion is developed after exposure to light, leaving an image on the film. There are various kinds of black and white and color film with different sensitivities. Film is the basis for the cinema and still photography industries and has been manufactured for many years in the same format. Several width standards are used for various applications: 70 mm film is used for wide-screen cinema; 35 mm is usually used for fea-

ture films and commercials; 16 mm, once widely used for news coverage and documentaries, today is almost obsolete; 8 mm and super 8 mm are no longer in use. Both 35 mm and 16 mm perforated film can be transferred to video by telecine machines, and some TV programs are still shot on film. Most experts believe that film is superior in picture quality to video.

film camera   A camera that photographs a large number of pictures per second on film. The camera consists of a lightproof housing that contains the mechanism that moves the film, a lens, viewfinder and a film magazine, usually detachable. The film is moved one frame each time by an electromechanical mechanism, then stops, the shutter is opened for a short time to expose the film to light and then the film is moved forward to the next frame. This process is repeated usually 24 or 25 times per second. After exposure in the camera, the film needs to be developed.

Film cameras used for feature film normally employ 35 mm film; 16 mm film is used for more mobile and less expensive work such as students' films and some nature photography. The 8 mm and super 8 mm film cameras are now obsolete and video camcorders are used instead.

film splicer *see* **splicer**

film-to-tape transfer   Transfer of images from film to videotape. The tool for such transfer is the telecine machine. Feature films are transferred to tape to be transmitted on TV, while some programs and commercials are produced on film and then transferred to tape. The amount of information on a 35 mm film is much larger than a video frame; therefore, the transfer produces a good-quality videotape. Reversing the process by transferring tape to film will produce poor-quality film. *See also* **telecine.**

filter (electrical) An electrical circuit used to forward some frequencies and to block others. There are many kinds of filters, the most common being low-pass, high-pass and band-pass. Such filters are used by most electronic instruments.

filter (optical) Glass or other transparent material used to alter the composition or intensity of light passing through. There are several kinds of filters: **(a)** Neutral density filters (ND): used to lower the intensity of light without any change in the color composition of the light. **(b)** Color temperature correction filters: used to change the color of light from daylight to artificial light and vice-versa in order to adjust it to the kind needed by the camera. **(c)** Coloring filters: used to change the color of the light. **(d)** Effects filters: used to add effects such as fog, stars and diffusion. **(e)** Polarizing filters: used to eliminate reflections from windows and shiny surfaces.

Filters are placed either on the front of the lens or behind the lens inside the camera's body. They are also used in lighting to modify color temperature of lamps and to create colored lighting. Filters used for lighting are placed over the lens or light output of the lamp. *See also* **color temperature; dichroic filter; neutral density (ND); polarizing filter.**

filter factor The amount of light that a given filter absorbs is expressed in percents or f-stops. An increase of exposure or lighting intensity is needed to compensate for the light loss.

filter wheel A flat wheel with several filters fixed in it. Used in video cameras to enable quick change of filters either by hand or by motor in large studio cameras. Usually ND and effects filters are mounted in the filter wheel.

fine cut The last stage of the process of film editing (sometimes this term is used for video editing as well). Comes after rough-cut stages. *See also* **rough cut.**

fisheye An extreme wide-angle lens, with strong barrel aberration and a highly curved front element. The focal length of this kind of lens is very short and the depth of field is long. The image is distorted, especially around the edges.

fish pole Microphone boom held by hand, usually in field production, sometimes in the studio. Modern fish poles come in different sizes and are made of carbon fibers folding to compact and lightweight units.

flag Small square sheet of metal used to shade camera lens or part of the scene. Flags are usually painted black and mounted on a stand. *See also* **French flag.**

flaps *see* **barn doors**

flare Light from a strong source coming into the camera lens, not in the normal path but reflected randomly from internal parts of the lens. Flare causes unwanted effects such as spots and beams of light, or the image of the light source multiplied several times in the picture. The internal parts of a lens are always made to be nonreflective, but when a strong light source is involved, the reflection cannot be totally eliminated.

flat (a) In reference to a picture or video signal, having insufficient contrast. (b) Dull, uninteresting.

flat lighting Low-contrast, uniform lighting with little or no highlight or lighting effects. Usually the result of using floodlights only when building the set lighting.

flat response Behavior of a system in which the output signal amplitude or bandwidth is identical to the input signal. The term *flat response* refers to a graph comparing output to input voltage. If there is no change, the graph will be flat.

flicker A phenomenon of TV, cinema and computer screens. Since the picture displayed consists of series of single frames appearing each for a fraction of a second, sometimes the eye notices the small interval between frames and the screen appears to be flickering. Flickering is a problem in cinema projectors as well. In cinema the way to eliminate flicker is to show every frame of the film twice. In TV the method is to divide every frame into two fields and to display them separately. The human eye can perceive a series of pictures as individual pictures up to the rate of approximately 40 pictures per second, depending on factors such as lighting conditions, brightness and contrast of the displayed pictures.

flip An effect created by digital picture manipulators in which a picture seems to be turned around its vertical axis.

flip-flop A family of basic electrical circuits that are used to form memory cells and other building blocks of analog and digital circuits.

floodlight A lighting instrument that produces a widespread diffused light. Floodlights are one of the basic lighting instruments found in every cinema or TV studio, used to create soft and uniform background lighting. Floodlights do not create harsh shadows like spotlights and therefore make people look better. *See also* **backlight; fill light.**

floor Studio or stage floor. The place where rehearsal, production or shooting takes place.

floor manager The person in charge of the studio staff and performers during rehearsals and recording or transmission. He or she also coordinates between the director in the control room and studio. The floor manager wears headphones connecting through the intercom system to the director and control rooms.

floor men/women Persons in charge of erecting and dismantling scenery, placing props and other activities in the studio or onstage.

floor plan Drawing of the stage or studio floor used for planning of scenery, lighting and camera location.

floppy disk A thin flexible disk coated with magnetic oxide in a protective cover. The cover shields the disk and yet enables the disk drive to rotate the disk and contact the surface to write and read data. The floppy disk is a popular means of storing and transporting data and software. The first standard floppy disks measured 8 inches. Today 5.25- and 3.5-inch disks are standard. A 3.5-inch floppy disk can have a capacity of up to 1.4 Mbytes.

fluff An error, usually verbal, made by talent during production.

fluid head Camera mounting head used to enable the camera to make pan and tilt movements in a very smooth and continuous way. This is achieved by forcing a fluid (usually oil) through narrow holes while moving. This arrangement does not allow any sudden movement.

fluorescent lamp Fluorescent lamps are vapor discharge lamps in which the glass tube is internally coated with a substance that fluoresces, thereby increasing the light output of the lamp. Lamps are normally long and tubular, up to eight feet in length. A fluorescent lamp is a very efficient kind of lamp, about three times the efficiency of a normal domestic tungsten lamp. Fluorescent lamps produce soft, low-intensity light used normally in public places, factories and hospitals.

fluorescent lighting Lately some manufacturers have begun making fluorescent lighting for TV studios. This kind of lighting saves a lot of power both in lighting and air-conditioning. Manufacturers produce fluorescent lamps with color temperatures of 3,200° K and 5,600° K needed for

production. New fluorescent lighting is dimable, flicker-free and has high frequency.

flutter Variations in movement speed of tape or other recording media occurring more than 15 times per second. Flutter causes distortion or vibration in the pitch of the reproduced sound. Can also cause problems in reproducing video signals recorded on tape. Measured in percentages of the nominal speed. *See also* **wow; wow and flutter.**

flyaway Portable satellite uplink unit built into flight cases. Cases are of a size that enables the equipment to be carried by a van or aircraft. Such an uplink unit is usually used for transmission of news to the home station via satellite from practically anywhere in the world. *See also* **uplink.**

flyback (a) The motion of an electron beam inside a picture tube of a video camera or a cathode ray tube from the end of a line or field back to the beginning. During this period the beam's intensity is reduced so that the retrace will not be visible. (b) A name for the high-voltage transformer used in TV sets.

flying erase An erase head in a video recorder mounted on the headwheel. A flying erase head is needed for frame-accurate erasure of video only for editing purposes.

flying spot An early method used by film and slide scanners to produce a video signal. A high-intensity CRT is placed on one side of the film and a light-sensitive photocell on the other side. A small bright spot scans the CRT screen. The light goes through the film and a focusing lens to the photocell. The voltage or current the photocell produces is relative to the transparency or brightness of the film in every given point. Flying spot film scanners produce sharp images, and some models are still used today. *See also* **telecine.**

FM *see* **frequency modulation**

f-number   Also known as relative aperture. A number representing the relative aperture of a lens. The f-number is equal to the focal length f divided by d, the effective diameter of the lens or iris. The bigger the f-number, the smaller the amount of light passing through the lens and vice-versa. The aperture of the lens diaphragm is indicated by f-numbers. The importance of the f-number is that it is an instrument to obtain the same aperture with different lenses. Two different lenses with the same f-number will deliver the same amount of light if the lighting conditions are the same. Usually f-numbers are written in the form f 8 or f/8.

FOB   Free on board. Commercial term meaning goods delivered and taxes paid to a specific location.

focal length   The distance from the lens by which an image of an object in infinity is formed. The longer the focal length, the larger or the more magnified the image will be and the field of view will be narrower. The shorter the focal length, the less magnified the image will be and the field of view will be wider. The focal length is normally engraved on the outside of the lens in a form such as f = 50 mm. In zoom lenses the focal length changes within certain limits, such as f = 50–200 mm (not to be confused with f-numbers). *See also* **field of view; f-number.**

focal plane   A virtual or real plane perpendicular to the optical axis of a lens on which a focused image is formed. In film cameras, the film is placed in the focal plane of the lens. In video cameras, the picture tubes or CCD units are placed at this plane.

focal point   A point on the optical axis of a lens to which parallel rays of light appear to converge or from which rays diverge to form a virtual focus.

focus   **(a)** A point to which light or sound waves converge. **(b)** The exact location of the object that will cause the lens to produce a sharp image at the plane of the light-sensitive device.

focusing   The camera lens creates an image of what is in front of it. This image is intended to be as sharp as possible on the plane of the light-sensitive device inside the camera. In video cameras this device can be a picture tube or a CCD element. In order to get a focused picture, the distance of the lens from the plane of the light-sensitive device must be correct, and it changes if the object changes its distance from the lens. Adjustment of the correct distance is done normally by moving the front cell of the lens forward and backward in a screwed mount. This adjustment is the actual focusing and it can be a continuous action if the object moves away or toward the camera lens. Sometimes, for artistic reasons, the image is defocused intentionally.

focusing ring   A ring around the lens housing used to focus or defocus the image by moving optical elements inside the lens (usually the front element) forward or back. The ring is grooved for a nonslip grip and several object distances are marked on it, from the minimum object distance of the lens to infinity. A mark on the lens barrel allows focusing according to a known object distance.

focus puller   A person in feature film productions whose job is to measure the distance from the lens to the object and to adjust the focus ring of the lens accordingly. If there is movement in the scene, the focus puller's job is to keep adjusting the focus while the camera is shooting to get a sharp image at all times.

fog filter   A filter used to create the impression that the scene is foggy. Sometimes used to hide wrinkles or other defects. Fog filters come in different degrees of fog and can be mounted on the front of the lens or, in studio cameras, on the filter wheel.

fog machine   A device used to produce fog on the set or in concerts. The use of fog onstage or in the studio makes light beams from spotlights highly visible. This phenomenon is used to enhance the effect of beams of colored or moving lights.

fold back   Sound played to musicians or singers by earphones in a recording studio, usually previously recorded by the same persons. Used when a multichannel recording is made in separate stages. A final mix is then performed to get the finished sound tracks. Sometimes fold back sound is sent to monitoring loudspeakers onstage or in the studio.

follow focus   To continuously keep in focus a moving object or person during shooting of film or video.

follow spot   A lamp that produces a strong focused light beam used to illuminate performers in theater, circus, cinema and television. The light beam from the follow spot is normally used to follow the performer wherever he goes in a round spot of light, when the background illumination is darker.
  The follow spot is a strong lamp with focusing lenses and an iris that determines the diameter of the light spot. Follow spots are mounted on a tripod or stand that allows movement (pan and tilt). An operator is needed to aim the beam in the right direction and follow the performer's movement in a steady way.

font   A shape or design of a complete family of letters and numbers. Different fonts are used in character generators, word processors and many other kinds of computer software. Every font has its own distinct shape and name and is usually copyrighted.

foot-candle   A unit of illumination, also called candela. The intensity of light on a surface at the distance of one foot away from a standard candle. Foot-candle is used mainly in studios to measure light levels.

footlights   Lights in a row on the contours of a studio set or at the front of stage or stairs.

footprint   The area on earth to which a satellite's transmission is aimed. The satellite's signal within the footprint can be received with a relatively small antenna. Outside the footprint a considerably larger antenna is needed to receive the signal. The footprint can be wide, covering a whole continent, or narrow, depending on the structure of the transmission antenna or dish.

4 fsc   Four times the frequency of the subcarrier. A number frequently used as a sampling rate for video signals.

4:1:1   A ratio of sampling frequencies in subcarrier frequency multiplication used in digitizing video signals. The first number is the luminance (Y) sampling rate, the second and third are for the color difference R – Y and B – Y signals. The 4 represents 13.5 MHz and the 1s represent each 3.75 MHz of sampling frequency. 4:1:1 is used by the DVC videocassette recording standard in NTSC. *See also* **DVC.**

4:2:0   A ratio of sampling frequencies in subcarrier frequency multiplication used in digitizing video signals. The 4 represents 13.5 MHz and the color difference signals are sampled at 6.75 MHz every other line, meaning one line is sampled at 4:2:2 and the next one at 4:0:0. 4:2:0 is used in PAL versions of DVC. *See also* **DVC.**

4:2:2   A ratio of sampling frequencies in subcarrier frequency multiplication. The first number is the luminance (Y) sampling rate, the second and third are for the color difference R – Y and B – Y signals. The 4 represents 13.5 MHz and the 2s represent each 6.75 MHz of sampling frequency. The 4:2:2 ratio is used in the ITU-R 601 high-quality standard for digital broadcast video. *See also: CCIR 601.*

4:2:2:4   Same as 4:2:2 with an added key channel sampled at the same rate as the luminance channel, which is 13.5 MHz for NTSC.

4:3   Traditional television screen aspect ratio.

4:4:4   Ratio of sampling rates used in some computer-based equipment. All three components (Y, R – Y, B – Y or RGB) are sampled at four times the subcarrier frequency. Offers superior quality, but it is not applicable in television equipment where the standard is 4:2:2.

4:4:4:4   Same as 4:4:4 but with an added key channel.

FPS   Frames per second. The number of frames displayed during one second of film projection or the number of frames exposed during one second of shooting. The standard film frame rate is 24 FPS. During projection, every frame is projected twice to reduce flickering of the screen. *See also* **PPS.**

frame   **(a)** In film, a single still picture. The film is a long strip consisting of many frames in sequence. The frames are pictures of the scene taken in constant time intervals. In order to achieve the illusion of continuous motion, a frame or picture rate of at least 40 pictures per second (PPS) is needed. To save film, it is shot at a lower rate and every frame is projected twice. In cinema, 35 mm film has 24 pictures per second. **(b)** In TV, a set of lines that hold the information of one complete picture scanned from top to bottom (525 lines in NTSC). A TV frame consists of two fields, one for the odd lines interlaced together with the other one for even lines. The separation to two fields is to double the rate of pictures presented on the TV screen per second, in order to prevent flickering of the screen. In NTSC the frame rate is 30 per second and the field rate is 60 per second.

frame grab   An attribute of some graphics software designed to capture digitally a complete TV frame and process it or use it as background for graphics or characters. Still stores also grab frames to store them in memory or on disk.

frame store   A device that has a large memory and is capable of storing a complete TV frame. A frame store is usually part of a digital video effects unit or of a frame synchronizer. *See also* **video effects.**

framing   The arrangement of objects in the TV frame or the manner in which the cameraperson sets the frame to cover an object or objects.

freelancer   A professional who is not a member of the station or production house staff and is hired per job or assignment.

freeze frame *see* **still frame**

French flag   Small square sheet of metal connected to a flexible, adjustable arm used to shade a camera lens or part of the scene. Flags are usually painted black and mounted on a stand.

frequency   The number of full cycles of a periodic waveform or other phenomena in a given period of time. Frequency is normally measured in

cycles per second or "hertz." The hertz is low frequency relative to frequencies used in radio and especially in TV. For high frequencies, terms such as *kilo* (1,000), *mega* (1,000,000) and *giga* (1,000,000,000) are used. For example, 1 Khz is 1,000 hertz, or one thousand cycles per second.

frequency modulation   A signal such as audio or video modulates or changes the frequency of a periodic wave or carrier (normally a sine wave) by way of multiplication. The result is a carrier with changes in frequency according to the changes in the intensity of the video or audio signal. The carrier is transmitted and after it reaches its destination, the original signal is retrieved by demodulation. Frequency modulation is highly immune to interference, since interference usually affects the amplitude or envelope of the carrier wave rather than the frequency. *See also* **amplitude modulation; demodulation; modulation.**

frequency response   The ability of a circuit or device to handle different frequencies applied to it without change. Special test signals are used for measurement of frequency response. The test signal has different frequencies that cover the specific frequency range at the same level. The test signal is applied to the input of the device under test and the output is measured. For example, a video distribution amplifier has to deliver to every output all the frequencies included in the video signal as they are applied to its input. If one or more frequencies are suppressed, the picture produced by that signal will lack detail, chroma or other components.

fresnel lens A specially constructed, short focal-length lens used mainly as a condenser for spotlights. Short-focus lenses are normally thick and heavy. The fresnel lens is an arrangement of concentric glass rings, each one having a different part of the convex. In each ring the thickness is reduced to a minimum, thus reducing the overall mass of the lens. Because of their reduced width, fresnel lenses better resist the intense heat in studio lights. Fresnel lenses do not create a precise or sharp image, which in the case of spotlights is an advantage because it blurs the image of the lamp filament. Spotlights are also called fresnel lights.

fresnel spotlight A spotlight using a fresnel lens to focus the light beam. *See also* **fresnel lens.**

friction head A camera tripod head that provides smooth horizontal and vertical movement. The smoothness of movement is obtained by means of friction plates. The pressure on the friction plates is applied by external knobs that allow adjustment to fit the needs of the camera operator. *See also* **fluid head.**

front porch The part of a video signal between the end of active video and the beginning of horizontal synchronization pulse in every line.

frost A kind of diffuser for studio lights.

f-stop Numbers calibrating the ring adjusting the opening of a diaphragm in a lens. The ring usually moves with stops and the numbers denote the f-number for each stop. *See also* **f-number.**

fsc Subcarrier frequency or f-subcarrier. Some frequencies such as sampling rates are measured in multiplication of the subcarrier frequency.

FTFT Film/tape/film/tape. A process of editing video footage transferred from film. In order to save time and money, the footage is transferred to video in a one-lite process with no special attention to picture quality. The video material is edited off-line. At the next stage only the footage used in the editing is transferred again from film to tape, this time with full attention to picture quality and color correction. A master is then edited in an on-line process from the high-quality video material. This way, costly color-correction time is saved. *See also* **off-line; on-line; one-lite.**

full track A ¼-inch audiotape in which the entire tape width is used for one track, to distinguish from stereo or half-track formats that use the same tape width.

gaffer A chief lighting electrician in film productions in the studio and in outside locations.

gaffer grip A metal grip used for mounting or hanging lighting equipment.

gaffer tape An adhesive, isolating, strong and very useful tape used by gaffers and many others on a film or TV set for countless jobs. Width of the tape is usually two inches (5cm).

gain Ratio or amount of amplification or attenuation. Gain is mentioned mainly in relation to amplifiers or amplifier stages and antennas and is measured in decibels. *See also* **dB.**

gain before threshold   Gain of an audio compressor for input levels under the threshold level, measured in dB. *See also* **compressor.**

gain reduction   In an audio compressor, reduction of audio input levels above threshold level, measured in dB. *See also* **compressor.**

gamma   The slope of a curve in a logarithmic graph representing the relationship between the amount of light a light-sensitive element in a video camera receives and the output of the video signal it produces. In video cameras, gamma is adjustable normally in the range of 0.4 to 1. In practice, in a video camera the gamma adjustment determines the brightness of mid-range light levels of the scenes in the output picture. Picture tubes in TV sets have a fixed gamma value that is larger than 1.

The value of gamma for the complete chain beginning with the video camera and ending with the TV set should be close to 1, meaning that there is a linear relationship between light levels on the scene and the light levels reproduced on the TV screen. A number different from 1 will indicate a nonlinear light reproduction and contrast distortion. Because the gamma value of the screen is larger than 1, the gamma value of the camera signal has to be smaller than 1 to get a linear light transfer at the end of the path.

gap *see* **head gap**

gate   (a) Part of a cine camera or projector that holds the film in place and allows precise and smooth movement of the film without scratching it.

The gate is made very precisely and determines the size of the frame according to international standards. **(b)** A logic device, one of the important building blocks of digital electronic circuits. A gate is a circuit having some inputs (normally between one and ten) and one output. Every gate performs a logical operation such as AND, NAND, OR, NOR, XOR and invert. The inputs are presented with either a high voltage (logical 1) or a low voltage (logical 0) individually. The output state depends on the state of the inputs and the logical function it has to perform. For example, in an OR gate the output will be high if one of the inputs is high. In an AND gate the output will be high if all inputs are high. In computerized and other complex digital circuits, large numbers of gates are employed.

geared head   A camera tripod head in which the horizontal and vertical movements are provided through gears driven manually by a crank. This kind of head provides very precise movement and is normally used with cine cameras. Geared heads are not built for fast movements. *See also* **fluid head; friction head.**

gel   Thin plastic color filter used in front of floodlights or spotlights to change the hue of the light output. Gels come in many colors and are used to match or to correct a specific color temperature of light and to create different lighting effects. The name *gel* comes from the early filters that used to be made of gelatin.

generation   A term used to describe one cycle of recording a signal such as video or audio on tape. In the process of postproduction, sometimes the signals are transferred from tape to tape several times, each time for another purpose, to shorten, to add graphics, to add translation and so on. In every playback from one machine and recording onto another, the signals deteriorate. In the planning of a production, efforts are made to keep the number of generations to a minimum. In digital recording equipment, the amount of degradation is very small and therefore the issue of generation is less significant.

generation loss   Loss of quality in duplicated film, video or audio. In each generation or copy there is degradation of signal quality, mainly in analog systems. In digital signal processing and recording, generation loss is less crucial. *See also* **generation.**

genlock   Generator lock. Synchronization of a device to an external signal. In a studio or editing room, all devices that produce video signals, such as cameras, VCRs and character generators, must be genlocked to allow mixing of their output signals. The reference signal comes from a sync generator or other source of stable video signal. One sync generator can be locked to another if one feeds the other with a reference signal to lock onto.

geostationary orbit   Orbit of a satellite at the altitude of approximately 22,250 miles, parallel with the equator. At this altitude, the satellite travels with the earth's rotation and stays at the same place in relation to the ground. This kind of orbit is used by many communication satellites, allowing them to serve as stationary radio, telephone, data and TV global relay stations in space.

geosynchronous orbit *see* **geostationary orbit**

ghosting   In TV sets, duplication of the image on the screen. It usually occurs as a result of reflection of the transmitted signal from houses or hills. The reflected signal is received shortly after the direct signal, creating another image close to the primary one. Similar effects can be caused in studios and other facilities by open-ended or unterminated cables.

giga-   Prefix meaning billion (1,000,000,000). Used in conjunction with several units such as GByte (Gigabyte) and GHz (Gigahertz). *See also* **byte.**

glitch   A momentary interruption in continuity of a video signal, usually during playback or transmission.

GMT   Greenwich Mean Time. The time at longitude 0°, which is used for coordination of international exchange of all satellite communications.

gobo   **(a)** In film production, a flag or metal flap used to shade or prevent light from reaching certain areas in the scene. **(b)** In TV productions, a cutout used as foreground, normally for live action. **(c)** In audio, an absorbing partition used for acoustical separation between musical instruments or other sound sources.

good night   A term used to announce that a transmission is over, meaning usually, "Thank you for your services and you can switch off the equipment now." Normally used in communications between TV stations and switching and satellite stations while coordinating a transmission.

GPI General purpose interface. A two-wire interface used to trigger equipment such as digital effects units, video switchers and audio mixers. Usually the trigger is a contact closure between the two wires. GPIs are widely used in editing rooms to send a command from the editing controller to start effects and fades at the correct timing determined by the editor.

grades (in monitors) Video monitors are divided into three groups:

Grade 1: Very precise picture monitors with fine detail, low registration error and other aberrations. Grade 1 monitors are used by engineers for evaluation of video signals in studios and control rooms.

Grade 2: Medium quality; still produce very good pictures for general purpose in control rooms, editing rooms and studios.

Grade 3: Simple monitors; sometimes home receivers in which the quality of the picture does not reflect the quality of the signal fed to the monitor.

grain reduction In film-to-tape transfer, the use of electronic equipment to reduce film grain. The same equipment is normally used to reduce noise as well. *See also* **noise reducer.**

graphic equalizer A device comprised of a series of filters used to change the level of different frequencies in an audio signal. The difference in frequency between filters in professional graphic equalizers is usually ⅓ or ⅔ octave and the frequencies range from the low end of the hearing spectrum at 50 Hz up to the upper end at 16 kHz. The filters normally allow changes in the range of plus or minus 12 dB. The sliders of the filters are arranged side by side, where the low-frequency filters are on the left and the high-frequency filters are on the right. The position of the slider's buttons form a graph of the response of the equalizer across the frequency range, thus making it easy to see what kind of equalizing is applied, if any.

Graphic equalizers are used to correct imperfect frequency response of microphones and other audio equipment, to improve sound of singers and narrators and to make a certain instrument in an orchestra more or less noticeable. Graphic equalizers play an important part in audio recording, transmission and public address.

graphics Artwork done either by hand or with the aid of a computer, such as captions, drawings, graphs and photographs, used as background or inserts in TV programs.

gray scale A test chart having a series of panels in gray shades ranging from black to white in several steps (normally 5 to 11). A gray scale chart is used to check and adjust black and white and color cameras. With this chart, in color cameras the three color channels are checked to have the same response to the different luminance levels of the chart. Black level, gamma, gain and flare correction are adjusted for the R, G and B channels of the camera. If these parameters are correctly adjusted according to the gray scale, the color reproduction of the camera will be correct.

green One of the three primary additive colors (RGB) used in TV to produce all other hues.

grid Metal framework built above studio spaces for suspension of lighting equipment and scenery. In large studios there are catwalks on top of the grid so that equipment such as electrical wiring can be reached in relative comfort.

grille (crosshatch) (a) A test pattern generated by an electronic test generator as a video signal, used to test and align picture monitors. The grille is a black and white signal, having white horizontal and vertical lines on a black background. The monitor's geometry and registration (in color monitors) are checked using the grille. (b) A test chart put in front of a video camera to check geometry and registration (in color cameras only).

grip A person in a film production responsible for moving the camera on the tracks and sometimes also for constructing various platforms and other installations to hold the camera. Sometimes a grip is to be found in outside TV productions as well.

ground A part in electrical and electronic equipment wiring that is always in zero voltage. Utility system power sockets have one contact that is grounded. The utility system ground wiring is usually connected to metal pipes or girders that have contact with the earth.

Grounding of electrical equipment is essential to avoid flow of electrical current from a device through a person's body to the floor. Such flow can be harmful and even lethal. If the device and the floor have the same electrical potential, no current will flow. Housings of electrical devices are connected to ground, especially if they are made of conductive material such as metal.

ground loop Two or more ground connections or paths that exist in one system. Slight voltage differences between grounding points can cause interference in audio and video equipment, such as hum (in picture and sound) or noise in audio equipment.

ground row A series of cyclorama lights or spotlights lighting a cyclorama or scenery from ground level.

group delay A distortion of video signals occurring when passing through a device, system or line. Group delay is a difference in delay between components of different frequency. Group delay affects the sharpness of vertical lines in the TV picture by causing overshoots, undershoots and ringing in the video signal. Group delay is measured in nanoseconds (nsec).

grouping Controlling a group of channels or VCAs (voltage controlled amplifiers) with a single fader.

group master In audio consoles, a fader controlling the signal level for a group of channels.

group shot A camera shot that frames a whole group of people, as distinguished from other shots such as two-shot and three-shot.

guard band Space between tracks recorded on magnetic tape to avoid crosstalk.

guide path In tape machines, the path of the tape threaded between guides and posts leading the tape around the headwheel or other fixed heads.

guide track   A track of sound recorded temporarily, to help locate other tracks in place.

gun mike   A highly directional microphone used mostly outdoors. The gun mike is usually a condenser microphone with a long body, hence the name "gun." Also known as "shotgun microphone," the gun mike is very efficient in noisy environments because of its ability to collect audio signals from a specific direction and to conceal sounds coming from all other directions.

gyro zoom   Name for a lens with a built-in image stabilizer. This kind of lens is used mainly in sports and news, for shots taken in motion from cars, helicopters, boats or from the shoulder, in uneasy situations. Gyro zooms in general are able to eliminate a considerable amount of vibration in the picture.

H   Short for horizontal, which is frequently used in relation to TV and video (horizontal line, deflection, frequency, scan and phase).

half track   A two-channel, two-track audio recording format for ¼"-wide magnetic tape. Frequently used for stereo recording.

hand-held camera   A camera used without a mounting device such as a tripod or pedestal. The camera usually rests on the camera operator's shoulder, sometimes held overhead in crowded areas. Other positions are used for special purposes. Shooting from a hand-held camera is not a desirable practice if there are other choices; normally used for news and sports only. *See also* **steadicam.**

hand signals   Visual signals given to performers on the set, usually by the floor manager; also called cues. Hand signals are used during recording or transmission instead of vocal communications that will be picked up by the microphones. Standard signals are used for a variety of time, direction and other cues to indicate action such as standby, keep talking, speak up, roll tape, ten seconds and cut.

hard disk   The main storage device for digital data in computers. A hard disk comprises one or several metal disks coated with oxide. The disk rotates while magnetic heads in contact with the disk record or read data from the disk. Information on the disk is dense and capacity of magnetic hard disks can be several gigabytes for a standard disk fitted in a desktop computer. An important specification of a hard disk besides capacity is its access time. *See also* **access time.**

hard light   A spotlight producing strong highlights and dark shadows (as distinguished from soft light).

hardware   A general name for equipment, especially in the field of computers, to distinguish from software.

harmonic   A frequency that is a whole-number multiplication of a basic frequency. If the basic frequency is f, the harmonics will be 2f, 3f, 4f and so on. Theoretically, the number of harmonics is endless and they decay proportionately as the frequency grows higher. Harmonics are sometimes unwanted phenomena and other times put to use in circuits such as frequency multipliers.

harmonic distortion   Distortion of audio signals in which spurious harmonics are added to the original frequencies of the audio, usually after amplification. Harmonic distortion is measured as the percentage of spurious harmonics added to a pure sine wave or tone.

HDTV   High-definition television. An improved format for television. The amount of detail is five times that in current TV formats. Aspect ratio of HDTV is 16:9, meaning the screen is much wider. The number of picture lines in the European system is 1,250 and the field rate is 50. The intended standard for the U.S. is 1,125/60.

HDTV is a quantum leap in terms of picture quality, but the problems involved are complicated. All equipment needed for production and post-production in HDTV is highly expensive and home receivers are very expensive as well. There is a problem of compatibility with current home TV receivers that are not able to display HDTV signals at all, even in NTSC quality. There is a problem of wider transmission bands needed for HDTV, which in densely populated areas are not to be found.

HDTV transmissions will probably be digital and compressed, using MPEG 2; however, there is no agreement for a world standard. Detailed technical specification of HDTV can be found in SMPTE 260M and CCIR Rep. 801-4 papers.

HE *see* **head end**

head clogging   In video recording and playback equipment, the accumulation of dirt or oxide from the tape on the video head. This can cause disruption or loss of picture during playback and faulty recording that cannot be played back. To discover such a situation, a "confidence head" that plays back from tape during recording is used.

head end   In cable TV or closed-circuit television (CCTV), the end of the cable or cable network from which the signals are fed; in cable TV normally the transmission center.

head gap   A narrow space between the poles of a magnetic record head. Magnetizing of tape ferric oxide or metal particles takes place where the tape is in contact with the tape. The width of the gap in one of the factors that determines the maximum frequency that can be recorded on tape.

headphones   A device used to listen to audio privately, without disturbing others. Headphones are two earphones mounted on a framework to fit the head comfortably, holding the two earphones in place, covering one's ears. Headphones are connected by a wire, usually with a PL-55 connector at the end. This kind of connector can be plugged into most home audio appliances and to professional audio equipment as well. Stereo headphones are well suited for listening to stereo sound because of the good separation between the two earphones.

headroom   **(a)** The space in a camera shot between the top of a person's head and the upper end of the frame. **(b)** Range between the upper levels of audio signals to a level that will cause distortion and overload.

headset   An arrangement of earphones, sometimes including also a microphone, used in radio and TV studios. Headsets are normally used in places where open microphones are present so as not to interfere with program sound. Headsets enable the user to listen to intercom and program sound, sometimes each fed to another ear. Headsets are used by personnel such as stage managers, camera persons and boom operators. Most headsets include a microphone insensitive to ambient noise to enable bidirectional communications. Most headsets used in TV work are padded to provide isolation from environmental noise or strong music such as a rock band. This isolation is sometimes vital for the TV crew to hear the control room.

heatsink A metal body mostly made of aluminum connected to electronic components to increase heat dissipation. Some electrical components dissipate a large amount of heat relative to their size. A heatsink is then essential to the component's proper operation. The component passes most of the heat it produces to the heatsink, which passes it to the surrounding air. A component designed to operate attached to a certain heatsink will be damaged or completely destroyed if it operates without one.

helical scan A method used by most videotape recorders today for scanning the tape by the video heads. The heads are mounted on a drum and the tape is wrapped around the drum at a slant. While the tape is pulled forward and the drum is rotating, the head records a diagonal track along the tape.

HI 8 Consumer video format using 8-mm tape cassettes for recording of audio and video. HI 8 is an improved version of the 8-mm format.

HI-FI High fidelity. A term used to describe audio systems that delivered good quality sound. The fidelity was similar to the original sound. This term was used mainly in the 1950s and 1960s.

high-definition Having a large number of detail or "pixels" (picture cells) in a picture. The higher the definition, the more information you can get from the picture and the more disk space or tape length you need to store the picture.

Also the name of a relatively new transmission format. *See also* **HDTV.**

high impedance In audio, an impedance of a circuit that is larger than a couple of kilo-ohms.

hiss Term used by audio engineers to describe the sound that thermal and random noise recorded on tape makes when the tape is played, to distinguish from other noises. Some degree of noise is always present in audio recordings generated by various electrical components and amplified.

Hi-vision Trade name for an HDTV (High-Definition Television) system employed in Japan. This system has an aspect ratio of 16:9. Line rate is 1125 and field rate is 60 per second. This system is not at present recognized by the FCC. *See also* **HDTV.**

HMI Halogen metal iodine. Highly efficient, high-intensity light, usually a spotlight. HMI is normally used for outside shooting of film and video productions. It produces daylight 5,600° K light and is bulky because of a heavy transformer it needs to produce its working voltages.

hoist An electrically powered fixture used in large studios to lift studio lights up and down according to needs. Usually the lights are lowered for maintenance and adjustment and then raised again.

home cinema Also called "home theater." A trend in which a large-screen TV (the larger the better) and a surround sound system are used at home to view feature films. This is to make the home viewing experience as close as possible to the full-size cinema hall. Films are recorded on laserdisk or videotape. TV size is usually 33" diagonal or larger. The sound system normally consists of five or six speakers driven by a specialized amplifier. Regular TV programs also benefit from such an installation. *See also* **surround sound.**

hood Cover used to shade picture monitors and viewfinders from sunlight or other strong light. The hood helps camera operators see through the viewfinder more clearly.

hop A signal sent to a satellite and back to earth. Sometimes two or more "hops" are needed to send a TV signal between two very distant points on the globe.

horizontal blanking A period of time between turning off the electron beam in a picture tube after it has finished scanning a horizontal picture line from left to right until it gets back to the left side of the screen to start the scanning of the next line. The beam is turned off so that it will not be visible on the screen during this period. In the composite video signal, sync and burst are present during the horizontal blanking interval. *See also* **CRT, composite video.**

horizontal frequency The number of horizontal scan lines per second. In NTSC it is 15,734 Hz; in PAL, 15,625 Hz.

horizontal period The period of time taken to scan a complete horizontal picture line. In NTSC it is some 63.56 microseconds and in PAL, 64 microseconds.

horizontal phase The phase relationship between the horizontal sync pulses of two video signals. Correct horizontal timing between different sources in a facility such as a TV studio or editing room is essential for the ability to switch and mix together various video sources. If horizontal phase is misadjusted, horizontal shifts and color changes will occur during switching and mixing of sources.

horizontal resolution The maximum amount of detail one horizontal line can hold. Horizontal resolution is defined and tested as the ability to differentiate between a number of vertical black and white lines. The number of the lines determines the resolution.

There is a close relationship between resolution and frequency response. The better the resolution, the bigger the frequency response. If the frequency response of a system is lowered at some stage of a signal path, the resolution or detail of the picture will drop accordingly.

Horizontal resolution is one of the important characteristics of video cameras, monitors and TV sets.

horizontal sync   A pulse located between horizontal scan lines. Its function is to synchronize all video equipment to the same horizontal timing and mark the beginning of horizontal scan retrace.

horn   An efficient and usually large loudspeaker, used mainly for public address rather than home systems.

house lights   General lighting in a TV studio intended for everything but production. Since TV lighting draws a lot of current and produces a lot of heat, the life of expensive lightbulbs is short and air conditioning has to be used. The house lights used are normally fluorescent lights.

house number   A unique identification number given to tapes or cassettes inside a station or other facility. Sometimes bar-code labels are put on tapes with the house number to enable fast and error-free reading.

house sync   A synchronizing signal generated by a sync generator and fed to all video devices in the station or facility.

hot camera   A camera that is turned on, working.

hot-head   Camera mounted on a crane with a remote-controlled pan and tilt head. The light weight camera is operated remotely from the floor. This way a relatively long, light weight and inexpensive crane can be used.

hot mike   A connected, working mike.

hot spot   A spot in the picture where the light is extra strong or reflected from a glossy surface. A hot spot can cause an area that is washed out, with no detail. *See also* **washed out.**

hue   One of the three characteristics of color in television signals. In composite signals, the hue is determined by the phase of the subcarrier in each location along the line of picture information. Sometimes the hue adjustment in TV receivers is called tint. *See also* **pixel.**

hum   Distortion of audio or video signals by penetration of utility system frequency (60 Hz or 50 Hz). Since utility power lines are present in every kind of facility, measures must be taken to avoid induction from this frequency to signal lines or keep it under certain limits. Utility system frequency present in audio signals is an annoying humming sound, and in video signals it appears as waves normally moving slowly up or down the screen.

hum bucker   A coil or circuit used to cancel unwanted hum from video signals. The hum bucker is inserted into the video path.

hum filter   An electronic circuit used to attenuate hum frequency in audio signals. Audio information is attenuated in this frequency as well.

HUT   Household using television. A term used in television and advertising, usually in relation to rating and share calculations.

hybrid   A circuit board incorporating different kinds of electrical components such as thick film and surface mount. Hybrids are used to minimize space, weight and power consumption and to increase reliability.

hybrid satellite   A satellite employing both C-band and Ku-band transponders. *See also* **C-band; Ku-band.**

hyperband   Frequency band of 300 MHz to 450 MHz used in cable television. This band carries 26 TV channels in NTSC or 21 channels in PAL. Not all TV receivers are equipped to receive hyperband frequencies.

hyper cardioid   Microphone with sensitivity pattern similar to the cardioid, but narrower, more directional and less sensitive to sounds coming from off-center. Unlike the cardioid, the hyper cardioid has some sensitivity to sounds from the back of the microphone. *See also* **cardioid.**

hysteresis loop   In magnetic media, a graph describing the magnetism left versus the magnetic force invested to obtain it.

Hz   Hertz. A unit of frequency. One hertz stands for one complete cycle of a periodic waveform. Hz is usually used with a prefix such as KHz (kilohertz—$1,000H_3$), MHz (megahertz—1,000,000) or GHz (gigahertz—$1,000,000,000H_2$) to denote high frequencies.

I   One of two color difference signals in the NTSC standard. In RGB terms: I = 0.6R-0.28G-0.32B. The I signal contains mainly cyan and orange.

Iconoscope   The first picture pickup tube used to build an electronic TV camera, developed by Zworykin in 1933. *See also* **camera tube; Zworykin.**

idler   *see* **pinch roller**

IDTV   Improved definition television. *See also* **EDTV.**

IFB   Interrupted feedback system. A small earpiece worn by talent during live transmission. This enables the talent to be in aural contact with people—such as the director and producer—in the control room. Usually the earpiece is concealed and the audience watching the program is not aware of its existence. Program sound that does not originate from the studio, such as phone calls and prerecorded music, can be fed through the IFB to the talent in the studio. IFBs are used both in the studio and in outside broadcasting. For reporters in the field, IFB is vital to keep in contact with the station during transmission.

image enhancer   An instrument used to improve picture characteristics such as contrast, chroma levels, hue and detail.

image intensifier   An instrument used to intensify or increase the level of weak video signals. With the increase of signal level, the inherent noise level rises as well.

image orthicon   Picture pickup tube used in early black and white studio cameras. The image orthicon is a large tube employing oversized, heavy deflection coils and dedicated circuitry. *See also* **camera tube.**

imaging device   A light-sensitive device capable of converting an image—created usually by a lens—

into an electronic signal. Imaging devices are the heart of all video cameras. The quality of the imaging process is the most important factor that determines the quality of the picture produced by the video camera. The current imaging device for video cameras is the CCD (Charged Coupled Device). Before that the camera pickup tube was used. Some applications such as HDTV still use tubes. *See also* **camera tube; CCD.**

Imax A film format 70 mm wide projected on a large, wide screen. In some places Imax is projected onto a domelike screen that nearly surrounds the audience. Combined with a multitrack sound system, this kind of projection puts the audience in the middle of the action.

impedance Resistance of an electric circuit to the flow of alternating current. Impedance is measured in ohms.

incandescent light Light produced by a hot metal-filament lightbulb, the kind used in households.

incident light Sunlight or artificial light falling on a subject from external sources of illumination.

independent broadcast station Radio or TV commercial broadcast station, with no affiliation to a national network or private chain of stations. Usually financed by sale of air time.

industrial A degree or level of sophistication, quality, durability and price, distinguished from the higher broadcast and lower consumer levels. Industrial-level equipment is usually used when professional quality is needed, but the material is not going to be broadcast. *See also:* **broadcast quality; consumer.**

inky dinky Low-power, small size fresnel spotlight used in the studio. Usually 600 watts or less. Also called "inkie."

inlay Part of a video image inserted into another. The inlay can be inserted by means of various effects, such as wipe or key.

in-line console An audio mixing console in which every input module is used as an output as well. These modules are called "input/output modules" or "I/O modules." Module outputs are used to feed multitrack recording machines. Grouping of channels and all other standard mixing console features are present as well. In-line consoles offer possibilities and flexibility in operation such as multichannel recording and transmission at the same time. *See also* **I/O module.**

in-line picture tube A picture tube in which the three electron guns are arranged in a line. Every pixel on the screen is made of three small parallel stripes of color—red, green and blue. This is to distinguish from Delta tubes where the electron guns are arranged in a triangle. In-Line tubes are the most common picture tube in use because of their high contrast. *See also* **cathode ray tube.**

in-point In magnetic audio- and videotape editing, the point in an existing recording from which new material is added or inserted. The position of the in-points has to be set for both the recorder and player. In videotape editing systems the position of the in-points (and out-points) is identified by time-code numbers. *See also:* **editing, out-point; time-code.**

input sensitivity The level or amount of signal a device needs at its input for normal operation. High sensitivity means a small signal is needed and low sensitivity means a large amplitude input signal is needed.

A preamplifier is a high-input sensitivity circuit that can be used to overcome the low-input sensitivity of a power amplifier. The preamplifier will bring the relatively small microphone level of several millivolts up to line level, which will allow the power amplifier to produce the desired output power.

insert edit A method of video editing in which video, audio tracks and time code are added on the tape inside an existing recording, without interruption, to make smooth edits. Insert editing requires a prior continuous recording on the tape and definite in and out points. Unlike assembly edits, inserts enable editing of video only or a specific audio channel. *See also* **assembly edit.**

insertion loss/gain Variation of gain or signal level in a line, path or circuit due to insertion of a passive or active component such as a pad, filter or amplifier.

insert shot Visual material such as photographs, drawings or graphics inserted during editing of a program into a scene.

instantaneous editing Switching between video sources or combining them together while a live event or program takes place. This kind of editing is technically performed by a video switcher. Instantaneous editing is a common practice in taping and transmission of TV programs. It saves time if the program is intended for editing and it is the only way to bring to the viewer a variety of video sources in live programs.

instant replay Immediate playback of important moments in sports events. Usually played back from a VCR dedicated to replays.

intensity modulation (IM) Modulation method usually used in fiber-optic transmission systems. The analog signal level directly modulates the light source intensity.

intercom A communications system enabling speech to be sent and received at the same time between different points. Normally intercom systems use wires to connect from point to point. In cases where the user has to be mobile, wireless intercom is preferred. Some stations are rack or table mounted units and others are belt packs. In television stations, intercoms are located in almost every studio, control room or other facility. In most places loudspeaker stations are used. In recording studios, headsets are used to prevent penetration of intercom sound to microphones. The size of intercom systems varies from two to several hundred. Modern intercom systems are computerized and allow quick reconfiguration.

interface (a) Appropriate connection between two circuits or systems in terms of level, impedance, protocol, baud rate and many more signal characteristics. (b) A circuit or component connecting two circuits. An interface is used to adapt the level, impedance, protocol and other output characteristics of one circuit to the input of another.

interior (INT) Shot or scene taken inside a studio or other indoor space as opposed to exterior.

interlace The method in which two sets of TV scan lines (fields) are combined into one frame. Interlace of two fields is used to double the frequency of pictures presented to the viewer's eye in order to increase continuity and decrease flickering of the screen. *See also* **field.**

intermittent movement Movement of film in a camera or projector. The film stops, a frame is exposed or projected and the film moves again, while magnetic tape movement, which is continuous.

intermodulation distortion Distortion of a complex audio signal in which the sum and difference aspects of the basic signal frequencies are present.

interpolation Calculation and averaging of picture information or pixels in digital images. In the process of moving and resizing images, interpolation is needed to calculate the new parameters of pixels with consideration to neighboring picture elements. When interpolation is not used, the result is artifacts and a less "transparent" image. *See also* **artifacts; pixel.**

I/O Input/Output.

I/O module The module of the in-line audio console. The I/O module

normally consists of a line/microphone input, microphone amplifier, level control, input routing, signal processing (equalizer and slide fader), stereo panning and a line output. The I/O module is connected to mixing, routing and monitoring buses within the console.

IPS **(a)** Inches per second. The speed at which tape travels in tape machines in relation to recording heads. Every audio and video recording format has a fixed IPS rate. In ¼-inch audiotapes, standard speeds are 7½ and 15 IPS. Two-inch tape machines use 15 IPS speed and Betacam tapes move at 4 IPS. **(b)** Instructions per second. The number of instructions a computer or computerized system can perform per second. One of the ways to measure of the power or speed of a computer. Usually millions of instructions per second (MIPS) or billions (BIPS) are performed in modern computers.

IR Infrared. An invisible part of the spectrum beyond the red, approximately in the region between 7,000 and 150,000 angstrom. Infrared radiation penetrates clouds and haze more easily than visible light. Hot materials or bodies emit infrared rays.

IRD Integrated receiver decoder. Unit planned to be used at the receiving end of digital video broadcasting (DVB) transmissions, to do the tuning and decoding of audio and video signals from the MPEG-2 data stream, as well as service information and text. All decoded signals will be fed to the TV receiver or monitor. *See also:* **DVB; MPEG.**

IRE Institute of Radio Engineers (USA). Also a unit for measurement of video level in the NTSC system. The video signal luminance part from sync tip to peak white is divided into 140 IRE units.

iris   A diaphragm that consists of metal leaves or blades attached between two rings in a lens. It moves to control and adjust the size of the opening that allows light to enter the camera. The number of leaves is normally between 5 and 12; more leaves means a more circular shape of the opening. *See also* **diaphragm.**

ISDN   Integrated Services Digital Network. A service using existing telephone copper wiring networks for transmission of digital data. ISDN provides a dial-up medium for high-quality audio, video, text and computer file transfer. International tabletop conference, telesurveillance, transaction services, interconnection between local area networks and internet access are only some of possible uses of ISDN.

The basic rate interface (BRI) is the standard ISDN interface, providing two 64-Kbit/sec "B" (bearer) channels and one "D" (data) channel used for signaling with a 16-Kbit/sec bit rate. The overall bandwidth of a BRI unit (using one two-wire copper line) is 144 Kbit/sec. Eight different devices such as modems, telephones and fax machines can be used simultaneously when connected to a single BRI interface.

Full bandwidth audio is transferred successfully by ISDN between radio and TV stations. Full bandwidth video can be transferred via ISDN systems with the aid of MPEG-2 compression. A larger configuration called primary rate interface (PRI) is also in use. In the U.S. it consists of 23 "B" chan-

nels, each of 64 Kbit/sec, and one "D" channel with a 64 Kbit/sec. In Europe the PRI configuration consists of 30 "B" channels capable of delivering up to 2 Mbit/sec. The primary rate interface is normally carried by coax or fiber-optic cables.

ISO   International Standardization Organization.

iso (camera)   Isolated camera. When recording a program on tape, usually the output of the video switcher that switches between the different cameras and other sources is recorded. *Iso* means recording a particular camera output on a separate, additional VCR. The advantage is the ability to use the iso material during editing as inserts in case of a problem during recording on the main VCR. Usually a camera shooting a cover shot is selected for iso recording. Sometimes when an event is very important and cannot be repeated, every camera is recorded separately.

ITC   Independent Television Commission. Regulatory body for all independent programming in the United Kingdom. Deals with both technical and legal issues.

ITS   International Teleproduction Society. A U.S. association of members of the TV industry, with a branch in the UK. ITS promotes the use of video for a variety of purposes.

ITU   International Telecommunications Union. A United Nations regulatory committee that sets standards for all forms of communication. ITU-R (previously CCIR) is occupied with RF spectrum regulations. ITU-T (previously CCITT) sets standards for telecommunications.

ITU-R 656 *see* **CCIR 656**

ITU-R BT.601-2 *see* **CCIR 601**

jack bay *see* **patch bay**

jack field *see* **patch bay**

jam sync (a) Locking of a time code generator to an external time code or sync signal. (b) The process of restoration of lost or damaged time code on tape. A time code generator is locked to the videotape recording sync and time code is recorded (inserted) on tape.

jelly Gelatin color-correction filter used in lighting.

jenny Slang for an electrical power generator.

jingle A short piece of music used mainly for commercials. Jingles are usually made cheerful and catchy to get listeners' attention.

jitter Variations in a signal in respect to time, caused mainly during reproduction of signals from magnetic tape or other media. Insignificant jitter is caused by almost every device handling signals. Jitter is measured in time units such as nanoseconds or milliseconds.

jog Movement of videotape frame by frame or field by field forward or backward. Jogging is useful for searching a particular frame during viewing or editing. Normally the jog action is done by turning a search dial in one direction or the other.

joystick An electromechanical device that translates movement of the hand to movement of images on a video or computer screen in 2-D or 3-D. Joysticks are used in digital effects to move and rotate pictures and in video switchers to locate wipe patterns. The concept of the joystick is taken from the much larger control stick in aircraft.

JPEG Joint Photographic Experts Group. A standard for data compression of still pictures based on DCT compression. Compression rates between 5 and 100 are used in three levels of encoding quality: baseline, extended and lossless. Some video equipment uses JPEG for data compression, but its inability to do interfield compression makes it inferior to more advanced video compression techniques such as MPEG. *See also* **compression video; compression ratio; DCT; MPEG.**

juice Slang for electrical power used in film and video productions, mostly for lighting.

jukebox A device that allows automated access and use of a large number of records or CDs for playback. The jukebox consists of a storage area and a mechanical arm that moves CDs to the built-in player and back. Jukeboxes are used in places where fast access to large numbers of audio segments is needed.

jump cut In film and videotape editing, a dissonant edit or discontinuity. For example, if a person is located in the left side of a room at a given time and one frame later he appears in the right side of the room, this means a jump cut has been performed. Even more common, during the editing of an interview, when a word or sentence is removed the person in the picture jumps position slightly. Sometimes jump cuts are used as a trick where objects or persons appear or disappear "mysteriously."

jumping cue   A performer starting action ahead of cue.

junior   A 2 KW fresnel spotlight used in film and TV studios.

K   (a) Kelvin degrees used to measure color temperature (color of light) or the temperature scale in degrees Celsius starting at absolute zero ($-273°$ C $= 0°$ K). *See also* **color temperature. (b)** In computers, 1 K = 1,024 bytes of memory or data. *See also* **byte. (c)** Kilo. One thousand, as in kilogram (Kg), kilohertz (KHz) or kilovolt (KV).

ka-band   Frequency band of 18 to 20 GHz used in satellite communications.

key   (a) An effect used by video switchers in which a "hole" is cut in a video picture according to color or luminance and another signal is inserted instead. **(b)** The signal by which a "hole" is cut and some part of a video picture is replaced, or an audio signal controlling the levels of compressors or expanders. Video switchers and some audio equipment have special inputs for key signals. *See also* **chroma key; luminance key; video switcher.**

key frame   In digital video effects, complex movement of frames in terms of size position and rotation is determined in steps, one at a time. Every step starts with a key frame and the effects unit moves objects or frames from one key frame to the next in a continuous movement or trajectory. *See also* **digital effects.**

keying signal   A control waveform or voltage used to switch or control the level of another signal such as audio or video. *See also* **key.**

key light   Main illumination used to light an object or person in film and TV. The key light is normally positioned in the upper front, a little bit off-center. High intensity is used for the key lights relative to fill and backlights. Spotlights are usually used for key lights. *See also* **backlight; fill light; spot light.**

K-factor   A series of measurements used to scale the amount of different factors of linear distortion and to evaluate video signal quality in general. There are several K-factor measurements: K2T, Kpuls/bar, Kbar and K50 Hz. K-factor is measured with the help of a special test signal and a graticule put on a waveform monitor's screen. Some advanced computerized measurement equipment executes these tests automatically, but the test signal is always needed.

knee function   An attribute to be found in modern TV cameras in the signal processing circuits. Knee function was developed in order to take care of the large contrast between darker areas and highlights of a scene. The camera response to light is changed in such a way that from a specific level up, the camera will be less sensitive to light. This causes the sensitivity curve of the camera to have a "knee" at the point where the sensitivity changes. The knee function allows inclusion in the picture of illumination levels up to 600 percent higher than before compressed in the upper 10 percent of the video signal. Before knee function circuits, it was very common even in professional TV pictures to see highlights such as clouds washed out.

knee shot   A medium camera shot showing one or more persons from the knees up to over the head.

ku-band   Frequency band of 10.7 GHz to 12.75 GHz used for satellite communications and direct satellite broadcasting (DSB).

lab   Laboratory. Place where film is processed or where maintenance of audio and video equipment is performed. Research and development of new technologies also takes place in laboratories.

lag   Displacement and/or smear of a bright object moving against a dark background in a TV picture. Lag occurs mainly in tube cameras under low light conditions. Modern CCD cameras normally have no noticeable lag.

lambert   A unit of brightness of light reflected from an illuminated body. It equals one lumen per square centimeter.

LAN   Local area network. A connection between a number of computers in a restricted area. The network allows sharing of data and software between all connected computers. A "server" computer equipped with a special software is used to manage the network. Network interface cards in each computer make the connection and interface from the computer to the network.

lanyard microphone   A small microphone strapped to the neck, similar to a lavaliere microphone.

lapel   A small microphone clipped to the lapel.

Larsen effect   Feedback from a loudspeaker to a microphone and back, common in public address systems. Can be avoided by lower gain of the system, use of more directional microphones or different placement of microphones versus speakers.

laterna magica   Magic lantern. Very old device used for projection of slides.

lavaliere mike   Also called neck mike. A small microphone that can be attached to a person's jacket, blouse or tie. Some lavaliere microphones are wireless. A small battery-operated belt-pack transmitter sends the microphone signal to a receiver located usually in the sound control room. Lavaliere microphones deliver audio quality that is sufficient for speech and they have the advantage of being highly portable. Sometimes movement of the person causes the microphone to rub against the cloth to which it is clipped, thereby causing undesirable noise.

LCD   Liquid crystal display. Display used normally for small, battery-operated instruments and toys including very small portable TV sets. LCD displays consume very little power and rely on external illumination because they do not emit their own light.

lead-acid battery   A rechargeable battery normally used in cars and heavy machinery, sometimes also for photographic and video equipment. Lead-acid batteries are heavy, but inexpensive and do not suffer from the "memory effect" like nicad batteries. Lead-acid batteries contain a harmful acid that may cause burns to the skin and damage to equipment if not properly sealed.

leader   (a) A blank piece of film taped to the beginning of the actual material. Sometimes the leader is numbered in one-second intervals to allow accurate cueing. (b) A transparent piece of tape with a fixed length attached to both ends of a videotape inside a cassette. The transparent leader helps VCRs to identify the tape ends. (c) In audio, pieces of nonmagnetic tape spliced between audio segments (normally in ¼-inch tape) to allow quick visual allocation of the beginning of segments.

leakage   Unwanted penetration of sound to microphones, as in the following examples: (a) During recording of an orchestra, a microphone set to record one musical instrument collects sound from a neighboring instrument. (b) Sound from earphones used for intercom or playback of accompaniment is picked up by a microphone.

LED   Light-emitting diode. A light-emitting semiconductor used instead of very small lightbulbs in various instruments.

lens   An optical device composed of glass elements in a housing, forming an image on film or a light-sensitive device.

A single lens element, or simple lens, is a glass disk with one or both faces curved. If the lens is thicker at the middle, it is a converging lens. If the lens is thicker at the edges, it is a diverging lens. Modern lenses used for TV cameras are complex and include many glass elements made of different kinds of optical glass and different curves. Production of broadcast-quality lenses is a specialized task that requires a large amount of know-how. The number of manufacturers is limited to five or six.

As a result of their structure, lenses suffer from many kinds of imperfection while forming an image. These include astigmatism, barrel, coma and chromatic aberrations. To partly compensate for such aberrations, two or more elements with different optical attributes are joined together. The aberration correction is an expensive process that can more than double the price of the lens and therefore depends on the requirements needed for the specific use.

Most lenses used today for video cameras in the television industry, as well as in the industrial and consumer markets, are zoom lenses. A zoom lens offers a variable field of view (and a variable focal length) from wide angle to narrow angle or telephoto. The field of view is continuously variable and can be changed during shooting — an action known as "zoom in" or "zoom out." There are many kinds of zoom lenses for different uses and different kinds and sizes of cameras. A zoom lens is a complex and delicate device that contains optical, mechanical and electrical systems.

The most important attributes of a TV zoom lens are: (a) The resolution or amount of detail the lens can deliver. (b) Type and size of mount. (c) Widest field of view, narrowest field of view (field of view is measured in degrees) and the ratio between the two (zoom ratio). **(d)** Maximum aperture of the lens (f-number). **(e)** Minimum object distance from the lens. **(f)** Physical size and weight of the lens (especially important for hand-held or portable cameras). **(g)** The fitness of the lens to the perform its job in terms of minimal aberrations in the lens. **(h)** Servo functions included in the lens such as servo zoom and focus. **(i)** Existence of a range extender that can double the focal length. **(j)** Accessories supplied with the lens such as hoods, carrying cases, spare parts and grips.

The introduction of the CCD picture element and the HDTV format presented new challenges to lens manufacturers in terms of enhanced picture detail and reduced aberrations.

Lenses are very sensitive and must be kept covered at all times when not in use. Dust, dirt and fingerprints can be harmful to lenses. Damage can be caused during cleaning. *See also* **aberration; angular field of view; aperture; back focus; cap; diaphragm; f-number; focal length; focal plane; focus; focusing; focusing ring; fresnel lens; f-stop; iris; lens coating; maximum aperture; range extender; resolution; resolution chart; servo focus; servo zoom; shot box; telephoto lens; turret; wide-angle; zoom in; zoom lens; zoom out; zoom ratio.**

lens coating   A thin layer of coating applied to lenses in order to reduce glare, unwanted reflections and loss of light. For best results the layer of coating on the lens should be one-quarter of the wavelength of light. The refractive index of the coating should be the square root of the refractive index of the lens glass. Materials often used for coating are magnesium fluoride and bismuth oxide. Some lenses have a double layer of coating composed of two different materials for improved performance.

letterboxing   A method of displaying wide-screen TV picture on a conventional 4:3 aspect ratio TV receiver. Letterboxing is a way to overcome the aspect ratio difference without cutting away both sides of the picture. Black strips at the upper and lower edges of the TV screen indicate letterboxing. Many feature films today are transmitted on TV in letterboxed form.

level   **(a)** The amplitude or intensity of a signal or waveform. **(b)** One of several mix/effect units in a video switcher. **(c)** One of several "layers" of signals such as video, audio and timecode handled by a routing switcher.

lighting   The illumination used in film and TV studios and production locations. Lighting has two purposes, one technical and one artistic.

The first purpose is to provide the camera with sufficient light to produce a picture that is technically satisfactory. The amount needed varies according to the sensitivity of the camera and other factors. If the camera iris opens all the way, it will be difficult to focus the camera properly and focusing will become very critical, especially if the objects move around on the set. In TV studios the intensity of lighting is usually between 50 and 150 foot-candles. Sensitivity of cameras improves constantly and the amount of lighting needed drops accordingly.

The artistic role of lighting is to convey to the viewer the mood of the scene, the sensation of time of day, weather and season and the feeling of the nature of the place and the relationship between objects and the environment around them. By means of lighting people can be made to look older or younger and places to look scary or pleasant.

Most of the different lighting effects are made with a small number of relatively simple tools. There are a few kinds of floodlights that produce soft, scattered light and there are spotlights in several sizes that produce a narrow beam of light. Sometimes effects lights are used to produce special shapes. A lighting computer and a number of dimmers are used for switching lights and to control light output of each one of them separately or grouped together.

Basic lighting of a single subject such as a person or a still object consists of three lights: key light, which gives the basic lighting; fill light, which fills the shadows; and backlight, which is used to separate the object from the background. If many people or objects are to be properly illuminated, these three basic lights are needed for each of them and, if they also move from place to place on the set, things become even more complicated.

The person in charge of planning and execution of lighting and all its technical, artistic and safety factors is the lighting director. *See also* **baby; back light; barn doors; bounce (light); brute; camera light; C-clamp; cold lighting; color temperature; color temperature meter; cross light; cyclorama light; dimmer; fill light; filter (optical); flat lighting; floodlight; fluorescent lighting; fog machine; follow spot; foot candle; footlights; fresnel spotlight; gaffer;** **gaffer grip; gel; grid; ground row; hard light; HMI; hoist; inky dinky; junior; key light; lighting computer; light meter; mood lighting; senior; soft light; spotlight.**

lighting computer A dedicated computer specially built to control light sources via dimmers in the studio or onstage. The lighting computer can store in memory many lighting setups and retrieve them when required. Groups of dimmers can be set and controlled separately or together and "chasers" (running lights) can be created. Transition between sets of lights can be done either manually or automatically.

lighting contrast ratio The ratio between the two extreme light levels used to illuminate the performers or objects in the set, the key light and the fill light. A strong contrast makes the scene look dramatic.

lighting control A control desk used to control lights connected to dimmers. Sets of faders are used to control the output level of each dimmer. Transitions from one set to another can be made. Simple lighting controls are manual, while others are computerized. *See also* **fader; lighting computer.**

lighting plan A plan of the studio or location usually made by the lighting director. The plan indicates the kind and position of each light to be used, the direction of its light beam and the number of the power line or outlet it is connected to. The position of scenery, performers and cameras in the set are also indicated in the plan.

light meter An instrument that measures intensity of light. Used in still photography and film to set the iris and shutter. Lighting directors use light meters when setting up lighting for film and TV scenes. For TV work, light meters are normally calibrated in foot-candle or lux units. *See also* **foot-candle; lux.**

limbo A fabric background used in studios. Usually plain, gray or black.

limiter A device that limits signal level within certain standards or degrees. Limiters are also installed to avoid damage to transmitters and other level-sensitive equipment. Limiters tend to clip the upper part of the signal when it becomes too high and causes distortion. Compressors reduce the signal to size; many times, limiters and compressors are used in combination. *See also* **complimiter; compressor.**

line In television, pictures are scanned and displayed line by line horizontally, from left to right. The number of lines per picture (frame) and the duration of each line differs between the different TV standards. More lines in a picture means more vertical resolution. The amount of information in each line depends on many limiting factors. Among these factors are the resolution of the pickup tube, the number of light-sensitive elements per line in the CCD element of the camera or the overall bandwidth of the video system in use. In NTSC the number of scan lines is 525 per frame. In PAL the number of lines is 625 per frame.

Besides picture information, in every line there is a blanking period in which the scan of the line information is finished and is about to start again in the next line. In this interval are located a horizontal synchronizing pulse and a "burst" used as reference for the color information in that line. *See also* **burst; horizontal blanking; horizontal sync; video.**

linear distortion Distortion to waveforms that are independent of signal amplitude. Linear distortions are caused by systems that affect varying frequencies or, in other words, systems with a response that is not flat. Linear distortion can also be caused by external induction on equipment and lines, such as utility system frequency causing distortion (hum) on audio lines.

Linear distortions are classified into four categories in terms of time, for the measurement of video signals: **(a)** Short-time distortion: 100 nanoseconds to 1 microsecond. **(b)** Line-time distortion: 1 microsecond to 64 microseconds. **(c)** Field-time distortion: 64 microseconds to 20 milliseconds. **(d)** Long-time distortion: longer than 20 milliseconds. In this group are included chrominance to luminance gain and delay inequalities, group delay and frequency response. *See also* **nonlinear distortion.**

linear editing An editing method in which the edited segments must be recorded on tape in the exact order they will appear in the finished work. Electronic videotape editing, unlike film editing, is linear in the sense that it is not possible to take out a segment from a video sequence—the blank area has to be filled with some other material. Likewise, to insert a sequence inside a recorded portion means that another existing sequence will be erased. *See also* **editing; nonlinear editing.**

linear key   Key effect circuit in a video switcher that, rather than the usual hard switch between background and insert video, can also mix the two where the edges of the key signal are neither high nor low level. Linear key circuits produce key effects with smoother edges.

line level   In audio, a level of 1 volt or +4 dBm most commonly used to distinguish from microphone level, which is much lower. Line impedance is normally 600 ohms. Most interconnections between audio and video equipment are performed in line level. Lower microphone levels are amplified as soon as possible to line level. Higher levels are usually used only to drive speakers.

line-matching transformer   A transformer used to match two different impedances, used mostly in audio.

lineup time   The time needed for lineup of electronic equipment, including warm-up time to working temperature after switch on. Long lineup periods were needed for electronic equipment based on vacuum tubes, mainly cameras in TV studios (typically one hour or more) and OB vans. Modern solid-state and digital equipment needs very little lineup time, if any.

lip mike   A microphone specially built to work in noisy environments such as sports events. A bulge in the microphone body is pressed against the upper lip of the user to maintain optimum range from the capsule to the mouth.

lip sync   Synchronization between picture and sound, most noticeable when a person is talking. Sometimes picture or sound is delayed, or both are delayed but not equally. When video and sound travel in different ways, different delays are produced. A delay line has to be used to delay the faster of the two to match the other one.

live transmission   Radio or TV transmission in real time, not delayed or prerecorded in any way. Live transmission is very demanding for all talent and crew involved because there is no place for retakes and every mistake is aired as it occurs.

LNA   Low-noise amplifier. RF amplifier used for amplification of very weak signals such as satellite transmissions. To keep the signal-to-noise ratio within reasonable limits, the amplifier noise must be very low. LNAs are usually mounted as near as possible to the signal source, such as antenna or dish, to minimize pickup of interference by long cables.

LNB   Low-noise amplifier with a built-in down converter that converts the very high frequencies used in satellite communications to a lower one. *See also* **LNA.**

loading   Connection of a load or device that draws current to the output of a circuit or line. An antenna is a load connected to the transmitter. A speaker is a load connected to a power amplifier. If a load draws more current than the device is built to supply, overloading occurs.

location   A production site that is outside the studio in a place not meant for production, such as a street, a hotel, a forest or a train station.

logging   Writing down the content of a tape. Normally logging takes place as preparation for an editing session. All the raw material tapes are logged and every scene or take is written down with its content (in short) and its location on the tape. This process saves editing facilities time.

longitudinal   Tracks recorded along the tape. Opposite to transverse recording. Normally audio tracks are recorded longitudinally. *See also* **LTC.**

long-shot   Object shot from a distance or with a wide angle to look as if it is distant. Also a shot that includes everything happening on a stage or studio floor.

loop-through   A video input connection with an additional connector that is a tap off the input. A connection to another instrument can be made from the tap output connection. The loop-through output in the last instrument in the series has to be connected with a 75ohm terminator. A loop-through kind of connection allows feeding of a series of video instruments such as monitors with a single video source without the need for a distribution amplifier.

loudness   The intensity of sound as it is perceived by the human ear.

loudness control   In sound systems, circuits that compensate for the nonlinear nature of the human ear. Without loudness correction, sounds will suffer from considerable loss of bass response accompanied by slight loss of treble response. These losses will increase as the volume level decreases. As an inverse action, loudness correction is increased as the volume level goes down. Loudness correction boosts the low and high ends of the frequency band.

loudspeaker   A device that transforms electrical currents to sound waves or acoustical energy. The most common type of loudspeaker (moving coil) works as follows: a diaphragm is connected to a coil located in a fixed magnetic field. When electrical current flows through the coil it moves together with the diaphragm, which moves the air molecules around it, producing sound. Loudspeakers are widely used and they come in a variety of forms and characteristics to fulfill a variety of needs.

Usually a single loudspeaker cannot cover efficiently the complete audio range and several different loudspeakers are housed together, each covering a different part of the sound spectrum. Small loudspeakers are more efficient at high frequencies. Usually three kinds of loudspeakers are used: "tweeters" that cover the upper range, "midrange" for the medium range and "woofers" for lower range.

Important specifications of the loudspeaker are the impedance, the power rating and the frequency response. Mechanical dimensions and weight are important for housing and mounting the loudspeaker.

loudspeaker polar pattern   A graph of the loudspeaker sound intensity as it is measured from the different angles and distances around it.

loudspeaker radiation pattern
see **loudspeaker polar pattern**

loudspeaker transient response
The ability of a speaker to accurately
deliver short-time transients.

low impedance　　In audio, an impedance of 600 ohms or less, the standard for line inputs in professional
audio equipment.

LS　　Loudspeaker.

LSB　　Least significant bit. The last
bit from the left in a byte or binary
number. Also the bit with the lowest
value. *See also* **MSB.**

LTC　　Longitudinal time code. In
VTRs, VCRs and audiotape machines,
time code information recorded along
the tape in a special longitudinal track.
In VCRs, time code (VITC) is also
recorded inside the video information,
which is recorded in helical or slanted
tracks on the tape. An advantage of
LTC is that it is possible to read it
while the tape is in fast forward or
rewind motion. In speeds lower than
play speed (in forward or reverse),
normally it is not possible to read
LTC. *See also* **time code; VITC.**

lumen　　A unit of light flux. One
lumen is the amount of light flow that
falls on one square foot of surface at
a distance of one foot away from a
point source of one candlepower. One
lumen per square foot is one foot-candle, which is a British unit of illumination. One lumen per square meter is
one lux, which is an illumination unit
10.764 times smaller than one foot-
candle.

luminance　　Information included
in the video signal of differences in
brightness in the range between the
darkest and brightest parts of a TV
picture. Luminance signal holds the
information of the exact brightness of
every pixel or part of the picture. A
video signal including luminance information is sufficient to produce a
black and white picture. To produce a
color TV picture, chrominance signal
is needed in addition to luminance.
See also **chrominance.**

luminance key　　A method used in
television to replace parts of a TV picture with a picture signal coming from
another source. This operation is done
by a special circuit inside a video
switcher or a separate unit. Areas in
the picture with a certain luminance
level and up are replaced with picture
information coming from another
source (fill). The luminance level from
which the picture information will be
replaced can be adjusted. Luminance
key effects are independent of the picture color.

lux　　A unit of illumination. One
lumen per square meter is one lux,
which is 10.764 times smaller than one
foot-candle. Lux is used by lighting
directors in film and TV to measure
illumination levels.

M　　Mega. One million.

MII　　A component VCR format invented by Panasonic. Recording is on
½-inch tape. MII is a professional
color difference format using Y, B − Y,
R − Y signals. In this format there are
lightweight, portable recorders that
can be attached to a camera and a line
of studio recorders capable also of

editing. MII was introduced roughly at the same time as Betacam, but is less common.

MAC   Multiplexed analog component. A method of multiplexing the three channels of analog component video (Y, B – Y, R – Y) into a single channel of time compressed video. MAC is used to save bandwidth of channels in satellite transponders.

Macintosh   An Apple brand name for a computer widely used, mostly for graphics preprint work and multimedia. In TV, Macintosh is used mainly as a platform for audio and video postproduction software.

macro   (a) Feature of a lens that allows shooting objects very close to the lens while still retaining focus. The macro position of the lens is used to shoot small objects or fine detail from close range. Not all lenses are equipped with this function. (b) In computers, a series of several or many operations programmed to be performed by one keystroke.

magnetic tape   A tape made of a thin and strong base material such as polyester, coated with a layer of ferric oxide or metal particles. The particles on the tape are only several microinches in size. A magnetic field can be used to magnetize particles on the tape to a specific orientation. Analog signals and data can be recorded on the tape and retrieved later. Many types of magnetic tape are manufactured in different widths and lengths and various magnetic media, placed in a reel or cassette.

Magnetic tape is the most common way to store signals and information and by far the cheapest. The main rea-son that alternative recording techniques such as magnetic or video disk are employed is because magnetic tape does not have random access and sometimes it is a matter of several minutes to get from one end of the tape to the other.

Magnetic tape is used in machines such as audio recorders, video recorders and data recorders. Several methods of arranging the recorded tracks on tapes are used by different machines: longitudinal for analog audio tapes, quadraplex in obsolete 2" machines and helical scan in most digital audio and analog/digital video recorders. In video recorders a combination of helical scan and longitudinal tracks is used. *See also* **helical scan; longitudinal; metal evaporated tape; metal particle tape, quadraplex.**

magneto optical disk   A large capacity, low-price read/write disk that can be rewritten an infinite number of times, introduced in 1989. In the writing process, microscopic dots on a metallic layer of the disk are magnetized and given a magnetic orientation by means of a laser beam that heats the place while a magnetic head creates a magnetic field. To read the data from disk, the laser beam scans the dots. Every dot reflects the laser beam in a direction depending on the magnetic orientation (Kerr rotation).

There is an ISO standard for a removable cartridge containing a 5.25-inch disk (CD size). Capacity is several GBytes of data and is growing all the time. There is also a 12" size used by several manufacturers, with play time of about half an hour of broadcast-quality video and dual audio on each side.

master A video- or audiotape that is the original recording or original edited program. Copies can be made from the original or master, but the best quality will always be at the earliest generation, which is the master. In the age of digital recordings the question of master or copy is less crucial, since the difference is normally unnoticeable. In disk-based editing systems, a master of an edited program consists of original footage and editing decisions recorded separately on the disk.

master control room Controls and switches signals from several other control rooms in a TV station or other facility.

master SPG A sync pulse generator (SPG) that sends signals to all other generators in a facility or TV station on which to lock. All other SPGs are "slaves."

master module In an audio mixing console, a module that contains one or two faders that control the level of the mix bus output (the master output). Two outputs exist in case of a stereo mixing console.

master recording *see* **master.**

match frame In editing, frame-accurate rejoining of material. Match frame is an edit of two frames that were consecutive in the original material. If during video editing, for some reason, the recording from the player to the recorder has stopped, in order to continue the recording in a seamless way a match frame has to be performed. The same is true if one wants to change a cut in already edited material to a dissolve—one has to go back to a point before the start of dissolve and perform an invisible edit (match frame) and then make a dissolve from the player currently recorded to another source.

matrix A network of intersecting input and output leads. Every input can be connected to every output by mechanical contact or by an array of electronic switching circuits. Matrices can connect audio, video, time code and every other signal. The size of matrices vary from several inputs and one output to hundreds of inputs and hundreds of outputs. A matrix can save patch panels and a lot of wiring in complex facilities such as sophisticated editing rooms and studios.

matte A color video signal created by an electronic circuit. Luminance, chrominance and hue are adjusted to produce any desired color. *See also* **background generator.**

maximum aperture The biggest opening of the iris in a camera lens. This is the situation where the maximum amount of light enters the camera. The f-number will be the lowest possible.

MCU Master control unit. A unit that manages some other control devices. For example, in modern TV studios where several video cameras are used, each camera has a remote control unit to manipulate the different parameters. There is also a master control unit that operates all cameras and changes parameters for each camera separately or for all of them at the same time.

medium-shot A camera shot in which the subject is seen from a medium distance. In a medium-shot, a person will normally be seen from the waist up. Medium-shot covers the range between closeup and long-shot.

mega- One million. Denoted by a capital M. Used as a prefix letter with values such as byte (MBytes— 1,048,576 bytes), hertz (MHz) and watt (MW).

memory An array of cells that can store data and programs. Memories are vital in computers or other digital equipment. A single memory cell stores either a zero or a one. Data is arranged in the memory in bytes. The size of memory varies according to needs and can be as much as several gigabytes (1 GByte = 1,073,741,824 bytes) for a personal computer. The amount of memory needed to store one full frame of digital television sampled in accordance to CCIR 601 is 701 KBytes for 525 lines and 829 Kbytes for 625 lines.

Random access memories (RAM) allow access to every cell of the memory to store or retrieve data, in no particular order and without affecting other data. RAM is a read and write memory. There is a read-only memory (ROM), which is normally used to store data for initial startup of computers or other important data that should not be erased. There are read only memories that can be erased for reprogramming under certain conditions such as exposure to strong ultraviolet light. These are called PROM or EPROM (Erasable Programmable Read-Only Memory).

Solid-state chips, magnetic disks and tapes and optical disks are all ca-

pable of storing data, each of them having other features in terms of capacity, access time, physical size, durability, power consumption and so on. RAM solid-state chips are normally erased when computer power is switched off. Other storage devices such as disks are not dependent on power to keep the data stored. *See also* **byte; diskette; hard disk; optical disk; EPROM; RAM; ROM.**

menu Complex software uses menus as a means of navigating between many parts or modules. Normally when you get into the software you will get the main menu, from which you choose one item. This will bring you to the part you want or another menu page with more items to choose from, and so on. The number of menu stages you will have to go through depends on the complexity of the software.

metal evaporated tape Tape used for very dense recording of signals, normally digital. Metal evaporated tape has been adopted by the DVC ¼" video recording format. *See also* **DVC.**

metal particle tape Magnetic tape using metal particles instead of metal oxide. Audio and video signals recorded on metal tape have improved bandwidth, signal-to-noise ratio and dynamic range.

MHz Megahertz: 1,000,000 cycles per second.

micro- One millionth: 1/1,000,000. Micro- is denoted by the Greek lowercase letter μ (mu) and comes as a prefix letter in terms such as microfarad (μF), microvolt (μV) and microampere (μA).

microbar A pressure unit used for measurement of sound pressure: 1 microbar = 0.1 newtons/m^2 = 0.000,000,000,001 watts/m^2.

microphone A device or transducer used to convert sound waves into electrical signals. The microphone is used to pick up sounds and transform them into small electrical currents that can, after proper amplification, be used for recording or transmission. There are various kinds of microphones for different purposes in different quality and price levels. Microphones vary in sensitivity, pickup pattern and frequency band they deliver. Microphones are divided into several groups according to the principle of operation. Dynamic microphones use movement of a magnet attached to a membrane to induce electrical current in a coil. Condenser microphones are based on changes in capacitance of a variable capacitor. Some others use pizo-electric crystals to convert vibration to electrical current. *See also* **cardioid; condenser; dynamic microphone; gun-mike; hyper cardioid; lavaliere mike; omnidirectional; unidirectional.**

microphone line A cable connecting a microphone to any other equipment, carrying low-level microphone signals.

microphone mixer A device used to blend together several microphone signals. Mixers are used in studios and outside productions when more than one microphone is used. There are several channels to the mixer, each of which has a separate microphone input and means to control the signal level going from that channel to be mixed with others. The output from the mixer is normally amplified to approximately 1 volt (line level) and then fed to other equipment.

microwave High frequency of above 1 GHz used for directional, point-to-point terrestrial and satellite transmission and relay of TV, radio, telephony and data services.

microwave link A system that consists of a transmitter and a receiver both using the same microwave frequency to transmit TV, radio or telephone signals. Microwave links use highly directional dish antennas and relatively low transmission power normally in the range of 10 to 100 watts. Microwave links are used to transmit signals from remote news vans to the studio, from a station to a remote transmitter, from a helicopter to a ground station, from one station to another and from ground station to ground station via satellite. Mobile, compact microwave transmission units called "fly aways" are used to transmit from remote, temporary locations.

Miniature microwave units are sometimes installed on cameras to allow the camera operator freedom of movement. The transmitter of such a system has a nondirectional antenna.

MIDI Musical instrument digital interface. A standard protocol for interchange of data between computers and electronic musical instruments. The MIDI protocol contains data such as note numbers, duration, tempo, volume and control over effects processors and drums.

A numeric position in the MIDI protocol is assigned to every kind of instrument to insure that sound produced by synthesizers and computer audio cards from MIDI data—no matter where—will produce similar sound.

Files of MIDI data can be stored or sent via special cables or as computer data between electronic instruments. MIDI files take up substantially less storage space than digital audio files because the actual sound is produced by the electronic instrument according to the MIDI protocol information.

The basic MIDI standard agreed upon in 1980 is called "General MIDI System Level 1." It includes 128 note numbers and 16 instruments or note data channels. Expansions to General MIDI have been introduced by several manufacturers such as Roland—General Synthesis (GS)—and Yamaha—Expanded General (XG). These expansions include increased numbers of instrument channels, effects, and drum setups. A number of channels are used simultaneously to produce data for several instruments to play at the same time, as in an orchestra. Conversion of sound from acoustical instruments to MIDI data is also possible.

MIDI is used by professional musicians, audio engineers and multimedia creators to compose, store and distribute electronic music. MIDI is not limited to sound and is also used to control other devices that support MIDI protocol such as stage lighting, smoke generators, video projectors and explosion controllers.

midrange   In audio monitors, the speaker delivering the middle of the audio bandwidth.

milli- (m)   One thousandth: 1/1,000. Comes as a prefix letter to expressions such as milliwatt (mW), milliampere (mA) and millivolt (mV).

minijack   A small audio jack and socket 3.5 mm in diameter, often used for small portable audio equipment items such as disk and cassette players. Minijacks come in mono and stereo versions.

minimum object distance   The nearest distance from a camera lens at which an object can remain in focus. Minimum object distance is an important parameter of any lens. The longer the focal length of the lens, the greater will be the minimum object distance. In TV lenses this distance is normally in the neighborhood of three feet. Some lenses have a macro focus feature to enable closer object distance. *See also* **macro.**

mix-down   The reduction of the number of audio channels by the process of mixing several channels into only one or two.

mix-effect (M/E)   Main part of a video production switcher. A mix-effect is a unit capable of combining several video sources in different ways. Effects such as cut, dissolve, wipe, luminance and chroma key can be performed. Two or more crosspoint buses are used to select sources. Small switchers normally have one mix-effect unit, while large and complex production switchers may have up to four. In large switchers, the product of one mix-effect can be fed to another mix-effect to add an additional layer of effects and thus create complex, multilayer effects. *See also* **cut; dissolve; key; production switcher.**

mixer A circuit capable of mixing or combining several signals together. In broadcasting the term *mixer* is normally applied to a small audio mixing device with 3 to 12 inputs. Larger mixers are usually called "mixing consoles" or "audio consoles." In Europe a video switcher is also called mixer or vision mixer. *See also* **audio mixer; vision switcher.**

mix-minus An audio term that refers to a mix containing all sound sources except one. If in a news program a remote studio is included, the remote studio sends its sound to the news studio. The news studio in turn has to send sound to the remote, but care must be taken not to include the sound received from the remote, since this will cause feedback. The mix that includes the studio sources minus the incoming feed is a mix-minus.

modem An acronym for modulator-demodulator. A device that enables computers to send and receive data over telephone lines. Computer high-speed data stream is converted to a lower audio frequency and back on reception. Most modems today are built as an add-on card inserted into a slot in the computer. Some are self-contained and self-powered as a separate unit that is attached to the computer and a telephone line. Modems enable data transfer between computers as far as telephone lines go and connection to global networks such as the Internet. The speed of a modem is measured in baud rate (bits per second); a typical number is a baud rate of 28,800. Telephone lines have a very restricted bandwidth—normally no more than 5 KHz. Special data lines with higher baud rates can by installed by local telecommunication companies on request. *See also* **baud rate; ISDN.**

modulation A method used for transmission of signals over long distances. A carrier wave is modified by amplitude, phase or frequency according to the changes in the signal to be transmitted. Normally the carrier frequency has to be at least three times higher than the signal. Amplitude modulation (AM) was the first method of modulation to be used and is still in use. Frequency modulation (FM) came later and is more immune to interference. Modulation is used for transmission of modulated radio and TV signals from terrestrial transmitters and satellites, for transmission over fiber and coax cables and for recording signals on tape. *See also* **amplitude modulation; demodulation; frequency modulation; modulator.**

modulator A circuit that changes the amplitude, frequency or phase of a wave of constant frequency and amplitude, normally a sine wave (carrier wave). The information contained by the signal is transformed into changes in the carrier wave. The original information of the signal can be retrieved from the carrier wave by means of demodulation. *See also* **modulation.**

moiré effect An unwanted pattern appearing in video pictures. Moiré is caused by a high-frequency interference or information added to the picture signal. Moiré effects appear as a wavy pattern on the picture.

monitor (a) In audio, a self-contained loudspeaker that enables one to listen to audio signals. Also known as "audio monitor." **(b)** In video, a screen that displays video signals as visible pictures. Also known as "picture monitor" or "video monitor." In TV stations and control rooms, large numbers of video monitors are used to monitor the different video signals from cameras, tape machines, character generators and all other video sources. Video monitors come in different sizes and quality levels; some are black and white and others reproduce full color. They are similar to TV sets, the difference being that they usually are fed directly by a video signal and do not contain a tuner to receive signals from the air. **(c)** In test and measurement, a monitor is used display waveforms. The "waveform monitor" is an oscilloscope displaying video signals.

monochrome   Black and white. A video signal that contains luminance information only—no chrominance information is present. In the first years of television, monochrome was the only system available. Monochrome video is still in use in education and surveillance.

monophonic   Sound coming from a single source, as opposed to stereo or quadraphonic sound.

montage   A European name for film editing.

mood lighting   Lighting a set in a cinema or TV production to create a certain atmosphere or mood, rather than just lighting the set up for the cameras to be able to operate.

mosaic effect   An effect created by a digital effects generator in which the video picture is divided into uniform color squares. Each square has a color that is an average of the color of the picture in that area. The size and number of squares can be changed. The mosaic effect can be restricted to a certain area. *See also* **digital effects.**

motherboard   A relatively large printed circuit board to which most other boards in a device (especially microcomputers) are connected.

mounting equipment   Equipment such as stands, tripods, pedestals and cranes used to support audio and video equipment. *See also* **camera mount.**

mouse   One of the human-computer interfaces. A mouse is a small palm-size object that has press buttons and is rolled on the table or special surface (mouse pad). The mouse is wired to the computer and its movement causes a small arrow on the computer screen to move accordingly. When the arrow is placed in the appropriate place, a button can be pressed to operate a function. A mouse can perform other tasks such as drawing or drafting, depending on the software in use.

moving coil   **(a)** Moving coil loudspeaker: A coil attached to a diaphragm is placed in a constant magnetic field and when voltage is applied to the coil, it moves together with the diaphragm, creating air movements or sound. **(b)** Moving coil microphone: A coil attached to a diaphragm is placed in a constant magnetic field and when air waves (sound) move the diaphragm with the coil, voltage is created in the coil. This voltage is microphone-level audio.

MPEG Moving picture experts group. An international group of experts working to establish standards for the data compression of moving pictures and audio. MPEG is a continuation of JPEG to develop and add interfield compression. Similarities between successive frames of moving pictures allow for more compression to be obtained. MPEG is capable of delivering better quality pictures in high-compression rates than ever before. *See also* **compression; JPEG; MPEG 1; MPEG 2.**

MPEG 1 A standard designed to enable playback of video from CD-ROMs. However, data rate is not sufficient for broadcast-quality video.

MPEG 2 A standard for compression of digital video and audio signals with data rates ranging between 2 and 10 Mbits/sec. This wide range of data rates is designed to be used for a large number of formats, from the home VHS all the way to HDTV.

MPEG 2 has a good potential of becoming a common method of transmission and distribution of TV programs. It is also applicable for broadcasting of HDTV wide-bandwidth signals in standard TV channels. Encoding and decoding of MPEG 2 is relatively complex, which makes the hardware expensive. *See also* **HDTV.**

MSB Most significant bit. The first bit from the left in a byte or binary number. Also the bit with the highest value. *See also* **LSB.**

M-S recording Middle-sides recording. A stereo sound-recording technique in which two microphones are used: A directional cardioid microphone is pointed toward the center of an orchestra and a figure-eight microphone picks up the sides. The outputs of the two microphones are fed into a matrix that produces left and right outputs.

MTBF Mean time between failures. The assessed number of hours taken for a device to fail. A calculated measure of reliability of a device. MTBF depends on the reliability of each of the components included in that device. The more components included in the device, the lower the MTBF. The MTBF of a device will be smaller than that of the component with the shortest expected MTBF.

Digital and even electromechanical equipment today is highly reliable, and an MTBF of 500,000 hours is common. The existence of such high MTBF ratings does not mean that any device is guaranteed to work that period of time without failure.

multicellular horn An array of horn loudspeakers used mainly for public address. This arrangement is used to get a wide audio distribution pattern.

multicore A cable containing a number of different wires and smaller cables. Studio cameras were connected to the control room by multicore cables for many years, and some still are. Inside studio camera multicore cables there is wiring for utility system power, audio, video tally light and control. Most of today's studio cameras use triax cables instead. *See also* **triax.**

multilateral A satellite transmission intended to be received by many TV stations. *See also* **unilateral.**

multilayering   In audio and video editing, complex operations are sometimes done step-by-step each time some mix or effect is added. Every such step adds a layer and the signal goes through another generation. *See also* **generation.**

multimedia   The combination of graphics, still and video pictures, sound and text in one environment, normally applied to computers. Multimedia is created on computers equipped with special multimedia software to convey an idea, to teach or sell. Most multimedia environments are interactive, allowing the user to choose his own path in the presentation.

Multimedia presentations require a considerable amount of memory, due to the use of pictures and video. Compression techniques are used to reduce storage needed and CD-ROM disks are mostly used for presentation and use of multimedia works. Multimedia is used to create CD-ROMs with large amounts of interactive audiovisual information on almost every subject, for use in education, commerce, home entertainment and games.

multimicrophone technique   An audio recording technique using many microphones to cover an orchestra, as opposed to X-Y or M-S recording techniques.

multipattern microphone   A microphone with several switchable polar patterns such as cardioid, figure eight and omnidirectional.

multiplex   The combination of several signals into one composite signal, sometimes for transmission in the same frequency band or cable.

multiplexer   A device that combines a number of signals to form one composite signal.

multitrack   In reference to recording equipment, having the ability to record a number of audio channels on tape, usually a multiplication of 8 (up to 64 channels ordinarily). Multitrack machines are used in recording studios to record the different sources each on one track. The tracks, or channels, are fed to an audio console to be mixed together to a final mix, normally two-track stereo. The tape can be played back as many times as necessary until the mix is satisfactory. All tracks stay in sync because they are all recorded on the same piece of tape.

music library   A large number of various music segments indexed and ready for use, recorded on tape or disk. Music segments from libraries are mixed into film, radio and television programs as accompaniment or to create a certain mood.

Music libraries usually contain various kinds of music in different length to suit most kinds of short programs, commercials and promos. Normally the purchase price for the music library covers royalties for copyrights, and thus the music can be used without any extra costs.

music power   A short-time peak output power of an amplifier. Normally a strong external power supply is needed to perform this measurement. Music power is measured in watts.

mute   The action or mode of shutting down a channel in an audio console or a loudspeaker.

NAB National Association of Broadcasters. An American trade association of radio and television professionals. NAB maintains an information center and publishes books and newsletters such as *Radio Week*, *TV Today*, *Techcheck* and *NAB World* for international circulation. NAB organizes the definitive annual technological conference and exhibition (among others). NAB also offers members judicial representation. Several awards are sponsored by the NAB for community service, technical achievements, programming, research and more.

NABET National Alliance of Broadcast Employees and Technicians (USA).

nano- One billionth: 1/1,000,000,000. Nano- is used as a prefix to units such as nanosecond (ns), nanofarad (nF) and nanoampere (nA).

narrowcasting Transmission to a selected, narrow audience, as opposed to broadcasting.

NATAS National Academy of Television Arts and Sciences. An organization founded in 1957 for the support and promotion of all arts and sciences involved in television. The national academy presents the well-known annual Emmy Awards for outstanding achievements or contribution to television and publishes the *Television Quarterly*.

natural light Sunlight, direct or reflected, as opposed to artificial light.

NBT Next Big Thing. A new invention or major improvement of existing technology, at the final stages of research and development, supposed to be introduced in the near future. Useful phrase in the era of quantum-leap advancements in broadcast, computer and telecommunications technology.

NC17 A rating used to identify movies that allow no children under the age of 17.

ND (a) Neutral density. (b) Nondirectional. Usually refers to an antenna. *See also* **neutral density.**

near video on demand Video on demand is the ability to provide a program whenever a viewer wants it to start. Near video on demand provides that program within a reasonable time, such as ten minutes, due to technical limitations. *See also* **video on demand.**

neck-mike *see* **lavaliere mike**

needle drop A single use of copyrighted material such as music or score.

negative assembly *see* **negative cutting**

negative cutting Cutting and splicing of original negative footage of a film according to the edited work copy. A copy is used for initial editing so as not to scratch or harm the original in any way. The negative cutting is done in the lab with great care; from this edited negative all positive copies will be made.

network (a) A number of radio and/or TV stations under the same ownership, usually transmitting programs common to all stations. **(b)** A group of devices such as computers interconnected to share data or software. Computer networks are widely used to connect between users in a firm or organization sharing the same data base.

neutral density (ND) A term used for filters that have no effect on the color of light passing through them. Neutral density filters are used to decrease the amount of light entering the camera to protect its light-sensitive elements from excessive light or to reduce the depth of field of the camera. (If the amount of light is reduced, the iris has to be opened and the depth of field is then reduced). A special filter wheel is installed in most professional video cameras with several ND filters, each having a different percentage of light passing through, for use in different light conditions. ND filters are mostly used outside in daylight, rarely in the studio. *See also* **filter (optical).**

news camera Light-weight, portable and self contained TV camera used for stand-alone operation or as part of a larger layout at outside field productions. News cameras normally record the signal on an attached VCR or send it back to the studio by microwave or satellite link. *See also* **EFP; ENG.**

news flash A short news report of an event while it is happening or a short time after.

newsreel A short film of news events that used to be shown in cinemas, before the main film started. It was popular before television became popular.

N.G. No good. A term used for footage or takes in film and TV.

nibble Four binary bits.

nicad Nickel-cadmium. A kind of rechargeable battery commonly used for portable equipment. Nicad batteries suffer from a "memory" effect, meaning that the battery has to be completely discharged before recharged; otherwise capacity drops.

NICAM Near instantaneously companded audio multiplex. A digital audio system used or TV broadcasting. NICAM is used mainly in Europe and employs compression techniques. It is transmitted alongside the standard TV audio channels. NICAM is a major improvement to audio quality in television as it provides CD-quality sound.

night effect In cinematography, a method of filming night scenes during daytime by use of special filters. Also called "day for night."

19 mm Tape width of D1 and D2 digital videocassette formats.

nod shot In a TV program, usually a talk show, a reaction shot of someone who listens while another person talks. The length of such a shot is normally in the neighborhood of two seconds.

noise filter A filter built to eliminate noise existing in specific frequencies, such as the high end of the audio bandwidth. Noise filters are very limited and must be used with care so as not to filter out parts of the audio signal.

noise gate In audio recording, a use of the expander to prevent low background audio or noise from passing through. When the expander is set to a large expansion ratio and the threshold is set just below the lowest level of the instrument to be recorded, unwanted low-level leakage or noise will not pass through the expander. Audio signals higher than the threshold will go through.

noise reducer (NR) Noise reducers are used both in audio and video to improve the quality of signals in terms of S/N ratio. Noise reduction is especially important when noisy material from feeds with poor reception or old archive material is involved. When old audio recordings are used for the making of CDs, the use of noise reduction is recommended because digital media have a wider dynamic range and noise becomes more significant relative to the signal. In film-to-tape transfer of grainy film, NR can considerably improve the quality of the picture.

nondrop frame time code Since there are 29.97 frames a second in NTSC signals, it introduces a difference between time code numbers and real time of 3.6 seconds per one hour of video. Nondrop frame time code is successive but not consistent with real time. To solve the problem, two time code numbers are dropped every minute in a system called drop frame time code. Normally, nondrop frame time code is used.

nonlinear distortion A group of distortions to video signals that are amplitude-dependent. Nonlinear distortions are caused by either compression and clipping or cross-talk and intermodulation between luminance and chrominance signal portions. The main distortions in this category are: **(a)** Differential Phase—measured in degrees. **(b)** Differential Gain—measures in percents. **(c)** Luminance Nonlinearity—measured in percents. **(d)** Chrominance Nonlinear Phase—measured in degrees. **(e)** Chrominance Nonlinear Gain—measured in percents. **(f)** Chrominance-to-Luminance Intermodulation—measured in percents. **(g)** Sync Gain Distortion—measured in mV. *See also* **linear distortion.**

nonlinear editing An editing method in which the edited segments are recorded in an order that may differ from how they will appear in the finished work. Nonlinear editing has the advantage over linear editing of enabling last-minute changes to edited material. Film editing is nonlinear because segments can be put in or taken out at any given point of the film.

Modern disk editing is also nonlinear. During editing the only thing that really happens is that the editing list changes. The disk-based system is then able to "play" the edited segments in the required order, with clean cuts or transitions between segments. In disk editing, a lot of time is saved compared to tape editing by random access of material on the disk and no need for prerolling. Today, nonlinear editing is normally associated with disk editing. *See also* **editing; linear editing; random access.**

normal lens A film or TV camera lens that is not wide angle or telephoto.

notch filter   A circuit used to attenuate a specific, narrow frequency band.

NTSC   National Television Systems Committee. An American advisory group that created standards for broadcast engineering. NTSC is the current TV color transmission standard in North America, some parts of South America and Japan. A field rate of 59.94 fields per second is employed and in every frame there are 525 TV lines. Subcarrier frequency is constant at 3.579545 MHz. Amplitude of the subcarrier changes according to the instantaneous saturation of the color, and phase changes according to the instantaneous hue of the color.

Nyquist frequency (rate)   When converting from analog to digital, the lowest frequency needed for accurate and aliasing free conversion. Usually it is half of the highest frequency included in the signal to be sampled.

OB   (a) Outside broadcasting. A transmission done from a remote location from which there are no facilities such as a studio to transmit. An outside broadcast vehicle that has broadcast equipment installed is normally used. (b) Optical budgets. Outputs from a fiber-optics transmitter. The number of these cannot exceed a few.

object distance   The distance between a camera lens and the object at which it is aimed. The correct distance must be set on the focusing ring of the lens to obtain a sharp image.

OB van/truck   A vehicle equipped to perform radio or TV transmission from a remote location. TV OB vehicles come in different sizes, from a standard station wagon through vans to large trucks, according to the task. OB vehicles are equipped with cameras, switching equipment, monitoring, VCRs and microwave transmitters. In small news vans, usually one or two cameras are involved. Larger OB trucks used for sports and concerts employ large numbers of cameras, complex switching and monitoring, microphones and mixing consoles for audio and communication equipment such as intercom systems, cellular phones and transmission equipment.

octave   In audio, the interval between two frequencies f1 and f2, where f2 = 2f1.

off-axis coloration   (a) In microphone pickup, deterioration of sound quality or frequency response due to off-axis (off center, to the side of the microphone) pickup. (b) In loudspeakers, perceived sound frequency response will be deteriorated if the listener is off axis.

off camera   (a) In reference to a performer such as a narrator, being heard but not seen in a TV program. (b) Falling outside the camera's field of view.

off-line editing   Electronic video editing performed using inexpensive editing equipment to create an edit decision list (EDL). Broadcast-quality, well-equipped editing rooms are very expensive. The decisions about the kind and place of every edit sometimes take much longer than the actual time needed for the technical process of editing. To save the high cost of broadcast-quality editing, inexpensive editing equipment is used. The product of an off-line editing system is a list of edit decisions that contains full information about each edit. The EDL is then taken to the on-line editing room where the final broadcast-quality product is assembled in a relatively short time. Several off-line editing systems can feed one on-line system. Off-line editing, being much cheaper than on-line, relieves some of the pressure existing in more expensive systems to finish the job quickly. *See also* **editing; on-line editing.**

off mike An unintentional situation in which the adjustment of the microphone position has been changed or the person talking or performing has moved to the side or away from the microphone. In this case the sound will be faint or lacking in low-frequency response.

offstage Outside the visible part of the stage or studio.

off sync Out of synchronization. *See also* **sync.**

ohm (Ω) The unit of electrical resistance.

omnidirectional In reference to a microphone, having a pickup pattern that is shaped like a circle and equally sensitive to sound coming from all sides.

on-air In reference to a radio or TV program, in the process of transmission. In broadcast stations, the control room monitor of the transmitted signal is called on-air. Above studio doors there is a red "ON AIR" sign that can be lit when the studio is in transmission.

¼-inch Tape width widely used for audio open-reel tapes and the new DV standard for videocassettes.

1-inch Width of open-reel tape used for audio and video recording, mainly during the 1980s. One-inch machines are still used to play back existing material. *See also* **C-format; VTR.**

one-lite A simple telecine transfer from film to video with one setting of color parameters. No frame-by-frame or other color correction is used to save time and money. One-lite is normally used for material intended for off-line editing, where picture quality is not crucial and not for broadcast.

one-on-one recording In audio recording of many instruments and/or performers, a use of multitrack machines to record every instrument or performer on track, to be mixed in a later stage.

on-line editing Final editing of original video material in broadcast quality. On-line editing suites normally include elaborate broadcast-quality audio and video equipment. In the process of editing, effects can be made between sources. Graphics, digital video effects and characters can be added. Audio channels can be mixed and music, narration and audio effects can be mixed or edited in. Material edited in off-line systems can be quickly edited according to the EDL. *See also* **editing; off-line editing.**

open-circuit recording In microphones, the voltage produced by the microphone with no load connected or when connected to a high impedance load.

open loop gain   Gain of an operational amplifier without a feedback network. Typical open loop gain is 100,000.

open mike   Part of director's jargon requesting the sound engineer to open a channel in the mixing console to which a specific microphone used at that moment is connected. The specific signal is then fed through the console output to the audio and master control room monitoring systems for rehearsals or to record machines or transmission.

open reel   A reel of tape not protected by a housing of any kind (as opposed to a cassette).

operating system   A basic software used in computers to interface between the hardware and software of the computer. The operating system is loaded immediately after booting the computer—usually from the hard drive—to enable the use of other software. The operating system itself is not built to run applications computers usually include, such as word processing. The operating system makes the computer a standard tool that interprets a given set of instructions, even if there are some variations between different manufacturers.

Examples of the most common operating systems are MS-DOS for IBM-compatible PCs and System 8 for Apple Macintosh.

operational amplifier   A single-chip amplifier build to perform a variety of tasks in electronic circuits. The operational amplifier has many qualities of an ideal amplifier: high gain, high input impedance, low output impedance, high slew rate, high stability and low noise. The operational amplifier is an important building block that can perform many different tasks by the addition of several external components.

optical disk   Data storage disk using optical technology. Usually laser technology is used to write on the disk and read from it. Optical disks have a capacity suitable for storage of large files containing still pictures or video. Common sizes are the 5.25-inch (CD size) and the 3.5-inch removable disk. Optical disks are slower than magnetic hard drives but faster than floppy disks. They are fast enough to be used for real time video and audio.

Another member in the family of optical disks is the 12-inch laser disk. Laser disks can play some 45 minutes of video and stereo audio on each side, and the players are used as a home appliance to play back prerecorded disks. Laser disks are also used where some sequences have to be played repeatedly. Unlike tape cassettes, videodisks can be played a countless number of times without degradation.

Optical disks are "Write Once Read Many" ("WORM"). However, magneto optical disks (MO disks), which can be rewritten innumerable times, were introduced in 1989. *See also* **magneto optical disk.**

optical sound   Sound track used in some film prints. Audio is translated to changes in density of dye on film in the audio track. A lamp and photocell in the projector reproduce the sound signal, which is then amplified.

optical track *see* **optical sound**

orange filter   A filter used to convert daylight color temperature of 5,400° K to artificial tungsten 3,200° K light. Also known as #85 filter. Orange filters are used to convert color temperature of lighting equipment by covering the light output of studio lights with orange gelatin filters. Some small studio and ENG lights use dichroic filters that function the same way.

   In studio and portable video cameras, the orange filter is normally built into the filter wheel as one of the standard filters often used. In cine and still cameras, the filter is normally attached to the front of the lens. *See also* **color temperature; dichroic filter; filter wheel.**

orientation shot *see* **establishing shot**

out-point   In magnetic audio- and videotape editing, the point in an existing recording that is the end or the last frame of material being added or inserted. The position of the out-point has to be set for either the recorder or the player. In videotape editing systems the position of the out-points (and in-points) is identified by time code numbers. *See also* **editing; in-point; time-code.**

outtakes   Audio, video or film takes that are not included in the final film or program.

overdubbing   A practice in audio in which new or live material is mixed with prerecorded audio and recorded on another machine or another track of the same machine. Performers or musicians listen to the prerecorded material with the aid of earphones and do their part, which is mixed and recorded.

   The technique of overdubbing is used in TV for recording of substitution sound tracks for foreign language dialog. The existing music and effects are mixed with the new live dialog and recorded on one of the audio tracks on the videotape.

overlap   In editing, sound that belongs to the previous or next picture segment is left intentionally on all or part of the present picture segment. Sometimes a picture cut is "softened" by cutting the sound shortly after the picture.

overmodulation   Modulation of a carrier to an extent whereby the modulated signal will exceed its allocated bandwidth. In TV, overmodulation occurs when a high, nonstandard video signal is sent to a transmitter. The modulated video penetrates to the frequency allocated for audio. The result is low-frequency noise in the audio produced by the home receivers. Overmodulation can also lead to overloading transmitters and distortion of signals.

overscan   Enlarging the scanning of a CRT (TV picture tube) in such a way that the edges of the picture will be outside the screen. Home television sets are adjusted to overscan the picture to make sure that horizontal and vertical sync, test patterns and teletext signals will be cut out of the visible picture. Professional picture monitors sometimes have overscan and underscan possibilities.

over-the-shoulder   A camera shot taken from behind the back of one of the participants of a TV program. The shoulder and back of the head are included in the shot. Usually in this kind of shot a person talking is seen from behind the shoulder of another who is listening.

overtones   Audio frequencies that are too high to be heard by the human ear (over 20,000 Hz) but contribute to the overall quality of sound.

oxide tape   Conventional magnetic tape as opposed to metal particle tape, which has improved performance.

PA *see* **production assistant; public address.**

pad   A fixed-value resistive attenuator used in audio. Pads are used to bring down high audio levels to avoid overloading of devices such as audio consoles or amplifiers. Pads are normally small in size, passive and housed in a standard audio connector.

PAL   Phase alternating line. A television system widely used in Europe and most of the rest of the world, except North America and Japan. A field rate of 50 fields per second is employed and in every frame there are 625 TV lines. Subcarrier frequency is constant at 4.43361875 MHz. Amplitude of the subcarrier changes according to the instantaneous saturation of the color, and phase changes according to the instantaneous hue of the color at every point along the TV scan lines.

In PAL the bandwidth for the luminance signal is 5.5 MHz and for the color difference signals it is 1.3 Mhz.

Having been developed after NTSC, PAL has an improved ability to correct phase errors in the transmission path by reversing the color reference burst phase on alternate lines.

PAL ID   PAL identification. A control pulse usually produced by a sync pulse generator together with other control pulses, indicating the place where subcarrier phase inversion takes place.

PAL-M   A transmission standard unique to Brazil. It uses PAL but with a 525/60 line/field rate. In the TV stations, PAL equipment is normally used and the signal is converted to PAL-M before going to air.

PALplus   A 16:9 aspect ratio wide-screen transmission system developed to improve picture quality of existing TV transmission standards. In standard 4:3 PAL receivers, the PALplus picture can be displayed, but in "letterbox" form using 432 active TV lines only.

TV cameras must use 16:9 CCD chips or anamorphic lenses to produce 16:9 pictures. Wide-screen 16:9 monitors are available and some new PAL picture monitors are 16:9 switchable. Most other existing PAL production equipment is compatible with PAL-plus.

PALplus is already in use in several TV stations, mainly in Europe.

pan   A sweep of the camera movements. A turn of the camera from left to right or from right to left in a horizontal movement.

pan and scan   A method used for transmission of wide-screen feature films. Since the aspect ratio of the film is wider than the television aspect ratio, parts from the left or right of the film frame are not shown. The decision about which parts to leave out depends on the action in the frame. The part shown on TV is panned inside the film frame moving after the action. A disadvantage of this method is that the complete film frame can never be shown—some parts are always missing. *See also* **letterboxing.**

pan and tilt head   A mechanical device used both to support and enable free movement of a camera at the same time. The pan and tilt head is mounted between the tripod or pedestal and the camera. The head usually enables 360 degrees of pan movement and about 120 degrees of tilt movement. There are small pan and & tilt heads for fieldwork with lightweight portable cameras and larger heads for full-size studio cameras. The pan and tilt head must provide smooth movement and balance for the camera.

panning   In an audio mixing console, sending a mono audio feed to the right or left output of the console. On each channel in the console there usually is a panning control (potentiometer) that in center position sends the input equally to both outputs; turning the control one way or the other, partly or fully, will cause the audio to follow the appropriate output. Panning is important for the creation of a stereo "image." Every input to the audio console can be designated to the left or right output or to both continuously assignation. Panning control can be changed during recording or transmission, making the sound move from side to side, or "pan."

pan pot   In audio, a potentiometer used divide a signal between two destinations in a variable proportion, according to needs. Common mainly in audio mixing consoles in each input channel, it enables sending an input signal to the left or right master output of the console or every combination of the two.

pantograph   Foldable suspension for studio lights. Usually used in studios with a high ceiling. Pantographs enable the lights to be pulled down for adjustment or service.

parallel communication   Exchange of data or speech in several conductors at the same time. Digital words are sent in a number of conductors known as buses, each of which is the number of bits in the word (normally 8, 16, 32, 64), plus a ground wire, voltage supply wire and a shield.

Parallel communication is much faster than serial, but can only be carried by wires to relatively short distances. Communication between components in computers is parallel. Most communication between distant devices is serial.

parametric equalizer   An audio equalizer with a continuously variable point over the bandwidth at which boost or cut can be performed. Some parametric equalizers have control over the width (Q) of the frequency band to be boosted or cut.

passive satellite   A satellite used as a reflector for signals, with no active parts such as amplifiers or transmitters.

patch bay   A board including rows of connectors (normally female). To these connectors different devices and signals are connected. By using cords between the different connectors on the patch bay, a variety of interconnection and routing can be obtained. The cords (patch cords) usually have male connectors on both ends.

Various patch boards with different connectors are made for audio, video, time code and other kinds of signals. Patch bays are usually rack mounted or installed in audio consoles or control desks. *See also* **patch-cord.**

patch board *see* **patch bay**

patchcord   A flexible cable (jumper) normally a few feet long with connectors on both sides that fit the connectors on a patch board.

path   In computers, the location of a file within the disk system. The path consists of three parts: **(a)** The disk drive symbol (such as c:). **(b)** The subdirectory in which the file is located, including all subdirectories one has to go through to get to the desired directory (such as \games\chess). The different subdirectory names are separated by backslashes. **(c)** The full name of the wanted file (such as chess.exe). All these combined make the full path (in this example: c:\games\chess\chess.exe).

pause   In tape machines, a position where the tape has stopped rolling but is still in contact with heads. Pause position can be entered during recording or playback and enables fast restart when released.

PC   Personal computer. Name given by IBM to desktop computers intro-

duced in 1980. The PC used a 16-bit address bus that gave access to 1 Mbyte of memory, much larger than the old 64 Kbytes memory addresses. The first microprocessors used where 8086 and 8088 manufactured by Intel. The PC became very popular and clones were made in large numbers. Large amounts of software for PC or PC compatible computers where produced and still are today. The PC became very popular and dominant in the computer market. Every few years a new microprocessor is introduced, with improved performance and various desktop and portable laptop versions.

In broadcasting the PC has many applications, such as for character generators, audio editors, teleprompters and video editing systems.

PC board *see* **board**

PCM   Pulse code modulation. A modulation method used in ultra-high frequencies in radar and satellite communications. Composed of a series of pulses with varying lengths.

PD   **(a)** Program director. **(b)** Public domain. *See also* **public domain.**

peak reading meter *see* **PPM**

peak time *see* **prime time**

peak to peak (PP)   The amplitude of a given signal or waveform. The difference between lowest or most negative point of the signal (deep) and the highest or most positive point of the signal (peak).

peak white   The brightest possible part of a TV picture. *See also* **white level.**

pedestal (a) Heavy camera support mechanism used mainly in studios. The pedestal is equipped with wheels that allow smooth and quiet movement on the studio floor in all directions. There is a column on which the camera head is mounted. The column is collapsible to allow change in camera height. Camera weight is balanced by lead weights or pneumatically (via compressed air or nitrogen). (b) Camera movement up and down allowed by the pedestal. (c) The black level of a television video signal or picture. Black level in a TV picture determines the brightness of the picture. *See also* **camera mount; camera movement.**

perforation Row of holes at one or both sides of film. Perforation is standard for every film format and is used by film cameras and projectors to pull the film at a constant speed or number of frames per second. The number of perforations per frame is standard.

persistence (a) A quality of the human eye that allows it to see light for a short period of time (about 40 milliseconds) after its disappearance. Cinema and TV use this attribute to create the illusion of continuous movement by employing a series of still pictures. The number of pictures per second projected in cinema and fields per second in TV can be calculated to create continuity based on persistence of the eye. (b) In CRTs (picture tubes), the luminescent material emits light some time after the electron beam has moved on. In TV receivers, the picture tube has persistence calculated to increase the effect of a continuous picture and decrease flickering of the TV screen. *See also* **cathode ray tube.**

PGM Short for "program." Usually in the studio control room, "PGM" is written under the picture monitor that displays the final product of the studio, or the "program output."

phantom In audio, power supplied to microphones through the microphone cable from the mixer, console or special power supplies. The voltage supplied from mixers and consoles is normally 48 volts. Field batteries supply different voltages, mostly 18 volts. Being a DC voltage, it can be separated from the AC microphone signal even though it runs in the same wires.

phantom power supply A device supplying DC voltage to microphones through the signal line. Some phantom power supplies are battery operated for field use while others are utility-system powered. Modern audio consoles normally include phantom powering for each microphone input. *See also* **phantom.**

phase The instantaneous timing of one signal in relation to another. Phase is measured in degrees between periodical waveforms with identical frequency. One cycle represents 360°. If both signals reach the same peak at the same time, the phase between them is 0°. If they are half a cycle away, the phase difference is 180°.

In composite video signals, the phase between the subcarrier (chroma information) and the burst determines the color or hue that the signal will produce on the TV screen.

In audio care is normally taken not to cause phase reversal of one of two stereo signals. Phase reversal (180° difference) occurs when two wires in an audio cable are cross-wired. Such "antiphase" causes cancellation of the two signals if they are mixed or played together on speakers. *See also* **burst; chroma phase; phase cancellation.**

phase cancellation When two signals equal in frequency and amplitude but in a phase shift of 180°, mixed together or combined, the sum of the instantaneous levels will be zero.

In audio, where two sets of similar signals are frequently used as stereo pairs, accidental phase reversal of one of them will result in attenuation if the two are combined together. *See also* **phase.**

phasing **(a)** Adjustment of one video signal to match another reference signal, in terms of horizontal timing and subcarrier phase. All sources coming into a video switcher must be phased to the same reference to get smooth transition between sources. **(b)** Correct polarity between two stereo loudspeakers in a control room or home sound system. If the polarity of one of the speakers is reversed, interference and cancellation of sound will occur.

photoelectric cell A device that either produces an electrical voltage or changes its electrical resistance. Photoelectric cells are used for accurate measurement of light intensity in light meters and cameras. In old flying-spot slide scanners and telecines, a photoelectric cell was used to convert light going through the film into an electrical signal.

photometer *see* **light meter**

pickup tube *see* **camera tube**

picture composition Arrangement of objects, background and foreground in a picture to get an esthetic or "artistically correct" result.

picture monitor *see* **monitor**

pilot The first program in a series, made for demonstration and sales purposes.

pilot tone Control track recorded in double-system outside recording. Pilot tone is an accurate frequency signal recorded along the audio tracks in a separate track on tape. During playback or mixing, variations in speed are detected by frequency changes in the pilot tone and can be corrected while playing to stay in sync with the picture.

pinch roller In audio- and videotape machines, the capstan determines the speed of tape movement. The pinch roller, which is a rubber wheel, pushes the tape against the metal pivot of the capstan, providing nonslip grip of the tape during movement.

pincushion A kind of optical distortion of the image created by lenses. In this distortion, parallel lines at the edges of the frame bend away from the center of the frame. This bending happens both in horizontal and vertical. Pincushion distortion is corrected together with other distortions in compound lenses used for film and TV lenses.

pink noise In audio, a flat noise used to measure the response of a room or hall for the entire audio frequency band. Pink noise has an equal sound energy per octave. To produce pink noise, white noise is filtered through a -3 dB octave filter. *See also* **room equalization; white noise.**

PIP Picture-in-picture. The ability to see one TV picture within another picture. One picture is smaller and confined to a smaller frame inside the bigger one. PIP is useful in TV receivers having two tuners to see two stations at the same time. Some studio camera viewfinders also have a PIP function that enables the camera operator to see signals in addition to his own camera output, such as program or preview.

pixel Short for "picture cell" or "picture element." The smallest part of a TV picture or computer screen. Each pixel contains brightness, saturation and hue information. The number of pixels in a picture determine the quality of the picture in terms of resolution. Broadcast-quality TV pictures contain approximately 500,000 pixels, while consumer equipment delivers half that amount.

PL A ¼-inch plug and socket widely used in home and professional audio systems. PLs were first used for connecting telephone lines in switchboards in the early years of telephone. There are mono and stereo versions, with two or three contacts respectively, and there is also a smaller ⅛-inch mini-PL version used for compact equipment.

playback Reconstruction of audio and video signals recorded on tape or disk. Playback of the tape or disk has to match the movement and speed used for recording. A playback head reads the recorded tracks to read the recorded information.

playback head In audio- and videotape and disk recording equipment, a transducer used to reconstruct prerecorded audio by following prerecorded tracks of magnetized ferric oxide or metal particles on the magnetic media and producing an electrical current that is proportional to the level of magnetizing. The quality and condition of the head are critical to the playback process. *See also* **record head.**

player A device used to play back audio or video signals recorded on another device. The use of players saves money in places such as editing rooms where many VCRs are used and not all of them must have the capability of recording.

plug (a) A device used for easy connection of a cable to a socket. (b) Name for a commercial or short announcement on TV.

pluge (black set) Test signal specially made for adjustment of picture monitors. Pluge is a black and white signal with a gray scale for adjustment of monitor brightness. It contains three bars—blacker than black, black and whiter than black—in slight variations. Monitor brightness is adjusted so that only the whiter than black is visible. Often pluge comes with other test patterns to adjust additional picture monitor parameters such as contrast and color balance.

Plumbicon A Phillips brand name for a popular camera picture tube. Comes in ½-inch (13 mm), ⅔-inch (18 mm), 1-inch (25 mm) and 1⅓-inch (30 mm) diameters. The smaller tubes are used for small portable cameras and the larger for studio cameras. Most cameras manufactured today use CCDs instead of picture tubes. Some high-definition cameras are still manufactured with picture tubes as the light-sensitive element. *See also* **picture tube.**

PM *see* **production manager**

pointcasting *see* **point-to-point**

point of view camera   A very small video camera that can be mounted in places such as a race driver's cabin or a cyclist's, pilot's or skier's helmet. The signal from the camera is transmitted to the outside broadcast vehicle or studio. The camera allows viewers of the transmission to see the action from the point of view of the actor.

point source   (a) A light source of negligible size or a theoretical light source used for optical calculations. (b) A sound source of negligible size or a theoretical sound source used for acoustical planning and calculations.

point-to-multipoint   Broadcast from one point to multiple receivers or viewers. The transmission of a TV station to its viewers is a point-to-multipoint transmission.

point-to-point   Transmission of signals from one point to a single designated receiver, also called pointcasting. Transmission between relay stations or from an outside broadcast vehicle to the station is a point-to-point transmission.

polarity   Direction of an electrical (positive or negative) voltage or magnetic (south or north) field.

polarized light   Waves or vibrations of light that are limited to a single plane. Light is regarded as traveling in waves that vibrate in all directions at right angles to the direction of travel. Polarization of light occurs when light is reflected from polished surfaces such as glass. Some crystals will allow light through only if its waves move in a specific direction—all the rest will be absorbed. The light passing through such a material will be polarized.

polarizing filter   A filter that allows only light that vibrates in a specific angle to pass through. All other light waves will be absorbed. Polarizing filters are usually made of transparent plastic material treated by stretching to create an aligned molecular structure. Such filters are used in front of the camera lens to reduce reflections of light from water, shiny objects, windows and to reduce polarized light from the sky. They are mounted in a way that allows rotating of the filter to get the right angle.

Two polarizing filters one on top of the other can be used as a device to regulate the amount of light coming through in a continuous way. When one filter is rotated in relation to the other, the amount of light passing through will change. If both filters are aligned in the same direction, most of the light will pass. If there is a 90° difference, the light will be almost completely blocked.

polar pattern   A circular diagram describing direction and intensity.

Used as a way to describe the sensitivity of microphones to sound coming from all directions. Typical polar responses are the omnidirectional, cardioid, figure eight and unidirectional. Sound wave dissipation from speakers is also described by polar response diagrams.

polyester A material used in production of magnetic tape. The film coated with oxide or metal particles is made of polyester.

pop Sound effect generated by a microphone when consonants (such as b's, p's and t's) are pronounced or when there are sudden blasts of wind. A spongy cover called a "wind shield" is used to reduce such noises.

porch *see* **back porch; front porch**

portable camera A lightweight, self-powered and self-contained video camera. Also referred to as ENG camera, it often comes in one piece with a built-in VCR (Camcorder). Portable cameras can be connected as part of a larger system. They are also used in the studio connected by cable to CCU and the video switcher for hand-held operation to get angles that a camera mounted on a pedestal cannot get. *See also* **camcorder; camera; CCU; ENG; VCR.**

post-echo In an audio mixing console, a signal connected from the input channel after the input fader to the echo send line. Also the switch or switch position that sends the signal to the echo send line in this particular path.

posterization An effect in stills and video in which the number of col-

ors in the picture is limited to a very small number (typically six to ten colors). The result is an unnatural, posterlike or paintinglike picture.

postproduction The final stage of production work needed to complete a feature film or TV program after the shooting and recording have been completed. Postproduction consists mainly of editing and also addition of audio tracks such as narration, audio and video effects, titles, credits and making of copies for distribution. The preproduction and production stages of making a program must be done with the postproduction in mind; otherwise problems are bound to occur. Collection and taking care of equipment used in the production are also part of postproduction, and there are nontechnical postproduction jobs such as accounting. *See also* **preproduction; production.**

postrecording Audio recording for a TV program done after the completion of the visual part.

postsync Postsynchronization. When conditions on filming or recording location do not allow satisfactory dialog and effects recording quality, audio tracks are rerecorded in the postproduction stage, in studio-controlled conditions. Pictures taken on location are played back and the new audio tracks are recorded in sync with the picture.

pot Short for potentiometer. Potentiometers are used to regulate audio level and levels of other signals.

POV Point of view. A camera shot used to describe what a character in a program sees. For example, if that character is looking at a lion from a close distance, the point of view shot will be a closeup of the lion's head. *See also* **point of view camera.**

power consumption The total amount of electrical energy drawn by a circuit or device, measured in watts. Power consumption of different devices is important for calculation and planning of utility and other power supply systems. The power consumption of a system is the sum of the consumption of all the parts of the system.

power supply A device that delivers specific voltages and currents to a circuit or instrument. Power supplies draw power from utility systems, batteries or generators and produce the necessary voltages in either AC or DC according to the needs. Every power supply has a specific and limited current that can be drawn from it.

PPM Peak program meter. A method for measurement of audio levels that relates to momentary peaks of the signal rather than the average. PPMs have an advantage in that signal peaks can damage sensitive equipment such speakers, power amplifiers and transmitter stages. There are several PPM standards, with slight differences between them: BBC PPM, EBU PPM and a PPM standard used in Germany and Eastern Europe. The ITU has introduced a three-level test tone. In this sequence there are "peak permitted level," "alignment level" or "test level" and "measurement level." PPMs are widely used in England and Europe instead of VUs. *See also* **VU meter.**

PPS Pictures per second. In film, the speed or the number of frames shot or projected per second. Standard 35 mm cinema is shot in 25 PPS. To get slow-motion effects, film is shot at a higher PPS rate and then projected at standard speed.

PPV Pay per view. In cable television and direct broadcast satellite (DBS), some channels charge the viewer per program or movie, normally for specific programs only.

preamplifier In audio, an amplifier used to increase gain of weak signals from microphone level (~ 5 mV) or other low levels to line level (~ 1 V). Preamps amplify signals before they are input to the main or power amplifier—hence the name. Due to the small signals handled, preamplifiers must be shielded against penetration of interference. Like every other amplifier, preamps should deliver linear, distortion-free amplification to the extent possible.

pre-echo In an audio mixing console, a signal connected from the input channel before the input fader to the echo send line. Also the switch or switch position that sends the signal to the echo send line in this particular path.

preheat The period of time for warming up of electronic equipment, such as studio cameras, to reach working temperature. During this period of time, changes in equipment parameters may occur; therefore, use or adjustment of parameters should be only after a warm-up period. Preheat is used mainly on old, vacuum-tube based equipment. New IC (integrated circuit) based equipment is less sensitive to temperature changes and therefore needs shorter preheat—sometimes none.

prelay   In audio, preparing audio tracks for final mix by premixing, editing and laying tracks on videocassette audio tracks, multitrack tape or digital media.

prelisten   In audio consoles, a button located on each of the input modules that allows listening to the input signal before the processing is done by the channel, such as amplification and filtering.

premix   A mix of audio tracks made as preparation for a final mix. Premix is done to simplify the final mix to fewer channels of audio, sometimes because of equipment limitations.

preproduction   All work done before the actual shooting of a film or TV program. Preproduction includes financial planning, script writing, casting, rehearsals, wardrobe and rental or preparation of equipment and facilities. Proper preproduction work is vital for a successful production. Poor preproduction usually causes production to take longer than necessary and to cost more.

prerecorded   Of radio or TV program, recorded on tape ahead of its transmission. Most TV programs are prerecorded; there are few live programs.

prerecording   Early recording of audio parts of a TV program. The prerecorded audio is played back in the TV studio to be combined with the visual part. Prerecording is done to avoid expensive studio time or because TV studios are not always equipped for complex audio recordings.

preroll   Run-up time. In videotape editing, rolling the tape back a few seconds prior to the editing point. Preroll is needed to allow the mechanical and electrical parts of the tape transport to reach the correct speed and to lockup and synchronize with an external reference. Normally preroll time ranges between ten seconds in very old equipment to two to three seconds in more advanced equipment.

presence   In audio, a subjective term used to describe the quality of sound. Audio is said to have presence if the listener gets the feeling he is listening to a live performance rather than a recorded one.

preset monitor   *see*   **preview monitor**

pressure mike   *see*   **dynamic microphone**

pressure roller   *see*   **pinch roller**

preview   (a) The screening of a film to a selected audience before it is released to the public in order to test reaction. This enables last-minute changes in film content or distribution. (b) During video editing, a dry run of an edit or series of edits to show how that material will look after editing. The editing system switches the sources as if an edit has been performed.

preview bus   A row of buttons in a vision switcher used to select a signal for the preview monitor.

preview monitor A monitor in a control room usually located near the program monitor, used for evaluation of picture quality, framing and adjustment of effects.

primary area The area well covered by a radio or TV station, allowing good reception of the station's transmitters.

primary colors The three colors red, green and blue of the additive color system from which all other colors in TV systems are produced. Video cameras produce the three signals, one for each primary color, and then combine them to get the full-color picture. In television sets the color picture is composed of red, green and blue dots on the screen. Video projectors produce three beams of red, green and blue light that combined produce a color picture on the screen. They are distinguished from magenta, cyan and yellow, the primary colors of the subtractive color system, which is not used in television.

prime time Period of time during the day with the largest number of TV viewers. More attention is given to transmission by broadcasters during prime time. Commercial prices in network TV stations are the highest during prime time and most of the revenue is earned then.

Prime time is usually during early evening hours when adults are already home from work and children are still awake. Prime time in the United States is usually between 8 and 11 P.M. in the eastern and Pacific time zones and between 7 and 10 P.M. in the central and mountain time zones.

printer **(a)** A device that prints computer text and data on paper. Used in editing rooms to print edit lists. **(b)** A device used to print paper pictures from a video source. Used as quick way to produce paper pictures for continuity purposes, to print brochures and to release information to the press.

print through Transfer of information from one layer to the next in a magnetic tape spool. A faint ghost picture or sound can be generated or just minor disturbances. This unwanted phenomenon occurs after long storage time and sometimes results from high storage temperatures.

prism block A set of two prisms used in TV cameras to separate incoming light into the three primary colors. *See also* **beam splitter.**

processing amplifier (proc amp) A device used to stabilize and control different composite video signal parameters. Video processing amplifiers usually have low gain, but they can control black level, white level, chroma level, chroma phase, burst phase and sync phase independent of each other. Normally proc amps are used to strip the video signal from all synchronizing pulses and replace them with an internally generated set of pulses. Some amplifiers have an automatic gain capability that keeps the video level standard at all times. Processing amplifiers are normally used in control rooms and switching stations to correct small changes caused by long cables and transmission equipment.

producer Executive producer. A person in charge of the production process from the very early stages of script writing, financing, hiring of the crew and casting, through the production stages to the editing and distribution. Sometimes the producer is the creator and owner of the production and its products; in other cases the producer is an employee of a production house or TV station.

production assistant (PA)   Also called "gofer," a member of the production crew, usually at the entry level.

production manager (PM)   A person usually in charge of the production in the field, one level under the executive producer.

production schedule   A detailed planning of all production activities.

production switcher   A video switcher located in a production area such as a studio control room or a remote van. *See also* **video switcher.**

professional quality *see* **broadcast quality**

program   **(a)** Output signal from audio or video equipment intended for on-air transmission. **(b)** In computers, a set of instructions that tells the computer how to process, store and transfer data and how to operate different input-output devices.

programming   The planning and implementation of a program schedule in a radio or TV station or network. Programming determines the exact transmission schedule—which programs will be aired and at what time—for each day of the week, normally on a quarterly schedule. Pro-

gramming also includes long-term planning from one to three years ahead.

progressive scan   A TV scanning method with twice the number of lines in a standard TV picture. All lines are scanned in every field instead of only the odd or even in every field. Progressive scan provides better picture quality in large TV screens.

projection axis   The imaginary axis from the center of the projector lens to the center of the screen.

projection distance   The distance between the projection lens and the screen. Every change in video projection distance influences directly the image intensity and size. In projectors using a three-CRT system, a relatively long alignment process is needed after a change in projection distance.

projector (video)   A device used to screen or project a video picture on a surface or screen. Video projectors today are based on one of two different technologies: **(a)** CRT: Three high-intensity, small-diameter (usually 5-inch) CRTs are used, one for each primary color. A decoder circuit divides the video signal to be projected into the three primary colors, R, G and B, and each is sent to the corresponding CRT. Three lenses are used to project the picture from each CRT to the screen. Adjustment of such a projector is needed every time it or the screen is moved. The adjustment process to precisely align all three pictures takes considerable time. Usually internal test patterns are provided. **(b)** LCD (liquid crystal display): A lightbulb is used to produce white light. A system of dichroic mirrors separates the light from the light source into red, green and blue light beams. Each light beam goes through another LCD element. Each LCD unit has a resolution of about 500,000 pixels. Each pixel is a small element that can pass light or block all or part of it. All the pixels together produce the video picture, in this case a unicolor picture for each LCD panel. The pictures from the three LCD panels are combined by another set of dichroic mirrors. A projection lens throws the picture onto the screen.

Quality of a video projector is measured mainly by the light beam intensity, resolution, contrast ratio and brightness uniformity. They come in many sizes for uses that range from the home to projection in large halls. The intensity of a projector beam enables a large and bright picture to be formed that is measured in lumens. Video projectors can be used for front or rear projection. In front projection a higher picture intensity is achieved. Some projectors are built into a piece of furniture that looks like a very large TV set. There is a screen at the front—sometimes measuring 100 inches diagonally—and the projector is at the bottom, projecting to the screen with the help of a mirror.

Strong projectors are used in halls to produce pictures measuring as much as 30 feet diagonally, depending on the light conditions. If the room is sufficiently dark, the projection is more visible.

Projectors are also used to project high-quality HDTV signals and computer-generated images directly from the computer. *See also* **back projection; projection axis; projection distance.**

PROM   Programmable read-only memory. Computer memory used primarily to store initial data that should not be erased at any time. *See also* **EPROM.**

promo   Promotional announcement. Advertisement of a radio or TV station for its own programs, to enhance awareness and viewing. Promos are sometimes used as buffers in the transmission schedule to compensate for last-minute changes in the length of live transmissions. Promos are added or removed where necessary because they are not as vital in the transmission log as programs and commercials.

prompter *see* **teleprompter**

propagation   Dispersion of electromagnetic waves away from a transmitting source such as a transmitter.

props   Properties. All items and objects such as furniture, lamps, dishes, books, toys, office equipment and electronic or electrical equipment used on a cinema or TV set to make it look real and give it the intended style.

protection copy   A copy of an audio or video master tape or disk stored in safekeeping and intended for use in case of damage to or loss of the original.

proximity effect   An increase in low-frequency response when using cardioid microphones very close to the sound source.

proximity effect filter   A low-cut filter usually built into microphones that can be switched on to reduce low frequencies in strong wind or when used close to the mouth.

PSA Public service announcement. A noncommercial message transmitted on radio or TV for the benefit of the public.

P/S/N PAL, SECAM, NTSC. The three major existing television transmission standards. *See also* **NTSC; PAL; SECAM.**

PST **(a)** Pacific Standard Time. A time zone of the West Coast of the United States and part of Canada. **(b)** Preset. A monitor in TV studios used to watch sources or effects prior to airing. Also a row of buttons in a video switcher in which the next source to be aired through a wipe or dissolve is selected.

PT *see* **prime time.**

PTT Postal, Telegraph and Telephone authority. In many countries, PPT is a name for the body responsible for communication services for radio, television and computer data as well as telephone and telegraph.

PTV **(a)** Pay television. Specific channels in cable television that require separate payment to receive them, such as HBO and the Disney Channel. **(b)** Public television. Television owned by the government or community.

public address (PA) An audio system for delivering sound of a performance or recording to the audience in a studio, concert hall or theater. Public address systems consist of microphones connected to a mixing console that feeds a loudspeaker system.

public domain (PD) Software, music, script, literature or other material not protected or no longer protected by copyrights.

pulse A momentary change and return to a known voltage. Usually pulses have a simple and identifiable form. Pulses are used in electronic circuits to trigger and synchronize other circuits. The horizontal and vertical sync pulses cause the deflection circuits in a TV set to start the scanning of a line or field.

push-pull A final stage in audio power amplifiers based on two power transistors, each of which conducts during a different half of a sinewave, one during the positive and one during the negative half.

PVW Preview. *See also* **preview monitor.**

PZM Pressure zone microphone. A microphone that is attached to a surface such as a table or the floor to pick up sound waves. A PZM is used to record groups of people or musical instruments.

quadraphonic A sound recording system using four channels. To reproduce the sound, four loudspeakers are used: front left, front right, back left and back right.

quadraplex A method of video recording on magnetic tape. Four recording heads are mounted around a wheel that rotates at high speed. Each head records a number of picture lines on the tape perpendicular to the tape movement direction. This method was used in the first 2-inch broadcast-quality video recorders. *See also* **2-inch.**

quantizing The process of sampling an analog signal or waveform to produce a digital signal or a signal with reduced bandwidth and a "stepped" waveform made of discrete levels instead of the smooth original analog waveform. *See also* **sampling.**

quantizing noise Noise generated during the quantization process. Such noise is present in serial digital video signals.

quartz-iodine bulb Lightbulb used for TV lighting. Utilizes a tungsten filament encapsulated with a small amount of iodine in a glass or quartz tube. It has stable light intensity and color temperature characteristics.

quick plate A metal plate connecting the camera to the tripod head and allowing quick connection and release of the camera from the tripod.

quiescent noise Noise of a system when no signal is applied to its input; inherent noise.

R − Y One of the three color difference signals in component video. A subtraction of Y (luminance) from R (Red channel). *See also* **color difference signal; component video.**

rack Metal cabinet with shelves for housing of electronic equipment. A standard equipment rack is 19" wide internally at the front. Most audio and video equipment in studios and control rooms is mounted in racks.

rack mount A type of mounting equipment. Standard electronic equipment is built to fit in 19-inch racks. *See also* **rack.**

radiator **(a)** Part of a transmitter antenna that radiates radio-frequency electromagnetic radiation. **(b)** In audio, a loudspeaker radiating sound waves.

radio mike *see* **wireless mike**

RAM Random access memory. Memory in which data can be written and read in no particular (random) order. RAM is used in computers for temporary storage of data; it is erased when power is switched off.

ramp A video test pattern with a continuously rising voltage—from 0.3 V to 1 V during one horizontal line—used for gamma measurements. Some ramps are modulated and used to measure differential gain and phase.

R and D Research and development. Investment made by manufacturers and research laboratories to develop new theories, technologies and finally, products. Large manufacturers invest a considerable percentage of their revenue in R and D. Such research is effective after a long period of time, normally between one and five years, sometimes even more. R and D can be described as a continuous race to produce new products—faster, better and cheaper.

random access An attribute of memories and storage devices that allows data to be written and read in no particular order.

range extender In TV lenses, an option that allows doubling the focal length of the lens, normally by a factor of 2, sometimes 1.5. Range extension is done by an extra internal element in the lens system that can be switched in and out. Such extenders cause a decrease in the amount of light entering the camera, limiting the use to locations with daylight or strong artificial light. Range extenders are usually used in news, nature photography and sports.

raster   The illuminated pattern created by scan lines on the screen of a CRT.

rate conversion   The conversion from one sampling system to another or from one sample frequency to another.

rating   The percentage of the population that watches a specific program or channel. The estimated rating is determined by survey or through information provided by devices placed in viewer's homes that register which channel is watched, by how many people and at what times. Rating provides vital statistical information used in broadcasting and advertising to determine popularity of TV programs and prices of commercials.

raw material   Raw stock. Blank magnetic tape before it has been recorded, or film footage before exposure.

razorblade editing   Editing of magnetic tape, mainly audiotape, by cutting sequences away, adding material or rearranging the order. The cut pieces are spliced together, forming a new master tape. Razorblade editing in audio is slowly being replaced by electronic editing, together with the increased use of digital tape and disk recording.

Razorblade editing was also used in

the very early days of videotape recording.

R-DAT   Rotary digital audio tape. *See also* **DAT.**

reaction shot   A camera shot used to show the reaction of a person to an event on the set or during conversation with another person.

rear projection *see* **back projection**

rebroadcast   Delayed broadcast. Broadcast of an event after it takes place or a program transmitted at a later time by another station.

receiver   An electronic device that transforms radio or television transmissions into sound or picture. The receiver uses a tuner to select the wanted frequency and then retrieves the signal from the modulated carrier by a demodulation process. An audio signal is then amplified and transduced into sound by means of a loudspeaker, and a video signal is used to produce pictures on a CRT or another sort of screen. Picture reproduction is more complex than audio and requires more complex circuitry.

rechargeable battery   An electrical battery capable of being repeatedly recharged after discharge. Battery packs of all kinds, size and voltage rating are used for powering audio, video and lighting, mainly in portable equipment. Electrical specifications of rechargeable batteries consist of the rated voltage (most common is 12 volts) and the rated number of ampere/hours (Ah). After being discharged, rechargeable batteries can be charged again and brought to life by connecting them to a charger for a specified time. The most common kind is nickel-cadmium (nicad) batteries, although the old lead-acid and the latest nickel-metal-hydrate (Ni-MH) are also used, each having its own advantages and drawbacks.

recorder   A machine capable of recording audio or video, as opposed to a player, which can only play back.

record head   In audio- and video-tape and disk recording equipment, a transducer used to record audio or video signals. Electrical currents proportional to a momentary signal level induce a magnetic field to magnetize oxide or metal particles on the surface of the recording medium. The information recorded can be reconstructed in a later stage. The quality and condition of the head is critical to the recording process. *See also* **playback head.**

recording   Storing of data (such as audio and video) on magnetic or optic media in such a way that it can be retrieved later. In most cases, broadcast-quality signal is not recorded directly to the media but is modulated or digitized before recording.

recording speed   The number of inches per second (IPS) an audio- or videotape moves during recording.

recording studio *see* **sound studio**

recordist   A technician responsible for recording audio or video, usually in the field.

red   One of the three primary additive colors (RGB) used in TV to produce all other hues.

Reed Solomon   A mathematical code or process used for error detection in digital systems by creating parity words out of blocks of data. If the parity check indicates an error during the reading of the data, the system will look somewhere else for the missing data.

reel   Spool used for film or magnetic tape. Some equipment uses open reels; cassettes have a housing containing a supply reel and a take-up reel.

reference black   A surface with light reflection of 0 to 3 percent. Usually black velvet is used in camera test cards for black balance adjustment. *See also* **black balance.**

reference tone *see* **test tone**

reference white   White color reflecting 60 percent of light. Used for camera alignment cards to measure sensitivity under specific illumination (such as 1,500 lux) and for white balance adjustment. Also known as television white. *See also* **camera sensitivity; white balance.**

regenerated time code   Time code deteriorates every time it is being copied from one tape to another. After a few generations it can cause problems when trying to decode it. Therefore it is always recommended to regenerate time code by feeding it from the player into a time code reader/generator unit and sending the generator output time code into the recorder.

registration   In TV cameras, the accurate placement or overlap of the red, green and blue pictures. In cameras using picture tubes, registration has to be adjusted periodically and there is always a small error. In CCD cameras, the three picture elements are glued to the optical system and there are no registration adjustments.

relative aperture *see* **f-number**

relay station Transponder. A radio or TV receiver-transmitter arrangement used to receive a distant signal and retransmit it to cover additional area or to forward the signal to an additional relay station.

remote control The ability to affect functions of equipment from a distance, such as changing the audio level coming out of a TV set. Also the instrument used to control from a distance. Remote control units can be either wired or wireless. In TV, the term RCP is used for "remote control panel." Wireless remote control units are used mostly for audio and video home equipment and less in professional equipment. Studio TV cameras and studio lighting are controlled from the control room by wired control units. *See also* **camera control unit.**

remote van *see* **OB van**

rendering Processing of pictures and animation by a computer. Operations on high-resolution pictures and animation (especially in 3-D) in graphical software involve extensive calculations and mapping and therefore are usually time-consuming. The operators of such software normally leave the computer to do the rendering after the correct instructions or guidelines are set.

repeater (a) A set made up of receiver and transmitter used to receive weak or distant signals and transmit them at much greater power. A signal from a small hand-held radio, such as the type used by police officers, is usually received by a repeater and then transmitted with power sufficient to cover a large city. The frequencies received and transmitted are not the same. Repeaters are used for radio, TV and telephone communications and they can be either terrestrial or satellite based (transponders). (b) In fiber optics, a device that receives optical signals (light) from a line, retrieves the basic signal by demodulation, reshapes it and sends it modulated again to the next fiber line. All this is done to restore and compensate for losses in light beam intensity in long optical lines.

residual noise Noise level left in magnetic tape after it has been erased.

resolution The amount of fine detail or information present in an image. The higher the resolution, the sharper the image will be. Resolution is perhaps the most important attribute of an image. Higher resolution means a wider bandwidth is needed to transmit or record images and larger storage if the image is stored on tape or disk.

The number of picture elements (pixels) in a broadcast-quality NTSC picture is 720×487. PAL pictures have more active lines (575) and the resolution is higher. In HDTV the number is roughly 2000×1050, depending on the standard. Resolution of video equipment is measured in TV lines.

The resolution of TV pictures can

be degraded by every part of the production, postproduction and transmission chain, including the quality of the home receiver and quality of reception. *See also* **pixel; resolution chart.**

resolution chart A chart used to check and adjust resolution of cameras and lenses. The chart has groups of fine lines in different densities, each of them indicating a certain resolution.

resonance An electrical circuit or mechanical structure or device derived from a frequency that is equal to its natural vibration frequency (resonance frequency). In this case the system will vibrate more strongly than in other frequencies.

retrace The deflection of an electron beam inside a picture tube of a video camera or a cathode ray tube from the end of a line or field back to the beginning. During this period the beam's intensity is reduced so that the retrace will not be visible.

reverberation (reverb) Persistence of sound due to series of reflections inside a closed space after the original sound has ceased. Reverberation is a characteristic of the size and type of space in which it is created. In audio, for example, if a recording of a singer in a church is "sterile" and without reverberation, it will sound unnatural.

Electronic reverberation units allow adding reverb to audio channels with a variation of delay and decay times. Some reverberation units have a set of preprogrammed reverberations of certain places such as a concert hall, theater or church.

review In editing, a function that— by pressing a single button—allows one to go back and view the last edit performed on the editing system or VCR.

rewind Fast winding of tape backward, toward the beginning of the tape or recording. Most tape and cassette machines have a rewind button.

RF Radio frequency. Normally used for high-frequency carrier waves of radio or TV signals.

RF envelope The outer form of a modulated RF waveform. In amplitude modulation (AM), the information carried by the carrier is the actual shape of the envelope. In videotape recording systems, video is normally frequency modulated (FM) before being recorded on tape. In this case the RF envelope's shape indicates the quality of the recording on the tape.

RFI Radio frequency interference. Electromagnetic energy that is randomly dispersed, causing interference to electronic equipment and transmitted signals. RFI can originate from almost every electronic or electric system, such as computers or defective car ignition circuits.

RGB Red, green and blue. The three colors produced by video cameras, graphics and character generators. At the end of the path, the three colors are used to drive the three electron guns that make the color picture in the TV set.

RH Relative humidity. Must be kept low and constant when storing film and magnetic tape for long periods.

ringing   An oscillation causing ghosting in video signals and distortion of digital data stream pulses. Ringing is a transient phenomenon occurring due to restricted bandwidth or phase distortion. Different K-factor measurements are used to measure the amount of ringing in video signals.

rise time   The time needed by a waveform or pulse to rise from 10% to 90% of the full value.

RMS   Root mean square. Effective value of an AC voltage, as opposed to peak voltage. An RMS value of a periodic AC voltage is the square root of the average of the squares of the values along one cycle. For a sine wave, RMS is 0.707 of the peak voltage.

roll   (a) To start playing (of a videotape) or projection (of a film). (b) To move credits up or down the screen.

ROM   Read-only memory. A memory device that is written or programmed once and cannot be erased. In computers, programs and data needed for the initial operation of the computer are usually recorded on ROM-integrated circuits.

room acoustics   The sound-carrying behavior of a room, depending on the amount of absorption, echo and reverberation of sound waves. The room acoustics affect the quality of sound and the amount of room equalization needed. *See also* **room equalization.**

room equalization   A practice used in public address that adjusts the frequency response of signals sent to speakers to compensate for imperfections in acoustical characteristics of the specific room or hall. Normally the response of the signal sent to speakers is treated before amplification by means of a graphic equalizer. The room characteristics can be tested by sending pink noise to the speakers and measuring the sound response with a spectrum analyzer, or simply by a VU meter for every octave. *See also* **equalization; pink noise.**

room tone   The natural background sound present in a room or other space, such as a train station or forest, without the sound of actors or performers. Room tone is always present, originating from different sources in every environment. *See also* **ambiance.**

rotation point   In a compressor or expander input-to-output-level relationship curve, the point between unity gain and compression or expansion.

rough cut   Editing of film or video material in a quick and inaccurate way, with no effects included. Rough cuts are used to make decisions regarding content and length of the final work.

router   *see*   **routing switcher**

routing switcher   A device connecting incoming and outgoing signals. The number of signals can range between several and several hundred. Routing switchers are normally built as a matrix, in a way that allows connection of any incoming signal (source) to any output (destination) or to many or all outputs.

Routing switchers are used to switch signals such as audio, video,

RS-232 and the tally light between sources in studios, radio and TV stations, switching stations and postproduction facilities. Normally routing switchers are built to switch several kinds of signals (layers) such as video and stereo audio at the same time. The routing switcher is operated by control panels, either simple ones that determine which source will be sent to a specific destination or X-Y control units that govern all sources and destinations, normally a combination of the two kinds.

Patch panels are replaced in many facilities by routing switchers, the advantage being remote control of the routing device even by a telephone line, speed of switching (on air), no mechanical problems of bad contacts and the ability to display on a computer screen the status of the routing.

RP-125   Also called SMPTE 125M. Parallel digital interface for component video.

RS-232   A protocol used for serial, unbalanced asynchronous data transfer between computers. It consists of a start bit, seven or eight data bits, a parity bit and a stop bit.

RS-422   A standard balanced serial interface for control and data transfer over a range of up to 1000 ft/300m. Data is transferred over two twisted pairs for bidirectional operation and the end connectors are nine-way D-type. RS-422 is widely used in production and postproduction areas to interface between devices such as VCRs, editors, switches and audio consoles.

run-length coding   A data compression method. Highly efficient for storing picture information where large areas of the same color are present, such as certain kinds of computer-generated pictures. Not efficient for pictures from a video camera because of the random nature of picture information. Run-length coding stores pixel information with the number and location of the identical adjacent pixel.

run-through   A rehearsal shortened by doing only the beginning and end of long parts of a show. Entrance of artists and interviewees is checked, the audio, camera shots and lighting, and so on.

running time   Time from the beginning of a program during recording or a program on the air live.

run-up time *see* **preroll**

RX   Receive.

safe area   The area of a TV picture that will be seen on a home receiver screen. The edges around the picture as it is transmitted from the TV station are concealed on the home receiver screen. On the studio camera viewfinder screen there is a rectangular line marking the safe area to make sure that only the intended frame will be visible to the viewer at home.

Title generators also display the safe area on the operator's screen to ensure that all titles generated will be visible to the end user.

sales department   The department in a radio or TV station responsible for sales of advertisements and all contacts with clients. The sales department works closely with the traffic department for placement of commercials in transmission logs. In commercial stations and networks, the sales department is involved in programming.

sampling The measurements taken in the process of converting an analog signal to digital. Sampling is done in high frequency and every sample is given a value in the digital domain.

sampling rate Frequency of the samples taken in the process of converting an analog signal to digital. The sampling rate is expressed in Hz. For conversion of video signals to digital, millions of samples per second are needed.

SATCOM Satellite communication.

satellite communications Use of specially built space vehicles to deliver high-frequency signals over long distances. Communications satellites orbit the earth in geostationary orbits roughly 22,300 miles (35,680 km) above earth, each carrying a set of transponders. In this specific orbit, a satellite moves at the same pace as the earth's rotation and is always above the same location. Many satellites are "planted" in geostationary orbits, each covering a little less than half the globe.

Signals from an earth station at one end of a continent can be transmitted to a satellite and back to earth at the other end of the continent. Satellites provide global coverage over land and ocean delivering television, telephone, telex and data services. Satellites are also used for distribution of TV signals to vast areas, with no obstruction by mountains or buildings. Signals are received by small dishes. *See also* **direct broadcast satellite; geostationary orbit; SNG; transponder.**

Saticon A Hitachi Denshi brand name for a popular picture camera tube. Comes in ½" (13 mm), ⅔" (18 mm), 1" (25 mm) and 1⅓" (30 mm) diameters. The smaller tubes are used for small portable cameras and the larger for studio cameras. Most cameras manufactured today use CCDs instead of picture tubes. Some high-definition cameras are still manufactured with picture tubes as the light-sensitive element. *See also* **picture tube.**

saturation **(a)** A state of an amplifier or amplifier stage in which an increase in input signal amplitude will no longer cause an increase in output signal amplitude. Saturation causes distortion and therefore is usually an undesired state. In switching circuits, saturation is desirable. **(b)** Also referred to as "chroma" or "chroma gain." The amount of chrominance in a video signal or TV picture. Saturation of color in video signals such as NTSC is determined by the instantaneous amplitude of the subcarrier.

SC Subcarrier. A sine wave superimposed on the luminance picture information in composite video signals. The subcarrier wave holds the picture color information; when no subcarrier is present the picture will be black and white only. The amplitude of the subcarrier wave determines the saturation or intensity of the color; the phase in relation to the burst determines the hue of the color. The subcarrier and the burst both have the same fixed, accurate frequency, which for NTSC is 3.579545 MHz and for PAL is 4.43361875 MHz. *See also* **burst; hue; saturation.**

scaling   When converting signals from analog to digital, digital values are defined for the lowest and highest levels of the signal to be digitized. Scaling means to determine the way the digital domain is best used to contain signals in terms of dividing the available levels. In the ITU-R 601 standard for digital coding, black level is defined as 16 and white as 235 in the digital scale. In computer systems, scaling is normally 0 for black and 255 for peak white.

scanning   The movement of an electron beam over an area in a camera pickup tube or picture tube (CRT). The scanning starts at the upper left corner of the screen and moves line by line from left to right and downward, like reading a page of a book. In the pickup tube the electron beam gathers picture information, while in the CRT the beam creates the picture on the fluorescent screen in the same scanning. *See also* **CRT; pick-up tube.**

scene   Part of a feature film or TV program that takes place in a particular place and time.

scenery   Background used in cinema, TV and theater. Scenery creates a specific environment, real or imaginary. Scenery designers need to consider technical problems of sound, lighting and camera movement in addition to artistic considerations.

SC/H phase   Subcarrier to horizontal phase. Phase relationship between subcarrier and sync in composite video signals. In NTSC, zero crossing of subcarrier is aligned with the 50 percent point of the leading edge of sync. Incorrect SC/H phase can lead to instability during switching and editing.

scope   Short for oscilloscope. *See also* **vector scope; waveform monitor.**

SC phase   Subcarrier phase. The phase difference between the subcarrier sine wave and the burst at each TV line. This relationship determines the hue of the color in the TV picture.

scrambling *see* **encryption**

scratch track   Auxiliary audio track used for editing purposes only.

screen ratio *see* **aspect ratio**

scrim   Diffuser used in film and TV to soften light from spot- and floodlights. Translucent materials such as silk or a thin wire mesh fixed on a frame are used.

script   Written text, description of sound effects and picture content for a feature film, TV program or play. The script is used in preproduction for budget planning and casting, as well as design of scenery, dressing, lighting, props, makeup and technical facilities and requirements. Actors and performers study and rehearse the text.

  During production, the script is used by performers and crew for recording sessions. The director uses a script with added scene numbers, shot numbers and camera shots called a "shooting script."

scroll   Horizontal movement of titles across the screen as opposed to "roll," which is a vertical movement of text. Scroll usually moves text in one or two rows. It is useful for delivery of messages during a program, such as stock exchange rates or different announcements. Most character generators are capable of creating such movement in various speeds.

SCSI   Small computer systems interface. A widely used (parallel) interface with a high data rate. A 50-way bus can connect up to eight devices (including the controller). Devices such as magnetic disk drives, optical disk drives, tape drives and CD-ROM drives can be connected. SCSI has been improved with the years, and its maximum transfer rate has progressed:

Standard SCSI: 5 M transfers/sec.
Fast SCSI: 10 M transfers/sec.
Ultra SCSI: 20 M transfers/sec.
Each transfer is one byte or eight bits. There is a 16-bit "wide bus" version that can transfer a maximum of 40 M bytes per second. There are two types of bus—single ended and terminated—and two types of connectors. SCSI is limited in distance between devices; the overall length of the system has to be no longer than 20 feet. Because of its fast data rate, SCSI is suitable for nonlinear disk-based editing systems.

SDTV   Standard definition television. NTSC or PAL standard television format as opposed to high-definition television (HDTV).

SECAM   Sequential couleur avec memoire. A television transmission standard with 625 lines and 50 fields, used in France and the former Soviet Union countries. In this system color information is transmitted in two parts, one line containing the R – Y signal and the next line the B – Y. In the TV receiver there is a one-line delay. Direct and delayed color signals are combined to get the complete color information needed by the CRT. The SECAM system is more immune to differential phase and gain distortions than other transmission standards, but it has poor compatibility with black and white transmissions.

second unit   A camera crew additional to the main camera unit that shoots complementary shots.

selectivity   Ability of a tuner in a radio or TV receiver to tune to a selected frequency, among many other close frequencies.

self-erasure   A shortcoming of magnetic media such as tapes and disks. They may self-erase slowly over the years and lose the information recorded.

senior   A 5 KW studio quartz spotlight equipped with a fresnel lens.

separation light *see* **back light**

serial communication   The use of a single pair of wires to send and receive streams of sequential digital data, bit after bit. Serial communication is much slower than parallel but allows use of telephone lines and other two-wire lines. Serial communication can normally be carried to longer distances than parallel data.

serial control   Remote control of devices by means of serial communications. RS-422 is a serial control protocol commonly used in TV. *See also* **RS-422.**

serial digital interface (SDI) A standard for transmission of composite serial digital video and four embedded digital audio channels or component ITU-R 601. SDI uses standard 75 ohm coax cable and BNC connectors for distances of up to 900 feet. The use of existing cabling makes the transition from analog to digital much simpler. Most new broadcast video equipment is manufactured with SDI inputs/outputs, and many facilities such as TV stations, studios and editing rooms use SDI.

service manual Documentation containing technical drawings, theory of operation, test and alignment procedures and parts lists. Service manuals are vital for proper maintenance of electronic equipment. The quality of a device or system is measured also by the quality of documentation supplied.

servo focus Focusing system in which an electric motor inside the camera lens moves the focusing element of the lens. The camera operator moves a wheel that drives a small generator. The current produced by the generator goes to a servo amplifier inside the lens that drives the focusing motor. The advantage of such a system over mechanical systems is ease and smoothness of operation. Such an electrical system can also be used for distant, remote controlled cameras.

servo zoom Zoom system in which an electric motor inside the camera lens moves the zoom element of the lens. The camera operator moves a lever that drives a small potentiometer. The potentiometer is connected to a servo amplifier inside the lens that

drives the zoom motor. The advantage of such a system over mechanical systems is ease and smoothness of operation. Such an electrical system can also be used for distant, remote controlled cameras.

set The scenery and props used for a certain scene in cinema and TV. The set designer is normally responsible for construction, assembly and dressing of the set in the studio prior to shooting.

set designer An artist who designs scenery and props for TV programs and film.

set dressing Adding items to scenery that make it look real, such as furniture, carpets, books, pictures and everything that should be in that environment if it were an actual one.

setup (a) In video signals, the lowest part of active picture information that causes the screen to be black. In NTSC this part is specified as 7.5 IRE units (7.5 IRE units above blanking level). (b) An arrangement of a technical system. (c) Studio with crew, performers and equipment, all ready for a take.

shading Adjustment of the three color channels in a video camera to get equal illumination and color in the entire picture area.

shadow mask A dense grid installed in color picture tubes to force every electron gun's beam of electrons to hit only the corresponding fluorescent material dots.

share The percentage of television viewers who watch a specific program or channel. The estimated share is determined by survey or through information provided by devices placed in viewer's homes that register which channel is watched, by how many people and at what times. Share provides an important statistical information used in broadcasting and advertising to determine popularity of TV programs and prices of commercials.

sharpness Focus. A sharp picture is one with a large amount of detail—one that is not blurred.

shedding Loss of particles from magnetic tape emulsion, causing dropouts during playback and clogging of video and audio heads. *See also* **dropout; head clogging.**

shield Protection of electronic equipment and circuitry against penetration of stray radiation such as RF, utility system frequency and interference from electronic and electrical equipment. Wiring and circuitry pick up stray radiation and it is added to signals carried by circuitry, becoming part of the signal. To reduce such interference, sensitive circuits are encapsulated in metal-grounded housings and cables are surrounded by flexible foil or braided wiring. Shielding can reduce considerably the amount of radiation penetration, but normally it does not give 100 percent protection.

shielded cable A cable protected from stray radiation by aluminum foil or copper-braided wiring. The shielding is grounded at the end connector of the cable. Shielding of cables (and other circuitry) is essential especially where small signals such as microphone signals are used. Stray radia-

tion from transmitters, electronic and electrical equipment and utility system wiring can easily penetrate unshielded cables and become an unwanted part of the original signal.

shock mount A flexible mount used to connect a microphone to a stand or boom in order to isolate the microphone mechanically. Vibration and shock becomes part of the sound the microphone produces and might in severe cases damage the sensitive electromechanical parts of the microphone.

shooting The action of using a still, film or TV camera.

shooting ratio The ratio between the length of raw material used during production (film or tape) and the length of the finished work after editing. This ratio depends on the kind of program shot, the production budget and the efficiency and amount of planning invested.

shooting schedule A detailed planning of a film or TV production's timetable, including all facilities, equipment, crew and performers needed for each day and location.

shooting script The full text of a TV program or a motion picture film divided into scenes and camera shots. The shooting script is used by the director, performers and other crew members during all production stages.

short focal length lens A wide-angle lens. *See also* **wide-angle lens.**

shot One continuous segment of a program taken by a cine or TV camera. In film, shots are edited together by splicing pieces of tape. In TV, during transmission or recording, the production switcher alternates between different camera shots. Shots or takes can also be edited electronically. *See also* **electronic editing; take.**

shot box   A box attached to a zoom servo system that allows presetting of several zoom positions and moving from one to another by pressing a button. The speed of movement is also preset.

shotgun   A highly directional microphone. The capsule is mounted in a long fluted pipe that—together with its handle—looks like a gun.

shoulder pad   A camera accessory that helps comfortably mount a portable camera on the shoulder.

shunt   A bypass of resistors used to deflect part of an electrical current to an alternative path. Used mainly to protect sensitive measurement equipment from overcurrent.

shutter   **(a)** In still and movie film cameras, a small metal flap used to block the passage of light between lens and film. The shutter is opened for a short period of time to expose the film to light, normally once for each frame. There are several exposure times to suit different lighting conditions. **(b)** In some video cameras, a mechanical or electronic device that shortens the exposure of the CCD element to light. This allows improved slow-motion effects of material recorded by the camera. Normally the shutter in video cameras can work at several speeds. The higher the speed, the shorter the exposure time. Shutter operation causes the picture

produced by the camera to be darker, and one must compensate for this by opening the iris. Sometimes light conditions do not allow the use of shutters in video cameras.

shuttle   Fast rolling of tape from side to side in videotape machines. Usually the picture is visible and sound is heard during shuttle to help locate certain pieces.

side chain   A signal path parallel to the main path that is used to apply additional processing to the signal before routing it into the main path again. For instance, a digital effects unit is usually connected as a side chain of the main video switcher, where video is processed and sent back to the switcher.

side entry port   In microphones, apertures in the sides of the microphone housing to allow entry of sound waves to the back of the diaphragm. Used in unidirectional microphones for cancellation of diaphragm movement due to sound waves that come from directions other than the front.

signal   Variable electrical voltage carrying audio and video information. Other information such as computer data is also conveyed by electrical voltages.

signal-to-noise ratio (S/N, SNR)
A measure of the noise present in a signal in relation to the signal's amplitude. The ratio of the signal level to the noise level is measured in decibels (dB). Signal-to-noise ratio is one the important parameters of signal quality in audio, video and RF. Every amplification and almost every processing of signals adds noise. Noise

reduction is complex and not always possible.

sine wave   A periodical waveform very common in nature, in which the wave amplitude is proportional to the sine of the time variable. Radio and TV carriers are modulated sine waves. Most audio waveforms as well as burst and subcarrier in the composite video signal are also sine waves.

sitcom   Short for situation comedy.

16 mm   Small-format film used in television, mainly for news and documentaries. Also used by students and for low-budget feature films.

16:9   A wide-screen aspect ratio used by new TV transmission standards such as HDTV and PALplus.

skew   A distortion that sometimes occurs in the picture of tube-based cameras or CRTs in which the picture or one of the channels has the shape of a parallelogram.

skylight   A 5- or 10-KW light used for wide-area outdoor base lighting.

sky pan   A 5-KW halogen light used for high-intensity illumination.

SL   Sign language. A symbol indicating that a program has sign language on screen.

slap-back   An unwanted reflection of sound or echo from a surface in a room or hall.

slate   A small board used in film and TV to record the details of a shot. The slate is held in front of the camera at the beginning of the shot to help identify the shot in later stages of postproduction. It contains details such as scene number, take number and date. In film, a clapboard is attached to the slate to sync the sound to the picture during editing. Electronic slates that provide both visual information and an audible countdown are available today.

slave   A device linked to another master device and following its movements. One master can have several slaves. For example, one sync generator in one side of a building can be slaved to another in the other side. This way they will both produce all pulses, synced together.

slew rate   In amplifiers, the maximum rate of change in output voltage when working at the rated range. Usually rated as volts per microsecond $(V/\mu s)$.

slow motion   Projection or playback of film or video at reduced speed. If there is motion in the material, the reduced speed will cause the motion to slow down as well. This reduction in speed can continue until the film or video has come to a complete stop. At this stage the motion will stop as well and there will be a "freeze frame."

SLP   Super long play. Very slow-playing mode of VHS cassettes.

slug   Blank space in a program tape placed to mark the position of a commercial break. The length of the slug does not necessarily match the length of the commercial break—it can be just a marker. Often the transition to and from the slug is a fade-out and fade-in.

SM   Station manager. Refers usually to a radio or TV station.

smear   Blur of a picture. A smear often results from movement of the camera or the object during filming or taping. It makes objects look longer than they really are and blurred in the direction of movement.

SMPTE   Society of Motion Picture and Television Engineers. An American organization that sets standards for the television industry.

SNG   Satellite news gathering. The use of satellites to transmit live news from the field by a TV crew or outside broadcast vehicle. Special SNG vans are equipped with a satellite dish that transmits directly to the satellite. The transponder on the satellite transmits the signal back down to earth where it is picked up by a dish in the station. SNG equipment also comes in a "fly away," which is the satellite transmission equipment packed in a few flight cases.

   SNG allows direct transmission of events from practically anywhere on the globe in real time, and it is therefore widely used by news networks and other TV organizations.

snow   A layman's term for noise as it is seen on a TV screen.

SNV   Satellite news vehicle. A van or truck equipped with production and satellite transmission equipment. *See also* **SNG.**

soap opera   Name for a particular type of serial drama series usually transmitted during daytime.

soft focus   A picture in which the detail is slightly blurred or softened. Soft focus is sometimes intentional for a variety of artistic reasons, or it can be caused by bad focusing or degradation during processing of the video signals.

soft light   Studio light producing diffused, unfocused light. Soft light is used as a fill light for shadows cast by spotlights and as a base light to cover a wide area. Soft light comes out indirectly and is reflected from an uneven surface or goes through a diffusion filter.

software   In computers, a set of programs that enables the computer to compute or carry out all operations, including the communications and display within the computer. Without software, a computer is a completely useless object. Different kinds of software are used to perform different tasks. Software used for initial operation of the computer is stored in unerasable ROM memory chips, and others can be stored on hard disk, floppy disk and optical disk. The field of software is vast and rapidly growing.

soft wipe   A wipe effect with soft edges between pictures.

solar cell   A device that converts solar energy into electrical power. Solar cells are used to power satellites in space. Solar cells are semiconductors that produce steady and reliable electrical current as long as they are exposed to sun light.

solid state   A name for semiconductors using the transistor and integrated circuit technology that came after the vacuum tube technology, which used heated electrodes inside tubes containing gases to get amplification.

solo switch   In audio consoles, a switch usually present in every input module used to send the sound of that particular input channel to the monitoring system. When the solo switch is depressed, other signals are switched out of the monitoring system. The solo switch is a useful aid for the sound engineer to listen to just one of the many sources connected to the console, even during recording.

sound *see* **audio**

sound amplifier *see* **audio amplifier**

sound booth   Small soundproof room used for recording of narration, voice-over and for simultaneous translation.

sound console *see* **mixing console**

sound effects   Natural sounds such as animal sounds, street noise, footsteps and rain or thunder added to feature films and TV programs to make them sound more realistic and rich.

sound effects library   A collection of sound effects of all kinds recorded on tapes or CDs. Sound effects are normally categorized and arranged according to subjects for quick location.

sound engineer   Person with technical training involved in operating and maintenance of audio equipment.

sound head   In tape and cassette recorders, the head used for recording of audio.

sound lock   A chamber in sound and TV studios used for added isolation from outside noise, usually at the entrance door or sometimes along a wall adjoining another studio or hall.

sound mixer *see* **audio mixer**

sound perspective   In TV, adaptation of sound to the picture. For example, in an outdoor long-shot of a person, sounds from far away will be included, while in an indoor close-up of the same person, sounds will be adjusted accordingly.

sound studio   A facility specially made for recording and editing of sound. The space used for sound studios and attached control rooms needs to be acoustically treated (sound proofed) to prevent penetration of noise from the outside and to control the amount of echo from the walls. Equipment used in sound studios includes microphones, audio consoles and monitors, as well as recording and playback equipment. The microphones are located in the studio itself to pick up performers' sound and are wired to the mixing console, located in the control room together with the monitoring and recording equipment. Sound studios are used for recording music, narration and sound effects. In TV, normally the studio is used for recording of audio and video at the same time, while separate control rooms are used. *See also* **acoustics; audio console; audio monitor; microphone.**

soundtrack **(a)** Part of a magnetic tape or film devoted to sound. In film and videotape, one or more tracks of sound are used beside the larger part containing the picture. Location and width of sound tracks are precisely defined for each film or tape format. Some common videotape formats such as Betacam have four sound tracks. In less professional equipment, two sound tracks are usually used for stereo sound. **(b)** A recording of the musical part of a program, play or feature film. Such sound tracks are sometimes recorded and sold on cassettes or CDs.

source VTR A VTR (videotape recorder) feeding other VTRs during copying or editing.

speaker port In a loudspeaker cabinet, an opening used to improve efficiency and low-frequency response.

spider box A box with several utility system sockets for connection of different cables and instruments.

splice Joining of film or magnetic tape when it breaks or for editing purposes. Splicing is done by applying adhesive tape to join the two ends together. The ends must be correctly cut and joined to form a splice that will run smoothly through a projector.

splicer A mechanical instrument used for splicing of film. One of the main tools of the film editor. The splicer holds both ends of the film correctly in place while transparent adhesive tape is used to join the parts together. The splicer also cuts excess tape from the sides and from the film

perforation. Means are also provided by the splicer for correct positioning while cutting the film accurately between the frames.

splicing block A device used to aid splicing of magnetic tape (normally ¼-inch audiotape). On the splicing block there is a groove used to hold the tape in position while cutting or while adhesive tape is applied to hold the ends together. Some blocks contain a blade that cuts the tape at the correct angle.

splicing tape Adhesive tape used for joining film or tape ends. For joining film, the adhesive tape must be transparent. Some tapes for splicing audiotape are white or yellow so that when placed on the brown tape the splices can be easily located.

split edit An edit where picture and sound are not cut at the same place. Sometimes this kind of edit is used to "soften" the transition from one scene to another.

split focus A focus adjustment that is a compromise between two objects located at different distances from the camera lens to allow as sharp an image of both as possible.

split reel Film spool built from two separable flanges to allow quick loading of film.

split screen A way of putting two or more video pictures on one screen. The screen is divided by a wipe pattern created by a video switcher.

spool Reel used for film in projectors, telecines and editing equipment or for magnetic tape in VTR machines.

spotlight A light instrument producing directional light. Spotlights use a reflector and sometimes also a lens to produce a narrow light beam. Usually by moving the reflector backward and forward, the beam can be made wider or narrower. In cinema and TV productions, spotlights are widely used to illuminate restricted areas with light that will not "spill" to adjoining areas.

spreader A triangular mechanical device that holds the legs of a tripod in a constant spread. Sometimes on smooth surfaces the tripod legs tend to spread open, putting the camera in danger. The spreader helps to keep the tripod steady even on rocks and sand. In England it is also called "crow foot."

spring reverberation system A device used to produce reverberation effects similar to the natural reverberation of a hall. A coiled metal spring is suspended in a framework, with a driver on one side and a pickup element on the other. The audio applied to the driver sets the spring in motion and it is picked up on the other end, with the added reverberation. Today, compact electronic reverberation units give a much wider choice of echo and reverberation effects.

square wave A periodical, symmetrical waveform that moves between two equal length levels, with fast transition between them. A square wave is named after its square shape. It theoretically contains an endless number of sine waves that are the odd harmonics of the fundamental sine wave.

stage manager *see* **floor manager**

stage plan *see* **floor plan**

standard operating level A signal level agreed upon and commonly used, such as +4 dBu for recording audio levels.

standards conversion Conversion of video signals from one standard to another, such as from NTSC to PAL. Standards conversion is often used when programs are distributed to countries with a different transmission standard or during live transmission from one continent to another via satellite or other transmission lines. Standards conversion in broadcast quality is usually complex and needs expensive equipment.

standards converter An electronic device that converts TV signals from one standard to another, usually between the three common standards NTSC, PAL and SECAM. Standards conversion causes some degradation of the TV signal.

star filter Glass filter with lines engraved on it causing star effects on bright objects or light sources seen through it.

static signal processing Processing with steady parameters that are not dependent on signal level or other parameters. Most signal processing is static. *See also* **dynamic signal processing.**

Steadicam Trade name of a special mount for a portable camera. The Steadicam is strapped to the camera operator's body and absorbs vibration and movement caused by the operator's walking or running. Steadicam uses springs and shock absorbers and allows steady shots to be taken at all times. Use of the Steadicam is restricted in time because of its heavy weight added to the camera weight. It also needs special training to operate.

step-down transformer A device used to reduce electrical AC voltage.

stepped lens *see* **fresnel lens**

stereo A sound system intended to create natural sound by using two audio channels, left and right, each delivered to the corresponding side of the room or directly to the ear (by use of earphones). The two channels are normally created by microphones located on both sides of the orchestra or other sound source. Alternatively, sometimes during mixing, some audio channels are sent to the left and others to the right to create a stereo effect. The signal from each side is kept separate until it gets to the listener's ears. This way a sound with a sense of direction and depth is created.

stereo microphone A microphone with two sound-sensitive diaphragms housed in the same case. One of the capsules can be rotated 90° away from the other one. Both signals are separately fed out.

stereoscopic television A television system in which three-dimensional pictures can be obtained with the aid of special glasses. Still experimental.

still frame In videocassette recorders, when in play mode and the tape is not moving, the video heads scan the same field continuously and the result is a still picture. Still frames are used together with slow motion in sports and for retrieval of a certain frame from tape, but care must be taken because repeated scanning of the portion of a tape causes damage to it.

still store An electronic storage device for still video pictures. Normally several hundred pictures are stored on a disk, and each one of them can be retrieved at will. Still stores are mainly used in news studios, transmission centers and graphical environments.

stop frame *see* **still frame**

stopwatch Device widely used by TV production assistants to time all items before they are entered into programs and to count down toward the end of each segment for the benefit of the director and studio crew.

storyboard A series of drawings on special paper of the scenes of a commercial or program to be made. The drawings show what the frames should look like, provide information such as location, camera angle, the participants in the shot and the kind of background needed. Audio text and technical requirements are written below each drawing.

strobe An effect produced by digital effects units in which the video picture is frozen for preset periods of time, such as every six frames. This effect is visible mainly where there is motion, the result being a broken or jerky movement.

studio A large room or hall used for film or video shooting, providing a controlled environment in terms of temperature, lighting and acoustical conditions. The studio also provides all the necessary equipment ready for use and conveniently set up.

TV studios come in different sizes, from the size of a standard living room to ten thousand square feet and more. Facilities found in TV studios normally include the following: **(a)** Acoustical isolation from the outside world and acoustical treatment of the interior to prevent excessive resonance of sound. **(b)** Rigging and massive power supply for TV lighting. Power lines and outlets are located at many points in the studio ceiling and walls. **(c)** Powerful air conditioning that is able to deal with massive heat emission from lighting and other electrical equipment during all seasons of the year. This air conditioning must be very quiet so as not to be picked up by microphones. **(d)** A smooth and level floor that allows camera pedestals to move easily and quietly.

Around the studio additional space is needed for scenery and equipment storage, audio, video and lighting control rooms, dressing rooms and make-up rooms. Video equipment in a typical TV studio consists of cameras, VCRs, switching equipment, monitors, test and measurement equipment, effects and character generators. Audio equipment consists of a variety of microphones, mixing equipment, monitors and a variety of audio recording and playback equipment. Lighting equipment includes a variety of spotlights, floodlights effects lights and lighting control equipment such as dimmers and lighting computers. The quantity and sophistication of equipment differs according to the special needs of every studio, but there is a typical configuration in terms of the equipment layout and connection.

Normally all video sources such as cameras, VCRs, CGs, effects generators and external feeds from remote sources are connected to the main switcher. In parallel, all audio sources such as microphones, electronic musical instruments, tape and disk players, telephone lines, audio channels of VCRs and audio from external feeds are connected to the input of an audio switcher or mixing console. Both audio and video program outputs are sent to VCRs during recording or outside the studio for transmission.

Probably the most valuable asset of a TV studio is a well-trained and experienced technical and production team. A studio crew normally consists of a floor manager, floor men/women, camera operators, boom operators, electricians, a lighting director, audio engineers, video engineers, a CG operator and a technical director.

TV studios are expensive facilities to build, maintain and operate, even for large organizations. Especially in private facilities, studio usage is carefully planned for the most effective use.

studio camera   A large camera connected by cable to control equipment usually in a multicamera configuration, as distinguished from small hand-held cameras for fieldwork. In TV studios, several cameras may be connected to a switcher and monitors in the control room and operated by an engineer to maximize picture quality.

In studio cameras, size and weight are not as critical as in hand-held portable cameras as cameras are always mounted on pedestals or other mounting equipment. This allows for improvement of some camera functions such as more powerful and complex lenses, improved communications and more complex signal processing.

Hand-held (portable) cameras are also used in studios, usually for shots requiring angles that a camera mounted on a pedestal cannot perform (at least one such camera per studio). Portable cameras are sometimes used in small studios instead of studio cameras to save space and because of their considerably lower price. *See also* **camera.**

studio monitor   Video monitor placed in the studio for the benefit of the crew (mainly the floor manager) and performers. Monitors are connected most of the time to the program output of the studio—sometimes directly to a specific source, depending on the application.

subcarrier *see* **SC**

submaster   A tape or disk used in the process of making a master audio or video recording, at an earlier stage.

subtitling   The process of putting rows of text on the transmitted program's picture, usually the translation of a foreign language or sometimes transcription of the speech in the same language for the benefit of the hearing impaired.

subtractive color system   A method used in film and video to create a color image by subtracting or absorbing unwanted components from white light by a series of color filters. Filters used are usually in cyan, magenta and yellow, also known as minus red, minus green and minus blue, respectively. The output color depends on the amount of absorption of each filter and the combination of the three.

One example of a subtractive color system is LCD video projectors. Three LCD cyan, magenta and yellow elements filter out unwanted color components from a white light source. *See also* **additive color system; video projector.**

subwoofer   A loudspeaker built to deliver low frequencies in the range of 30Hz to 120Hz. Subwoofers are located at the center between the left and right speakers in a stereo or surround sound system. Subwoofers add extra depth to sound systems. Some of this sound cannot be heard, but it can be felt in parts of the body such as the stomach.

summing amplifier   An amplifier with two or more inputs used to mix the signal sources together to form one signal. At the same time, the input signals are amplified.

sun gun   A small, portable battery-operated light used for ENG work. The sun gun is just strong enough to illuminate a person's face during a short interview.

Super 8   An improved version of 8 mm film. The frame is larger by 50 percent and the number of frames per foot is reduced from 80 to 72. It was in consumer and industrial use until video became popular. Today it is obsolete, but a lot of hobbyist footage is still to be found.

super band   Frequency band of 230 MHz to 300 MHz used in cable television. This band carries 12 TV channels in NTSC or 10 channels in PAL. Not all TV receivers are equipped to receive super band frequencies.

super high frequency (SHF)
Frequency band of 3,000 to 30,000
MHz. Microwave links and satellite
transmissions of TV signals are within
this band.

superimposition In TV, imposi-
tion of one picture on top of another.
Normally a caption or graphics are superimposed over live video.

superstation A station distributing programs to cable networks or TV
stations via satellite.

Super VGA Super video graphics
array. A standard display card used in
IBM and compatible computers that
produces a graphics signal that is sent
out to feed the computer monitor. The
output signal is manufactured from
computer data.
    Super VGA (S-VGA) cards can dis-
play 256 colors in 640 × 200, 640 ×
350 and 640 × 480 pixels. With extended onboard memory (video
RAM), 800 × 600 and 1024 × 768 pixels can be displayed. Today in most
computers an extended number of colors such as 1,048,576 or 16,777,212 is
obtained by using an onboard memory.

supply voltage Voltage, usually
DC, provided by the power supply unit
to circuits in an instrument. *See also*
power supply.

surround sound An audio system used in cinema and the home to
create sound that is as similar as possible to sound in real life, which
comes from all directions. Five speakers are used to reproduce sound: center, front-right, front-left, back-right
and back-left. The speakers are connected to a special power amplifier.
Sometimes a subwoofer is added to
increase depth and low-frequency

presence. The signals for the different
speakers can be taken from an ordi-
nary stereo sound recording, or from
special recordings made for surround
sound. In some cinema systems, six
different audio channels are recorded
beside the visual part—one for each
speaker.

S-VHS Super Video Home System. A videocassette recording standard based on the consumer-level
VHS. Same size and shape as ½-inch
cassettes but with metal particle tape.
S-VHS involves Y/C recording with
improved picture resolution and signal-to-noise ratio. VHS cassettes will
play on S-VHS equipment, but S-VHS
cassettes will not play on VHS equipment. S-VHS is an industrial-level
format, used also by some cable television operators.

S-VHS-C A reduced-size cassette
for S-VHS that allows a considerable
reduction of camcorder size. The cassette has a maximum recording time
of 45 minutes. A special adapter is
needed to play the small cassette on a
standard S-VHS machine.

sweep (a) The deflection of an electron beam to scan a screen in a CRT.
(b) A gradual change in frequency
through a certain range. Sweep signals
are used in audio and video test signals
to test the response of a system to a
specific range of frequencies.

sweetening Mix down of sound
tracks with equalizing and added
effects.

switcher *see* **video switcher**

switching power supply A
power supply using high-frequency,
high-efficiency transformers for re-

duced weight and size. The high frequency is created by switching circuits.

switching station   A facility controlling a large number of communication lines such as radio, telephone and TV. Switching stations usually switch and connect signals to and from telephone exchanges, radio and TV stations and transmitter sites. Signals are interconnected by copper lines, fiber lines and terrestrial and satellite microwave links.

sync   Synchronizing pulse. In video signals, a pulse used to mark the beginning of a line (horizontal sync) or field (vertical sync). Synchronizing pulses enable proper timing and synchronization between sources and are vital to the proper operation of all video facilities as well as TV sets.

sync generator   A device producing synchronizing and timing pulses for video source equipment such as cameras and character generators. The pulses are used as building blocks for the construction of a video signal. A high level of frequency precision in the level of 0.0000025 percent is needed. Several pulses are normally produced:

Horizontal sync: the beginning of a line.

Vertical sync: the beginning of a field.

Horizontal blanking: length and location of line blanking.

Vertical blanking: length and location of field blanking.

Subcarrier: frequency and phase of subcarrier.

Burst flag: length and location of burst.

Color frame identification: the beginning of field one.

Sometimes a black and burst video signal is also produced. A different sync generator is needed for each transmission standard.

synchronization (sync)   Timing of one or more signals in accordance with a reference signal. Synchronization must be kept between audio and video in film or on magnetic tape. Another kind of synchronization is between video signals.

Video signals connected to a switcher must be synced for proper mixing. Remote sources coming into the station are normally synced to station reference by means of a frame synchronizer.

synchronizer   A device that locks the speed of an audio player to an external source such as another audio player or a videocassette recorder by controlling its speed. Normally time code or a sampling rate clock of digital audio is used to lock one device to another. Both signals are compared and the synchronizer calculates and consequently forces the slave machine to go faster or slower to match the speeds correctly.

synchronous orbit *see* **geostationary orbit**

sync level   The lowest tip of the video signal, 0.3 volts below black level and 0.7 volts below white level.

sync roll   (a) Synchronized playing of separate film and audio channels. (b) Simultaneous and locked playing of several VCRs, normally for editing purposes.

sync separator   A circuit that extracts the sync pulse from the composite video signal. Such a circuit is used in TV receivers to separate the sync signal and trigger the deflection circuits.

synopsis   A short form of a script. A description of the main story and characters of a full script, often used to present the script to decision makers without making them read the complete script, which usually take considerable time. *See also* **script.**

table stand   Small microphone support for tabletop use.

tabletop   A device built to be used on a desk or table, such as a computer. For some devices, *tabletop* indicates compactness.

tails out   In a reel of film or tape, a situation in which the first part to come out is the end of the program; the beginning is rolled at the center of the reel. In material intended for transmission, this is usually avoided because the time taken to roll the film or tape back to the beginning causes a delay in transmission.

take   **(a)** A fast switch or "cut" between sources in a video switcher. The actual switching between video signals occurs during the vertical blanking period and is therefore not visible on screen. **(b)** The action taken by an operator pressing a button to bring a source to air.

talent   An actor, singer, dancer or any other kind of performer who appears in a radio or TV program.

talk back *see* **intercom**

tally light   A red light mounted in the viewfinder and front of a camera. When turned on it means that the particular camera is "on air"—that is, the picture from this camera is either recorded on tape or transmitted live. In multicamera studio configurations the tally light is operated by the video switcher, and it appears also in the studio control room under each camera's monitor and on each camera control panel at the vision control desk. In ENG camcorders, the tally light comes on when the VCR is in record mode. Usually a two-wire contact closure is used to operate tally circuits. The tally light is important for the camera operator and for every crew member, as well as for the talent and audience in the studio.

tape *see* **magnetic tape**

tape guides   Polished metal posts in the tape transport system that keep the tape in its proper track during recording and playback. Several guides are positioned in various points along the tape's path.

tape speed   The speed of tape movement during recording in relation to stationary heads. Measured in inches or centimeters per second.

tape storage   Safe storage for magnetic tapes and cassettes (audio and video). Storage is fireproof and controlled in terms of temperature and humidity.

tape timer   Part of audio- and videotape and cassette machines that counts tape movement in time units. In old equipment it was mechanical, but in modern equipment it is electronic. The timer is used to measure recording and playback time and helps to get to a specific point on tape. Sometimes also capable of displaying tape remaining.

tape transport   The mechanical part of audio- and videotape or cassette machines. Consists of motors, wheels, gears and guides that handle the movement of tape during playback, recording and shuttle. The tape transport is a high-precision mechanism that moves the tape in different speeds and directions in a very delicate way.

targa (TGA)   A file format used in computers for storage and transfer of images. TGA was developed by Truevision and is currently used in both PCs and Macs.

target   (a) A light-sensitive part in camera pickup tubes. Light from the lens forms an image on the target and an electron beam scans the target to form a video signal. (b) Viewers for whom a program is intended, such as students, car owners or children of a certain age group (target audience).

TC   (a) Technical coordinator. (b) Telecine. (c) Time code.

TDM   Time division multiplex. Technique for transmission of multiple signals on one channel or line. Time-compressed portions of each signal are sent, each in a designated time division. At the other end of the line the reverse process is used to retrieve the original signals. TDM is used for video in the MAC standards, where time division, chrominance/luminance intermodulation and cross-color effects to be suppressed. *See also* **FDM.**

teaser   A short promotional piece used to create interest and draw attention to a specific program. Highlights of the program are usually edited to compose a teaser, with added graphics and sound.

technical director (TD)   A person in charge of maintenance and operation of technical production equipment and the technical and operational crew in production facilities such as studios and outside broadcast vehicles. In the United States, the TD also operates the video switcher during production. In Europe the technical director is more involved in quality control during production.

telecast   A television transmission.

telecaster   A television station or network.

telecine   Name of a machine and process of transferring images from film to video. Feature films are transferred to videotape to be broadcast on TV and some commercials and programs are produced on film and then transferred to tape for improved picture quality.

There are several methods of transferring pictures from film to tape. The simplest, used by hobbyists, is projecting the film on a screen and recording the images from the screen with a camcoder or camera and VCR. Flying spot machines use a spot of light coming off a cathode ray tube to scan the frame area. The light coming through the film is picked up by photocells and converted to video.

CCD-based telecines use a CCD element for each primary color to scan each frame line by line. Usually there are 1,024 pixels per line. The signal from the CCD elements is then converted to video.

Broadcast-quality machines are highly complex and include extensive color correction possibilities. Computerized circuits are used to correct each frame or scene differently.

Some telecines are capable of transferring negative film to standard positive video, and techniques such as noise and grain reduction and dirt and scratch concealment are employed. *See also* **color correction.**

telecom   Short for telecommunication. In some countries telecom is included in the name of the national or largest telecommunications company, such as British Telecom.

teleconverter   An add-on lens used in still photography to extend the range of a lens. Normally the extension is 1.5 or 2 times the focal length. Teleconverters cause a reduction in the amount of light entering the camera. In TV lenses the range extender is normally built into the lens.

telephone filter   A bandpass audio filter used to make a telephone-like sound out of full bandwidth sound by reducing its bandwidth.

telephone hybrid   A circuit used in audio to connect telephone lines to audio consoles and other audio equipment. The telephone hybrid circuit separates the incoming and outgoing telephone signals and interfaces between the levels and impedances of the line and audio equipment.

telefoto lens   A lens with a long focal length used for shooting distant events, mainly in news, nature and sports.

TelePrompTer   Device used by an announcer in TV to read his text while looking at the camera lens. The viewer at home is not meant to be aware of the fact that the announcer is reading his text from a screen.

The teleprompter is a picture monitor installed below the camera lens, facing up. A piece of glass is placed in front of the lens diagonally, allowing the lens to shoot through it and the monitor screen to reflect from it at the same time. The announcer looks at the glass and sees his text there. It seems to the viewer that the announcer looks at the camera or right at the viewer at home.

The monitor is fed with text from a computer or a small camera that is installed above a moving roll of paper with the text typed on it. The speed at which the text is rolled is crucial to the proper operation.

teletext   Alphanumerical information inserted into the transmitted TV signal. Teletext is used to provide the viewer with information such as weather, stock exchange rates, TV program guides and much more. This information is encoded into several TV lines during the vertical interval as digital data. The data is arranged in numbered pages that can be separately retrieved. A special decoder card is needed in the TV receiver to decode and display teletext information on the screen.

television   An electronic telecommunications system that enables real time transmission of audio and a stream of black and white or color pictures that are perceived by the human eye as a continuous motion picture. Television transmissions can be distributed by cable, terrestrial transmit-

ters or satellites and can be received
by low-cost, consumer receivers.

The principles that led to the development of modern television were
discovered, odd as it may seem, in the
nineteenth century. The first regular
black and white television broadcasting started in England in 1936 and in
the United States in 1941. Since then,
TV stations and viewers have mush-
roomed in number.

Television is widely used today for
distribution of educational, news, doc-
umentary and entertainment programs
worldwide. These programs are
watched by viewers all over the globe
for hours each day, making the
influence of television vast.

television standard   The transmission standard or technical parameters of the TV signal such as line
frequency, field rate and color system
according to an accepted standard
such as NTSC, PAL and SECAM.
Every country has adopted one of the
common standards, which compli-
cates the exchange of recorded material. Signals transmitted from one
country to another with different standards must be converted accordingly
by a standards converter somewhere
in between. *See also* **NTSC; PAL;
SECAM; standards converter.**

tera-   One trillion: 1,000,000,000,000.
A prefix, as in terabyte or Tbyte. One
terabyte is equal to 1,099,511,627,776
bytes.

termination   A resistive load connected to a line. Terminations are used
in video, computer and other high-frequency lines to prevent reflections. In
video, 75 ohm resistors are housed in
male BNC connectors used to termi-
nate lines.

terrestrial   Usually used in relation to transmitters, as opposed to
transmission via satellite.

test and measurement   A general name for various methods used to
evaluate and measure quality of signals and performance of equipment.
A large variety of special equipment is
used for T and M, usually of high accuracy, in broadcast fields as well as
others.

In broadcasting, audio and video
signals are monitored at every step of
the production process to ensure
proper quality. Perhaps more than in
many other fields, quality of broadcast
signals and the equipment used in the
process are watched very carefully.
The major reason is that the product is
distributed to a vast number of people
and another is that there is always
degradation along the distribution
path; therefore, "reserves" of quality
that are lost on the way to the viewer
but still leave adequate quality are
needed.

Digital acquisition, processing and
broadcast techniques improve signal
quality but introduce new T and M
problems.

The most useful equipment for T
and M in broadcasting includes specialized video waveform monitors,
vector scopes, standard oscilloscopes,
spectrum analyzers, ampere/volt/ohm/
watt meters, audio VU and PPM meters, audio and video precision monitors and computerized automatic
audio and video T and M equipment.

test generator   Also test signal
generator. A device producing test signals for audio or video. Test signals
are used for evaluation, measurement
and alignment of various kinds of

equipment. Several standard test signals are used to test characteristics of signal handling by the device being tested. The most common video test patterns are color bars, multiburst, pulse and bar and sine X/X.

test pattern   Test card. Printed test patterns put in front of the camera for alignment. Normally gray scales are used to adjust black balance, white balance flair correction and gamma. A crosshatch is used to check linearity (not necessary in CCD cameras), and a resolution chart that contains groups of lines in different densities is used to check the resolution available in the camera's output signal.

test signal   An audio or video signal containing special signals used for measurement, evaluation and maintenance of audio and video equipment performance instead of sound or picture. Most audio and video test signals are standard worldwide and are used in every recording, editing and transmission. *See also* **test generator.**

test tape   Tape or cassette containing test signals used for testing and maintenance of audio- and videotape and cassette recorders and players. Test tapes are normally produced by equipment manufacturers and supplied as optional accessories to items such as VCRs or audio machines. They normally contain precision recordings of several kinds of test signals.

test tone   A sine wave with given frequency and level used to test audio equipment.

theme   A melody recurrently appearing in a program in different versions and rhythms.

thermionic valve *see* **vacuum tube**

35 mm   The most common width of film used in still photography and the cinema industry.

threading   Placement of tape or film in its path in a recorder, VTR, telecine or projector. Since the introduction of video- and audiocassettes, threading of tape has been automatic.

3-D   Three-dimensional. A medium that has width, height and depth, such as some digital effects used for video and some animation software.

¾-inch   Three-quarter-inch video format also known as U-matic. *See also* **U-matic.**

three-shot   A camera shot with three persons in the frame.

threshold of hearing   The lowest sound level that a person can hear.

threshold of pain   A sound intensity at which the average human listener will start to feel physical pain.

THX   A standard for cinema and home-cinema audio developed by Lucasfilm that defines production, equipment and reproduction conditions for film audio.

TIFF   Tagged image file format. A file format for images stored digitally on computers. TIFF is a bit-map format originally used with Pcs and now used by Macs as well. TIFF is useful for file transfer of scanned images between computers in networks, on disk and by services such as the Internet.

tight shot A camera shot tightly framed on a person or object (extreme close-up).

tilt *see* **camera movement**

time base corrector (TBC) A device normally connected to the output of a videotape machine (or an integral part of one) that corrects time base error. TBC eliminates picture jitter and stabilizes the video signal by rebuilding the synchronizing pulses in a precise way.

time code (TC) A system that gives each frame in a recorded videotape a unique identification number. Time code is helpful in identifying audio and video material during playback, editing and transmission.

The format of time code is hours, minutes, seconds and frames, each with two characters, for a total of eight. In a continuous recording, different numbers can be given to each frame for up to 24 hours of recording. The frames are numbered in a consecutive order in relation to real time.

Time code is created by a circuit called time code generator, which can be an additional circuit inside a machine such as a VCR or a separate device. The code is a low-frequency digital serial signal that has to be recorded on tape together with the corresponding audio or video. Time code signals must be decoded to be displayed on a visible numeric display.

There are two ways of recording time code information on videotapes. One is as a longitudinal audio channel (longitudinal time code: LTC) and the other is as part of the video information (vertical-interval time code: VITC). Each method has its own ad-

vantages. LTC channels can be read at speeds from play speed to high fast forward and rewind speeds, while VITC can be read during slow motion and still frame. In most VCRs both methods are employed and the machine reads one of them, depending on the tape speed.

In most editing systems, time code is used by the edit controller to set edit points and locate material on tapes. Time code can be carried by the RS-422 protocol used to control machines in editing rooms from different machines to the edit controller and back.

Tapes intended to be used in the record machine in editing usually are recorded with continuous black and time code. Time code can be inserted on a tape after being recorded. Sometimes if an event is recorded simultaneously on a number of machines from several iso cameras identical time code is recorded on all tapes to help synchronize material during editing. *See also* **longitudinal; LTC; VITC.**

time-lapse video recorder A recorder with the capability to record single frames of video at a preset pace. If video is recorded at a frame rate that is slower than standard, the lapse in time results in a faster unfolding of events. This is used in shooting nature and scientific phenomena and in surveillance. An event or phenomenon taking several hours or even days can by reduced to a few seconds or minutes.

timeline Display used in audio and video editing workstations to show the different tracks in relation to time. Timelines are normally displayed on computer monitors. Several parallel lines are displayed, one representing real time and containing time or time code information. Others represent audio and video tracks and include information such as segment numbers, transitions and sometimes audio waveforms. Editing can be performed by moving segments or parts of segments from source material tracks to edited material tracks, either by keyboard operation or by use of a mouse. Edited material can be played back, while a marker is moving on the timeline to show the exact part being played. Normally, timelines can be expanded (in terms of time) to show longer segments or narrowed to show more detail.

time slot (TS)   A round time frame used in programming, such as an hour or half an hour. The time slot contains promos and commercials as well as the program—thus the actual program time is shorter.

timing   In a video facility such as a studio or editing room, synchronization of the different video sources to the same reference signal.

title   A caption in a TV program or film, usually at the opening or end.

title music   Music used as background for opening or closing titles in a film or TV program.

toe mark   Mark placed on the studio or stage floor to indicate position for performers or for placement of equipment, usually by taping a piece of gaffer's tape.

tone   A continuous sine wave used as an audio test signal. Test tones are recorded at the beginning of audio- and videotapes for level and adjust-

ment. In videotapes, tone is recorded together with color bars or other video test signals. Tone is also used for test and alignment of audio equipment.

tone control   Adjustments installed in audio equipment such as amplifiers or receivers to change the low (bass) and high (treble) audio characteristics. In the early days of audio equipment, these controls were used to eliminate hiss and hum. Today they are used to allow adjustment of audio quality to room acoustics and personal taste. *See also* **hiss; hum.**

tone generator   A device producing audio test signals, usually with the ability to produce tones in variable frequencies and levels. *See also* **tone.**

track   A line along a magnetic tape where a head has recorded. Separate tracks are allocated on the magnetic tape for the recording of video, audio and time code.

tracking   The ability of playback heads in tape machines to repeat or match the tracks previously recorded. Normally in VCRs there is a manual or automatic adjustment of the correct tracking. If tracking is incorrect, the picture will be distorted or completely lost.

traffic   A department in a broadcast station in charge of the daily transmission log, including placement of programs, commercials and promos.

transducer   A device that converts one form of energy to another. A resistor converts electricity to heat. A microphone capsule converts sound waves to electrical current.

transfer characteristic The behavior of a device in terms of output versus input characteristics.

transient A quick change or spike in utility system voltage that can cause damage to electronic equipment.

transistor A semiconductor capable of amplifying, buffering and switching. Most of modern electronics is based on transistor circuits.

transmission Distribution of audio, video and other information by the use of modulated radio frequency carrier waves in the air or modulated light in optical fibers. Transmission originates in a transmitter.

transmission standard *see* **television standard**

transmitter An electronic device that emits high-frequency radiation modulated by information such as audio or video. This radiation can be received from a distance and demodulated to retrieve the modulating signal. Transmitters are used for distribution of radio and television signals.

transponder A system mounted on a satellite to receive certain signals from earth, then amplify and transmit them back to earth. *See also* **repeater.**

trapeze An aberration of a picture in which the picture edges are not parallel. This aberration can be found in old (tube) video cameras and in CRTs.

treatment A description of a play or program less detailed than a full script, but longer than a synopsis. A treatment gives the background, character descriptions and highlights of the contents of the script. *See also* script; synopsis.

triangle *see* **spreader**

triax A coax cable with three conductors, one center lead and two surrounding screens or pipe-shaped conductors. Triax cables are used to connect professional video cameras to the camera control unit (CCU).

Trinitron A CRT (cathode ray tube) manufactured by Sony, used in television sets and computer monitors. Trinitron has high contrast and the screen is part of a cylinder rather than a sphere as in other CRT types. Its flat surface reduces reflection of light sources and glare in the screen.

tripod *see* **camera mount**

TRVO Television receive-only dish antenna. Used for domestic and TV station satellite reception.

TTL Transistor transistor logic. A family of integrated circuits powered by a voltage of 5 volts. TTL circuits draw large currents and tend to heat up. In the early days of integrated circuits, TTL was the fastest technology. Today C-MOS is faster and more power efficient.

tuner A circuit that isolates a particular single frequency band or channel transmitted on-air from the variety of frequencies existing. The tuner is a vital part of every radio or TV receiver.

tuning Adjusting the tuner for a specific station or frequency.

turret In old cameras, before zoom lenses, a round metal plate with a number of different lenses mounted on it. Turning the plate enabled each lens to be placed against the lens opening of the camera. In this way, different lenses of different focal length were used to get different field-of-view angles. The turret could be turned only when the camera was off-air.

TV Television.

TV lines A TV picture is made of lines scanning the picture from left right, line by line, downwards. In an NTSC video signal there are 575 lines per frame, most of them visible on-screen; some, however, exist during the vertical blanking interval. *See also* **video signal.**

tweeter A small loudspeaker in an audio monitor that delivers the high frequencies. *See also* **audio monitor.**

two-shot A camera shot with two persons or objects in the frame.

2-D Two-dimensional. A medium that appears to be flat, with only width and height—without depth.

2-inch Width of open-reel tape sued for audio and video recording in the early days of teleivsion. Some 2" tapes still exist in archives. *See also* **quadraplex; VTR.**

UHF Ultra-high frequency. The upper part of television transmission frequencies. Channels 14 to 83 in the United States, the frequency band between 470 MHz and 890 MHz.

U-matic A registered Sony name for a ¾-inch format of videocassette recorders. In this format two sizes of cassettes were available: a small one that fit in portable machines with a playing time of 20 minutes and a large one for studio use with a playing time of 60 minutes. U-matic was the first widely used cassette format; previously there were only open-reel machines such as 1-inch. U-matic video recorders were also the first portable machines used for ENG. *See also* **cassette; ENG.**

unbalanced (1) An audio system using two-conductor wiring, one for signal and one for ground. This system is used for large signals, where interference and noise are very small compared to the signal, such as loud-speaker lines. Most professional audio equipment uses balanced wiring, as opposed to nonprofessional audio systems. (2) The state of a camera before a mechanical adjustment is made to the camera head so that the center of gravity will be exactly above the tilt axis. This could allow the camera head to tilt or fall all the way over to one side, resulting in damage.

unidirectional A directional microphone with a narrow pickup pattern. Sound is picked up mainly from one direction. This kind of microphone is used in noisy environments or when the surrounding sound is of no relevance.

unilateral A satellite transmission intended for a single country or destination, as opposed to transmissions intended for many countries (multilateral).

unity gain No change in amplification. A device with unity gain is one in which the input and output levels are the same.

uplink A transmitter used to send signals to satellites. Uplinks are normally highly directional transmitters with a dish antenna. Some uplinks are mobile and are mounted on a trailer or truck for live programs or news broadcasts from the field. The signal sent by the uplink to the satellite is transmitted back to earth and picked up in the studio or an earth station. *See also* **dish; SNG.**

upstage The part of the stage that is farther away from the audience. In the studio, the side farther from the cameras.

user bits A set of eight hexadecimal (from 0 to f) digits that can be recorded on tape together with the time code signal. User bits are used to record a date, the number of a tape or other information.

vacuum tube Used as an amplification and switching device before the age of the transistor. Also called thermionic valves, they were usually made of glass, while large ones were made of metal. In some areas vacuum tubes have no substitute. High-power transmitters still use vacuum tubes; a CRT (TV picture tube) is still a vacuum tube. *See also* **CRT.**

variable play Playback of a videotape in speeds varying usually between normal play speed in reverse through still frame and up to a factor of three times in forward. To perform variable play, a VCR must be equipped with dynamic tracking heads. *See also* **dynamic tracking.**

vault Safe storage for film and magnetic tapes and cassettes (audio and video). Storage is fireproof and controlled in terms of temperature and humidity.

VCA Voltage-controlled amplifier. Amplification is controlled by applying an external voltage. This way, several amplifiers can be controlled at the same time by the same voltage.

VCA fader In audio mixing consoles, a fader that controls the audio level in an indirect way. The fader changes a control voltage that changes the gain of the console channel.

VCR Videocassette recorder. One of the most important items of equipment in the television industry. Videocassette recorders of many varieties are used to record, play and edit audio and video in the station and in the field. The VCR is a complex device that employs both precision mechanics and state-of-the-art electronics. Therefore broadcast-quality VCRs are highly expensive items.

A wide range of cassette formats are in use and each format usually has more than one cassette size. Small cassettes are used for lightweight portable VCRs and large as well as small cassettes are used in house for larger and more complex machines.

Before the VCR there was the VTR (videotape recorder), which filled the same needs but required more skilled operators and offered no portable machines (except for a few models that came out after cassettes already existed). The VCR offered many operational and technical advantages, such as eliminating the need to roll the tape to the beginning in order to take it off the machine, more audio channels and safe-guards against accidental erasing.

For every videocassette recording format, there are several models for different purposes: **(a)** Camcorder. Includes a camera and VCR, housed in one portable unit (small cassettes only). **(b)** Portable VCR. Used mainly for ENG and field acquisition (small cassettes only). **(c)** Studio player. Playback only of small and large cassettes. No editing facilities. **(d)** Studio recorder. Playback and recording of small and large cassettes. No editing facilities. **(e)** Editing player. A studio player with editing facilities. **(f)** Editing recorder. A studio recorder with editing facilities.Studio editing versions can be with or without dynamic tracking, which allows playback in slow-motion mode and still frame.

Many recording formats or standards are in use, some of them very popular and others limited to a relatively small number of users. Some formats offer better multilayering quality and are intended for high-end editing. Some formats are analog and others are digital (broadcast formats only): **(a)** U-matic: ¾-inch analog composite. The first widely used cassette format. Today still in use, mostly for nonbroadcast work. **(b)** M-II: ½-inch analog component. **(c)** Betacam/Betacam-SP: ½-inch analog component. The most common multipurpose format. **(d)** Digital Betacam: ½-inch digital component 2:1 compression. **(e)** D1: 19 mm (¾-inch) digital component 4:2:2. Highest quality, highest priced, large size machines. **(f)** D2: 19 mm (¾-inch) digital composite. **(g)** D3: ½-inch digital composite. **(h)** D5: ½-inch digital component 4:2:2 **(i)** DVC: ¼-inch digital component 4:1:1 5:1 compression. A consumer format with several professional versions. **(j)** S-VHS: ½-inch analog Y/C industrial level, some-times used in cable television for transmission.

Every facility or organization has to choose the right format or family of machines that will best suit its needs, which can be a difficult task. *See also* **4:2:2; Betacam-SP; camcorder; cassette; component; composite; compression; digital Betacam; DCV; dynamic tracking; D1; D2; D3; D5; editing; M-II; multilayering; S-VHS; VTR.**

VDA Video distribution amplifier. A video amplifier with one input and many outputs of the same signal. The purpose is to distribute exactly the same signal to many different instruments. The amplification is unity gain. The number of outputs is usually between four and ten. The VDA is an important building block of studios, editing rooms and transmission facilities. Some video distribution amplifiers include cable equalization and delay capabilities. *See also* **cable equalization; delay.**

vector scope An oscilloscope specially made for vector display of color components of video signals. Verctor scopes have a circular display where chroma level and phase can be measured. There is a round scale marked in degrees. Special marks are provided for evaluating standard color bar signals. Normally vector scopes are used together with waveform monitors, because other video signal components cannot be displayed.

vertical blanking A period of time between fields in video signals. Once the scanning beam in the CRT has finished scanning the lower part of the screen, it has to be deflected to start scanning the screen from the top (the next field). At the blanking intervals the beam intensity is brought down so that it will not be visible on the screen. The exact length of blanking intervals is defined by the different transmission standards, such as NTSC. The length of the blanking period, several lines, depends on the transmission standard.

vertical frequency   The number of fields per second in a video signal. In NTSC this frequency is 59.94 Hz; in PAL it is 50 Hz.

vertical interval   A period of time between two fields. The electron beam of picture tubes in cameras, monitors and TV receivers is turned off during this time to avoid the retrace being visible. The vertical sync is positioned in this interval and also time code (VITC), test signals (VITS) and teletext can be inserted in the blanked TV lines. *See also* **vertical sync; VITC, VITS.**

vertical sync   A period of 2.5 TV lines used to trigger the vertical deflection circuits in video monitors and TV sets. During this period, the average voltage of the video signal is lower than the rest of the field.

VGA   Video graphics array. A popular, standard display card used in PC and compatible computers that produces a graphics signal sent out to feed the computer monitor. The output signal is composed of computer data. VGA cards can display 256 colors in a resolution of 320×200 pixels or 16 colors in a 640×480 resolution. A larger number of colors can be obtained by using onboard memory. *See also* **Super VGA.**

VHF   Very high frequency. Frequency range between 47 and 230 MHz, used in TV broadcasting for channels 2 to 12. Also used for many purposes other than television.

VHS   Video home system. A common consumer-level ½-inch tape videocassette recorder. Used in TV for copies of raw material and programs to enable viewing at home but not for transmission.

video   A signal carrying a stream of TV pictures (frames) coded in a standard way. Used by TV sets and picture monitors to reproduce the coded pictures in high fidelity to the original. A single video signal originating in one camera can be transmitted and received by millions of viewers in many countries in real time. Video can be carried by cables, recorded, played back or transmitted by terrestrial and satellite transmitters all around the globe. The term *video* is also widely used as a short name for a videocassette and a videocassette recorder (VCR). *See also* **video signal.**

video assist   A small video camera attached to a motion picture film camera. Both cameras are fed from one lens, with an extension for the video camera. Unlike the film camera, the video camera has real time results. This arrangement allows the director and other crew members to see what the main camera is filming in terms of framing, picture composition and camera movements. This video output can also be recorded and edited.

video conference   Bidirectional communication method in which video and audio are used to conduct meetings between two locations distant from each other. The signals are carried by cable, satellite, data lines and today even by services such as the Internet. Video conferences are mostly used for business and medical purposes.

video disk A data storage device using optical and magneto optical techniques to store audio and video on disk. There are different kinds of video disk devices on the market: read only players that can play prerecorded disks; write once read many devices that can record once on every blank disk and devices that can rewrite on the same disk many times (1,000,000 times).

The disks currently used are 12-inch double-sided disks that can record half an hour of video and dual audio on each side. Video disk technology allows random access to every frame on the disk as well as external computer control that calls for use of video disks in automated and interactive applications.

Video disks have a long life without degradation of signal. This technology is therefore suitable for applications where a piece of video has to be played many times, such as a station ID or a program played in a museum many times a day for years.

Efforts are being made to develop a 5.25-inch disk with a capacity of one and a half hours or more, using MPEG-2 compression techniques and improved laser techniques.

video engineer A person with a technical education specializing in video equipment, in charge of one or more of the following: planning and installation of video facilities, maintenance of video equipment, daily operating, quality control of video signals and training of video equipment operators. Video engineering requires a long specialized training period after engineering studies, since video equipment employs a variety of old and new technologies.

video mixer A European term for video switcher.

video on demand (VOD) In cable TV, a service that provides every viewer with the program or movie wanted and at any time according to demand. This kind of service requires a vast amount of storage to be provided by servers. *See also* **near video on demand.**

video retinal display A revolutionary display in which picture information is projected directly into the eye, onto the retina, instead of using light reflected or emitted by a screen. The advantages are the ability to produce very high resolutions that use the full capacity of the eye and the ability to make this display transparent for superimposition on the normal vision. Due to its high cost, this display is limited in the early stages to military use, but there is no doubt that television-related uses will be developed in time.

video server A mass storage device for digital audio and video data. The server needs to have enormous capacity, fast access time and normally a number of inputs and outputs. A video server must handle extensive files of data in a continuous way. Currently, video servers are used in networks, serving video-on-demand facilities, postproduction, news and transmission.

New improvements to servers are presented all the time and new uses for video servers are implemented. The trend is that video servers will eventually replace all videotape or cassette recording machines.

video signal An electrical signal that carries picture information. Video is produced by television cameras and then recorded, edited and transmitted on-air (together with audio) for home reception. At the beginning of television, video carried black and white pictures only. Later on color was added to same basic signal to retain its compatibility with old home receivers.

The composite video signal is the most common form of video and is also the only form that the standard TV home receivers can use. Standard video signals have an amplitude of 1 volt peak-to-peak. The upper 0.7 volt is used for picture information and the lower 0.3 volt for synchronizing pulses.

The video signal is basically a serial signal that delivers the picture information line-by-line, field-by-field. In addition to picture information, the video signal always includes line and field synchronizing pulses and sometimes additional information such as time code, test signals and teletext.

Various devices are used in TV facilities to produce, process, record and switch video signals.

Video is a complex and high-frequency signal and therefore subject to deterioration and distortion. A variety of test and measurement equipment is used in the production, postproduction and transmission stages to monitor the quality of the signal. Today digital techniques are employed to deal with video signals, and improved video standards such as PALplus and HDTV are already in use. *See also* **black burst; black level; component analog; component digital; component video; composite analog; composite digital; composite sync; composite video; HDTV; PALplus; sync level; vertical interval; white level.**

video sunglasses Miniature video camera hidden in ordinary-looking sunglasses. The lens and CCD unit are in the glasses and additional camera circuitry and a miniature recorder are held in a pocket or taped somewhere on the body. Used primarily by intelligence and detective agencies; adopted also by TV for undercover investigative work of reporters.

video switcher Production switcher. A device capable of combining and switching a large number of video signal sources. In principle a video switcher has many video inputs and one output. The different inputs can be simply switched (cut) one at a time to the output or combined with some other inputs in various ways and then sent to the output.

There is a unit in switchers called mix-effect (M/E). Each such unit can combine two or three video sources to create an effect such as superimposition of two video inputs, a dissolve between two sources, a luminance or chroma key effect or a wipe transition between sources. Depending on the size of the switcher, the number of mix-effect units ranges normally between one and four. M/E units can be chained in a way that the output of one M/E is connected to another M/E as an input. This way, more complex effects can be created. At the end of the path, for example, there usually is a downstream keyer, which is keyer used to superimpose titles on what has been created by the mix-effect units.

A special output to the switcher called preview or preset is displayed on a monitor near the operator and used to prepare and adjust effects before being taken on-air.

The video switcher is an important tool for production, postproduction and transmission. During production in the studio or outside, the switcher handles all camera, VCR, character generator and effects signals and produces one composite output that is recorded and/or transmitted. In the editing room, the switcher handles incoming feeds from the source VCRs, effects generator and character generator and delivers the processed output to the record VCR. In transmission, the switcher sends to air usually one main source, with the ability to cut or make other more complex transitions from one source to another. Superimposition of titles during transmission is also possible. Operating a complex video switcher (vision control) with many inputs is a demanding job, especially during live transmission. *See also* **chroma key; cut; dissolve; downstream keyer; luminance key; mix-effect; preview.**

video toaster   A post production software and hardware that provides editing, mixing, effects and characters in one Amiga-based unit.

viewfinder   In video cameras a small screen (CRT) used by the camera operator to monitor the camera output picture. In hand-held cameras the screen size is usually 1.5 inches and in large studio cameras it is usually between 5 inches and 7 inches (diagonal). In addition to the camera picture, other signals (external) can be sent to the viewfinder such as the production switcher output to help the camera operator match his picture to other sources in the studio. In film and still cameras, the viewfinder is an optical device that lets the operator see the same field of view the lens sees.

virtual studio   A studio in which there is no real background or foreground scenery—instead there is a computer-generated image (virtual set). Performers in the studio usually have a blue background and chroma key techniques are involved. The difference from simple chroma key is that in a virtual studio the cameras can move and the computer generated background will move accordingly, creating a perfect and natural illusion, as if the performer is inside the virtual set.

Objects in the computer-generated image can be defined as background or foreground and in the final picture the scene will respond accordingly. If a person moves where a part of the "scenery" is defined as foreground, he will be hidden behind it. If the same object is changed in definition to background, it will appear to be behind the person in the studio.

In a virtual studio it is possible to create imaginary but convincing environments, limited only by the creativity and imagination of the artists involved. It can also be changed frequently, saving the need to build, maintain and store expensive scenery. Virtual studio techniques are young and promising.

vision mixer *see* **video switcher**

visual   The pictorial part of a film or TV program, excluding sound.

visual aids Articles such as charts, graphs, films, models, photographs and slides used during production for enhancement of program subjects.

visuals Slides, drawings and still photographs used as aids in a film or TV production.

VITC Vertical interval time code. Time code information inserted in a video signal in specific lines during the vertical interval. VITC is always frame-accurate. *See also* **time code.**

VITS Vertical interval test signal. Single lines of various test signals can be inserted in a video signal during vertical interval. VITS is inserted in the signal at the source of transmission and monitoring of the signal can be done anywhere along the transmission path, in switching stations, earth stations and cable TV facilities. The VITS signals are received at the viewer's end together with the TV picture, but they are located at the upper edge of the frame, normally outside the visible area. In every transmission standard there are TV lines allocated for VITS.

voice coil In dynamic microphones and loudspeakers, a coil connected to a diaphragm moving in a constant magnetic field. In the microphone, a low-level audio signal is induced in the coil when it is moved by sound waves, while in the loudspeaker high-level audio signals applied to the coil create a magnetic force that moves the diaphragm, creating sound.

volt The unit for measurement of electrical potential difference. Most battery cells produce 1.2 to 1.5 volts of voltage. Denoted by the letter V.

volume indicator *see* **VU meter**

VTR Video tape recorder. An audio and video recorder using tape on open reels. VTRs were in use before the development of cassettes. The first broadcast-quality machine was based on 2-inch wide tape (5 cm). The next generation was based on 1-inch-wide tape. These machines are still in use for playback of archive material. *See also* **2-inch; 1-inch.**

VTR operator A trained engineer who operates videotape and videocassette recorders in TV facilities. Besides operating the machines, this job includes monitoring of audio and video levels, audio and video connections and some simple editing.

VU meter Volume units meter. An audio-level meter designed to respond to audio levels like the human ear, to the mean value (RMS). Short-time peaks in signal level are not indicated by VU meters. VU meters normally have a scale in dB, starting at –20 dB and going up to +3 dB. The 0 dB level is the normal level. VU meters are an essential tool for audio recording, playback, mixing and transmission.

wall box A box attached to a studio wall with connections for audio or video equipment. In large studios several wall boxes are installed on different sides to allow easy access. Microphone lines, wired intercom and camera cables are all connected from studio control rooms to the studio floor through wall boxes. They allow different combinations of connections to be made according to needs and disconnection of equipment for maintenance or safekeeping.

WAN Wide area network. A connection between a number of computers distributed between several locations. Connection between locations is through telephone lines, data lines and fiber-optic lines. The network allows sharing of data and software between all computers connected. Special software is needed to manage the network, server computer and network interface cards in each computer.

washed out Having a white or faded appearance as a result of excessive lighting or because the iris is too wide.

watt (W) A unit of electrical power. The multiplication of the voltage across a device by the direct current that flows through it is the power expended on that device. *See also* **power consumption.**

waveform monitor A specialized oscilloscope built for evaluation and measurement of video signals. A video waveform display can be compared to a scale on the screen showing the standard video levels. Waveform monitors are common equipment in TV studios and other video facilities.

Since not all video components can be displayed on waveform monitors, they are normally used in conjunction with vector scopes.

wavelength In a periodical waveform, the length of one complete cycle.

wedge mount A quick attachment of cameras to the pan and tilt head, mounted on a tripod, pedestal or crane. A female wedge is mounted to the head and the male wedge to the camera. To attach the camera to the head, the two wedge parts are joined together and locked. *See also* **camera head; mounting equipment.**

wet sound Sound with a considerable amount of reverberation added.

WFM *see* **waveform monitor**

white balance An adjustment made in video cameras. This adjustment is made by pressing the white balance button on the camera after placing a white card in front of it.

The gain of each of the three color channels (red, green and blue) is adjusted internally so that the camera output picture will reproduce the correct object colors. This adjustment has to be repeated every time the location of the shooting or the lighting is changed.

Every change in color of the light — or color temperature — means another mixture of RGB signal levels; hence the need for readjustment of white balance. *See also* **camera.**

white bar Part of the video test signal used to measure signal level and transitions from black to white and white to black. During these transitions, sometimes ringing, overshooting and undershooting occur.

white level In video signals, the maximum level of the part of the picture with luminance information, which is 1 volt from the sync tip. This level represents white picture information, while lower levels represent darker parts of the picture down to 0.3 volts from the sync tip, which is black. *See also* **video.**

white noise   An audio signal with equal energy for each frequency of sound bandwidth. If measured by octave, every octave has twice the energy of the previous one, since by definition it has twice the number of frequencies as the previous one.

White noise is heard as a high-frequency noise or "hiss." *See also* **octave; pink noise.**

wide-angle lens   In a normal camera lens, usually the widest angle of view is between 55° and 60° horizontally. Angles wider than that are considered wide angle.

Wide-angle lenses are used in small studios or constricted places where the camera cannot be taken back to cover a wide area. A wide-angle lens can cover wider shots and creates the impression of a larger space.

wide-band noise   In audio, noise present over many or all audio bandwidth frequencies. White noise and pink noise belong to this category. *See also* **pink noise; white noise.**

wide-screen   A TV transmission format that is wider than the conventional 4:3. An aspect ratio of 16:9 is used in PALplus and HDTV formats. One of the main reasons is to accommodate wide-screen feature films. Reception of wide-screen formats is possible only with an appropriate receiver. PALplus is compatible with conventional PAL in that it is received in a letterboxed format on a standard PAL receiver. *See also* **letterboxing.**

wind machine   A large and powerful fan used in film and TV productions to create wind on the set. Often a car engine is used to drive the fan.

wind-shield   The European term for windscreen.

windscreen   A microphone cover used to guard against low-frequency wind noises and air blasts from plosive consonants (such as *ps* and *ts*).

winging   Directing a TV program without rehearsals.

wipe   A transition from one TV picture to another made in video switchers. In a wipe, the transition between pictures is gradual, with one picture spreading on the screen from one point or several, depending on the shape. All kinds of shapes are used: a circle that starts as a small dot and spreads all over the screen revealing another picture, as well as squares, diamonds, stars, stripes and many more.

The pace of the transition is controlled by the operator, and the wipe can also be stopped to place parts of two pictures in the frame at the same time. *See also* video switcher.

wireless   Communications between two or more devices with no wires connecting them. Radio and TV are wireless (except cable TV).

wireless mike   A microphone with a transmitter in the same housing or connected to a small belt-pack transmitter. The microphone signal is transmitted to a receiver located elsewhere in the audio control room or near the recorder (in ENG work).

Normally VHF or UHF bands are used and care must be taken when selecting the frequency to avoid interference from other equipment.

Wireless microphones allow freedom of movement to program participants and performers in the studio or on shooting location.

woofer A loudspeaker in an audio monitor that delivers the low frequencies of the sound.

WORM Write-once-read-many. Applies to devices such as CD-ROMs and some kinds of memories that are written only once and can be read as many times as necessary.

wow Low-frequency audio distortion originating in deviations in play speed of tape machines and record players. In CD players the wow is negligible.

wow and flutter Low- and high-frequency deviations in tape speed causing distortion in the audio signal played. Usually appearing together in equipment specification, both measured in percents. *See also* **flutter; wow.**

wrap "It's a wrap!" is a term used to announce that a production or transmission is finished and equipment can be switched off—or packed in the case of outside production—and the crew is released.

WYSIWYG What you see is what you get. Used normally in relation to computer displays that show how the material in question really looks, such as a word processor that can show on screen how the printed page will look.

XCU Extreme close-up (ECU). *See also* **extreme close-up.**

XFMR Transformer.

XLR A connector common in broadcast equipment. Its three-lead version is used in audio for balanced lines. All professional microphones use XLR connectors.

Four-lead XLR connectors are used for 12 V power supply cables and the five-lead version is useful for headsets of intercom systems. Other versions are less frequently used.

XMTR Transmitter. *See also* **transmitter.**

XPT *see* **crosspoint**

XTALK *see* **crosstalk**

Y *see* **luminance**

Y/C A nonprofessional video standard where luminance is separated from chrominance. used in formats such as S-VHS, VHS, HI-8 and video 8.

Y/C delay Delay between luminance and chrominance channels in component video systems, measured normally in nanoseconds (ns).

Y, Cr, Cb Luminance and color difference signals used in the digital ITU-R 601 coding. Cr and Cb are digitized $R - Y$ and $B - Y$ signals. Luminance is sampled at 13.5 MHz and color difference signals are sampled at 6,75 MHz.

YIQ The analog luminance (Y) and the two-color difference components used in color coding of NTSC and M formats.

yoke An arrangement of horizontal and vertical deflection coils mounted on the CRT neck in video monitors and television sets.

YUV PAL components luminance and two subcarrier modulation axes. The UV color components can be converted to $R - Y$ and $B - Y$ color difference component according to the following formulae: $U = 0.493 (B - Y)$ and $V = 0.877 (R - Y)$.

zero timing point   In a video facility, a reference point to which all video sources are timed. Normally such a point is the input of the main switching device, such as switcher or router.

zits   A popular name for flaws in a digitally processed picture.

zoom in   A term used in directing and camera work. The camera operator changes the focal length to a narrower field of view, making the object look larger and closer. This change in framing is often made while the camera is on-air.

zoom lens   A lens with variable focal length. A zoom lens is normally much larger and more complex than a fixed-focus lens. Moving elements inside the lens allow the focal length change to be controlled mechanically or electronically from the outside. In studio TV cameras the zoom lens has replaced a number of fixed focal length lenses used before for each camera. Today's technology allows one lens to cover the range between a 70° wide-angle field of view and 1.5° long telephoto. Different sizes of lenses are used for studio cameras and hand-held cameras. In portable cameras the weight of the lens is kept to a minimum in the neighborhood of two pounds, thereby limiting the amount of features included. In studio cameras the weight of the lens is less significant; it can weigh as much as 25 pounds and be much larger in size. *See also* **zoom range; zoom ratio.**

zoom out   A term used in directing and camera work. The camera operator changes the focal length to a wider field of view, making the object look smaller and more distant. This change in framing is often made while the camera is on-air.

zoom range   The range between the widest field of view and the narrowest in a zoom lens. The zoom range of a lens is usually stated, in the form of 8×12, where 8 is the focal length in the widest position and 12 is the zoom ratio. The same data can sometimes appear as $8 - 92$, where 92 is longest focal length in the narrowest position. *See also* **zoom ratio.**

zoom ratio   The ratio between the widest field of view and the narrowest in a zoom lens. Portable TV cameras usually use lenses with a zoom ratio between 12 and 17, while in studio lenses the ratio starts usually at 15 and can be as high as 50. A zoom ratio of 50 means that with the same lens, in a football game for example, a tight close-up of a player and a long-shot of the whole field can be made with same camera and lens, with all the angles between (without moving the camera from its position). Therefore, lenses with a large zoom ratio are often used for sports events. *See also* **zoom range.**

Zworykin, Vladimir K.   American physicist and engineer born in Russia (1889–1982). The inventor and developer of the Iconoscope, a light-sensitive picture pickup tube that was used as the heart of the first generation of all-electronic TV cameras to produce a video signal.